D0092720

TO FOLLOW
THE WATER

TO FOLLOW
THE WATER

Exploring the Sea to Discover Climate

From the Gulf Stream to the Blue Beyond

DALLAS MURPHY

BASIC
BOOKS

A MEMBER OF THE PERSEUS BOOKS GROUP

NEW YORK

Published by Basic Books,
A Member of the Perseus Books Group

Books published by Basic Books are available at special
discounts for bulk purchases in the United States by corporations,
institutions, and other organizations. For more information,
please contact the Special Markets Department at the
Perseus Books Group, 2300 Chestnut St., Suite 200,
Philadelphia, PA 19103, or call (800) 255-1514,
or e-mail special.markets@perseusbooks.com.

Text design by Cynthia Young
Interior graphics by Nan North

Set in 10-point ITC Century Book
Library of Congress Cataloging-in-Publication Data
Murphy, Dallas.
To follow the water : exploring the sea to discover climate /
Dallas Murphy.
p.   cm.
Includes bibliographical references.
ISBN-10: 1-58243-350-X (alk. paper)
ISBN-13: 978-1-58243-350-9 (alk. paper)
1. Ocean-atmosphere interaction—Popular works.   2. Ocean
circulation—Popular works.   3. Climatic changes—Popular works.
I. Title.

GC190.2.M87 2007
551.5'246--dc22
2007016359

ISBN-10: 1-58243-350-X
ISBN–13: 978-1-58243-350-9

10   9   8   7   6   5   4   3   2   1

For Annabella

CONTENTS

NOTE

A S THE STORY GOES, a promising young doctoral candidate in physical oceanography sits nervously at his oral exam before a committee of prominent ocean scientists. Instead of quizzing him on the principles of ocean circulation, one of the elder scientists, a famous figure in the field, asks: "Now that you've completed your course work and have been to sea aboard research vessels, how would you describe the oceanographer's primary job?"

Surprised, the student pauses, ponders, and replies: "To follow the water."

When I first heard the story, I understood that it was probably apocryphal, a device composed consciously to sum up the science. But at the time I didn't fully appreciate its implied point: that "to follow the water" is a lot easier said than done. As Carl Wunsch, an actual famous figure in the field, put it, "One of the reasons oceanography has a flavor all its own lies in the brute difficulty of observing the Ocean."

INTRODUCTION

"Come on," said Chief Scientist Molly Baringer, gathering audience members from both labs for tonight's movie, that climatological dust-up *The Day After Tomorrow*. "It'll be fun."

This was our last night out after thirty days at sea aboard the research vessel *Ronald H. Brown*, now steaming for her homeport of Charleston, South Carolina. All aboard were weary, glassy-eyed, and ready to walk on solid Earth. I was thinking about having a last look at the nighttime ocean, then bed. "Is this like the Italian kids who go to the opera to boo the tenor?" I asked.

"Exactly," said Molly.

It was a hot ticket. The audience—officers, crew, technicians, volunteers, and scientists—overflowed the chairs in the ship's lounge onto the floor, shoulder to shoulder. We could tell from swelling minor-key background music as the credits rolled that something bad was about to happen. Our hero, Jack, a climatologist with the National Oceanographic and Atmospheric Administration (NOAA) is speaking at a climate-change conference in New Delhi, India, where it is snowing. Jack warns the audience that if we continue our greenhouse gas emissions, global warming will melt the polar ice caps, and all that freshwater will sever the worldwide ocean circulation. If that happens, then we're looking at another ice age.

Someone asks Jack to explain the seeming paradox. How can global warming cause an ice age? Our climate, Jack begins, is highly fragile, and the ocean— But he is interrupted by the trollish U.S. vice president, intentionally resembling Dick Cheney, who snarls,

"Our economy is also fragile. You *scientists* [intoning the word as it were *syphilitics*] would do well to remember that."

The exchange doesn't get far before Jack, not one to suffer fools, shouts back, "Mr. Vice President, if we don't act now, it may be too late!"

Well, of course it's already too late.

Cut to: mega-tornadoes tearing through Los Angeles, obliterating the Hollywood sign and other symbols of civilization. Reports of disaster are reaching NOAA headquarters from all over the globe. Sea levels have risen twenty-five feet in *half an hour*; hurricanes are forming *over land*; a five-story wall of water submerges Lower Manhattan, sweeping away East Coast icons of permanence. *Finally*, giant storms cover the entire Earth. When they clear, Jack pronounces, "We will be in a new ice age."

We were amused that Jack was a NOAA scientist. The *Ronald H. Brown* is a NOAA ship (pronounced "Noah"), Molly a real NOAA scientist. To understand the long-term circulation of the North Atlantic as it relates to climate change had been the purpose of this expedition, now concluding with computer-generated images of climatic doom. The real scientists giggled or moaned softly at the oceanographic gibberish between Jack and the other cinematic scientists, but in the darkened room, once the "science" had been dispensed with, the ship rolling gently, they began to nod off. Just before joining his colleagues in sleep, the German ocean theorist Jochem Marotzke sitting beside me turned and said, "All this, it's nonsense, of course. But at least the movie puts the ocean into the climate."

I escaped a headache from the Doomsday din and the soggy human part of the plot by fleeing topside. White caps rolled out beyond *Brown*'s quarter wave, but with the wind, the Gulf Stream, and the ship all heading in the same northerly direction, her motion was subdued, almost gentle.

The ocean *has* been left out.

Yet a concept of climate that ignores the ocean makes no more sense than one that excludes the air. Flowing great distances, like global blood vessels, ocean currents stabilize our climate by transporting heat from where there is too much to where there is too little. One reason why the ocean has been left out of the climate-change discussion is that its internal mechanisms and its interactions with the atmosphere are stunningly complex. That the ocean has been left out has helped pitch the discussion toward unproductive, distracting extremes—either global warming is bunk or sea levels are about to rise twenty feet—and to frame the issue as if it were a matter of opinion, like the place of prayer in public schools.

Climate and climate change are strictly matters of science. Only scientists can figure out what is actually going on; only they can inform us. And only from oceanographers can we learn anything real about the ocean's role in climate. But as yet, and for various reasons, we don't talk very effectively with scientists, or they with us. This book seeks to aid the cause of communication by introducing the ocean's astounding dynamics and the bright people who devote their lives to understanding its ways and means. This, then, is a story of discovery—first, for the sake of context, by marine explorers, but mainly by scientists. Here and now, oceanography has "come ashore," its practitioners' interests and ours intersecting around the climate we all share. Scientists haven't simply discovered the role of the ocean in the complex network we call climate; more than that, they are beginning to employ oceanographic techniques to predict climate change.

I can hear my friends in the field caution against overstatement. They aren't quite able to do that today, but they will be, if not tomorrow, then the day after. The time has come to talk.

Chapter 1

OUT THERE

L et's say, arbitrarily, that in the year 700 A.D. a monk is strolling a rocky crescent beach at the mouth of Bantry Bay in the far west of Ireland. The tide is coming in fast, and a scatter of rain is starting to fall. About to turn back, he notices something peculiar in the line of wet, black sea wrack at the high-tide line, and he picks it up. It is a heart-shaped bean with a hard, shiny brown shell about the size of a child's fist. He dries it, turns it over in his hand, and holds it to the light. He has never seen such a thing before. Did it come from lands across the Western Sea? Or from beneath the sea, the fruit of some aquatic plant ripped from its roots during yesterday's westerly gale? Is it a sign, a symbolic heart? He squints out at the horizon as if for an answer. Finding none, he glances back at the shiny little heart in his hand and marvels still again at the ineffable mystery of God's creation.

The sea-heart bean, technically *Entada gigas*, originates in the tropics where, the monk's Bible tells him, the seas boil, but enough sea-hearts made the ocean crossing to have been used as teething rings in medieval Europe and hollowed out to make snuffboxes during the Enlightenment. Ground to powder, they were taken as a tea to relieve constipation. Midwives used them as talismans in birthing rituals, blessing with good fortune infant and mother by carrying *gigas* so many times around the birthing bed in the direction of the sun, or something like that. Having come from across the unknown, the unknowable sea, they were attributed magical powers (or in the case of constipation, efficacious results). We called them lucky beans in southeast Florida where I grew up.

Other drift objects crossed the Atlantic and fetched up on the shores of Great Britain, Ireland, Spain, and Norway, coconuts and another variety of *Entada*, but none was so nautically well found as *gigas* for the voyage, its seed surrounded by a thin airspace for buoyancy and encased in a hard, impermeable shell for watertight integrity. The robust vine thrives on hundreds of sun-bright riverbanks between the Costa Rican rain forests and the Orinoco Delta, festooning its host trees with extravagant six-foot-long seedpods (Costa Ricans call them "monkey ladders"). When the season is right, the vine drops its pods to the forest floor or directly into the river, releasing the seeds. Most fetch up somewhere downstream. But to begin the long transatlantic voyage all *gigas* needs to do is reach the sea, where it will fall under the influence of the Caribbean Current that sweeps westward across the sea.

If *gigas* avoids lurking obstructions—the prominent bulge of the Mosquito Coast, the exposed reefs and sunbaked shallows between Nicaragua and Jamaica—if it hangs in the middle of the sea, then it will ride the current for nine hundred miles, all the way to the Yucatan Channel, the eighty-mile chokepoint between Mexico's Yucatan Peninsula and the western tip of Cuba. The full flow of the Caribbean Current, which has sprawled across the entire basin, must now squeeze through the bottleneck. When that happens, the physical laws describing the behavior of fluids require that the velocity of flow increase, just as it increases in a garden hose when you narrow the nozzle with your thumb. *Gigas* is swept right along, into the Gulf of Mexico.

Geography offers to water only one exit from the Gulf of Mexico, and it's called the Straits of Florida. Huge masses of water blast at dazzling velocity though this half-pipe trench between the arc of the

Florida Keys and the north coast of Cuba. The straits bend north-ward and, like riverbanks, direct the flow between the Bahamian shallows on the east side and the mainland coast of Florida on the west. (If it really were a river, it would contain a volume of water eighty times greater than all the rivers on Earth combined.)

This is the birthplace of the Gulf Stream, the most studied, investi-gated, probed, measured, and pondered strip of saltwater on the globe. Here in these tight reaches it's technically called the Florida Current, but that's just a matter of agreed-upon nomenclature. It's the Gulf Stream, and it's flowing north at three or four knots, some-times five. One billion cubic feet of seawater blow past Miami, Ft. Lauderdale, and Palm Beach *every second*. Remaining in the axis of the current away from the countercurrents that form on the inshore side of the Stream, the monk's *gigas* could cover 120 nautical miles a day (139 statute miles) by doing nothing but floating.

North of Grand Bahamas Island, the eastern "bank" of the Stream vanishes when the chain of shoals, reefs, and low-slung cays slide abruptly into deep water. Now with room to stretch on the seaward side, the current slows somewhat and widens, and the volume of transport nearly triples (to about 150 million cubic meters per sec-ond) as it draws in slightly cooler water from the Sargasso Sea and bears *gigas* north past the coasts of Georgia and South Carolina. Yet the Gulf Stream in this stretch is still constrained by land. The west-ern "bank," in the form of the continental shelf, remains. At the lati-tude of Charleston, the shallow, sprawling shelf edges the axis of the Stream one hundred miles offshore. In fact, all the way back up-stream to the Yucatan Channel, the current has been shaped, squeezed, or steered by land. While that "River in the Sea" is an over-worked and somewhat reductive metaphor, it's appropriate insofar as it implies the presence of solid banks. If it chanced to avoid the snags, continents, and countercurrents, *gigas* would likely make it

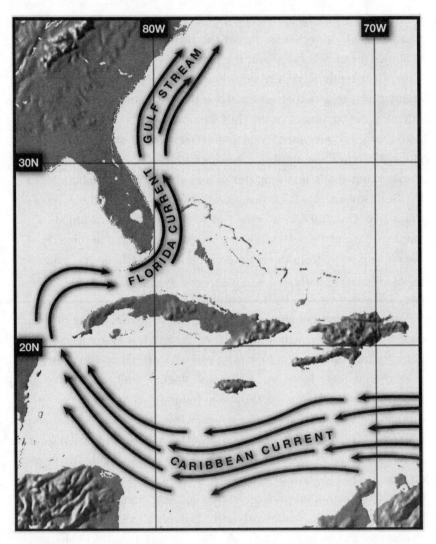

Origins of the Gulf Stream

all the way to Cape Hatteras. But there everything changes. The Gulf Stream puts to sea at Cape Hatteras, casts off all terrestrial association, and it will never again approach dry land.

In technical language, the Gulf Stream becomes a "free zonal jet" at Cape Hatteras. In utterly unscientific language, it seems to celebrate liberation with exuberant display. It wavers, undulates, and meanders. Over time, its net transport remains northeastward toward the Grand Banks. But in the short term, there's no predicting its whims. Today it might be a (relatively) simple, seventy-mile-wide jet of hot water flowing from west to east between the cold continental shelf water south of New England and the warm Sargasso Sea. Within a week, it might meander north or south, spurt to four knots, and then change its character from a narrow, unified stream to filaments of current flowing at different speeds. Then again by the end of the month, it might have reformed onto a straightforward easterly course lazing along at two knots. Or not.

And so the sea-heart bean, having drifted more than two thousand nautical miles, now faces its greatest "peril." Any of those meanders might cast it into the Sargasso Sea or out into the cold continental slope water to the north where even an evolved drifter like *gigas* will rot and finally sink. Likewise, *gigas* might be entrained in one of the huge eddies cast off by the main flow and go around and around, getting nowhere until it meets the same end. And then there is that other intrinsic impediment: Contrary to popular belief, the Gulf Stream does not go to Europe. This is no technicality, nor a matter of nomenclature like the Florida Current. To reach the shores of Ireland, Great Britain, or Norway, *gigas* must find its way into the North Atlantic Current, a sort of offshoot current from the Gulf Stream. The North Atlantic Current flows in fanlike tendrils of warm, salty water drifting languorously along the west-facing shores of Europe.

It is not in the nature of currents to end, as rivers end when they
empty into the sea. That would fly in the face of a most basic law of
nature, the conservation of mass. Having flowed in, water must flow
out. The North Atlantic Current does not end when it delivers its
warmth and its drift objects on the shores of Western Europe. The
current in some partially understood pattern circles the Arctic waters where, chilled in winter, it sinks to become part of the complex,
near fantastical deep circulation. Likewise, the Gulf Stream does not
end near the Grand Banks where it sheds the North Atlantic Current.
Remnants of the Gulf Stream meld into the slow, broad south-setting
Canary Current. When it reaches the tropics and falls under the influence of the Trade Winds, the Canary Current bends westward
melding into the North Equatorial Current, which sets back across
the Atlantic, through the Windward Islands passage and into the
Caribbean Sea—to complete the circle. How many sea-heart beans,
after a year at sea, fetched up at the mouth of the very river from
which they issued? Probably not many, but some, no doubt. The system is circular, and nature loves circles, perhaps nowhere so much
as in the oceans.

North Atlantic Surface Currents

Chapter 2

THE SEA OF DARKNESS

Even Geoffrey Chaucer (1343–1400) needed a survival gig to make ends meet before he hit it big with *Canterbury Tales*, and as these things go, his wasn't onerous—serving the royal household as a sort of high-level clerk and tutor combined. As part of his duties, or because he wanted to, Chaucer taught navigation. He had been interested in it all his life and referred to himself as "an unlearned compiler of old astrologians." These days, astrology doesn't come up very often when the subject is navigation, but in his day few Europeans thought of it in modern terms as a set of practical techniques to fix a ship's position in the open ocean. Under the syllabus of navigation, Chaucer told fantastic stories about mythic figures in imaginary oceans, because in the fourteenth century almost no one had ventured out into the real ocean. The Vikings, of course, had crossed the Atlantic, settling in Iceland and Greenland, and then sailed on to "discover" America in about the year 1000. But the Vikings did not record their discovery; nothing came of their settlements in Newfoundland or in Greenland, and Chaucer may never have heard of the Viking voyages.

Among his more enthusiastic, if unlikely, students was Princess Philippa, John of Gaunt's daughter and King Edward III's granddaughter. When Philippa became queen of Portugal by dint of marriage, she passed her navigation knowledge and her enthusiasm on to one of her young sons by the name of Henry. Exaggerating only slightly, one might say that the era of Western expansion we now call the Great Age of Discovery began with this young boy listening to his mother tell stories about the sea and the heavens she'd learned from Geoffrey Chaucer. The young student grew up to become Henry the Navigator.

Early in the 1420s, Henry founded the famous institution at Sagres, where Portugal shoulders its way out into the open Atlantic, "his great prototype of modern exploration," as historian Daniel Boorstin described it. A personally opaque fellow, Henry wrote nothing and, famously, never went anywhere. The only portrait I've ever seen shows a dark and brooding countenance exuding stern Christian rectitude. Henry had fought in the Crusades at the Battle of Cueta, and, celibate all his life, he died wearing a hair shirt. On the one hand, he was the stereotype of a medieval prince, on the other, a paradigm of Renaissance humanism. Cleareyed and pragmatic, Henry ignored prevailing Christian dogma about boiling seas and terrible monsters and, presumably, old astrologisms. Sagres was to be a sort of marine think tank, and in staffing it he ignored prevailing racial prejudice by inviting Jews, Genoese, Venetians, Germans, Scandinavians, Arabs, and Muslims, the finest cartographers, navigators, shipbuilders, and scholars from all over the known world, anyone who could help him fulfill his purpose.

Frustratingly, we don't know precisely what his purpose was. The simplest and most likely explanation was that he wanted to find a sea route to the East. Asia was well known to Europeans, who viewed it jealously and with un-Christian avarice. The East possessed everything Europeans wanted but had none of: pearls, satins, gold, silks, and spices, especially spices. The East even had the Garden of Eden, assumed at the time to be a real place. Asian goods had been trickling to the West over the ancient Silk Road to the end of the line at the eastern shore of the Mediterranean. From ports in present Lebanon and Israel, Italian middlemen distributed them to market, and the merchants who made their fortunes in the spice trade bankrolled the flowering of the Renaissance in Italy. Marco Polo had thoroughly stoked Europe's hot ambition for things Asian when, in 1295, he returned to Italy after spending seventeen years in China, and published *Travels*. His great journey and its first-person account showed those at home that the East was even grander, greater, and *wealthier* than they had imagined. But then shortly after *Travels* hit the best-seller list, the Moors closed the Silk Road due to the recent religious unpleasantness. Just like that they choked off Europe's only access to those things Europeans would not live without. The search for a sea route to Asia would become the whole point behind the unprecedented European expansion that Henry was pioneering. But Henry never said he was looking for a sea route to anywhere particular.

However, his strategy suggests that he had a specific idea to test. Between 1424 and 1434, he funded and dispatched fifteen voyages—all in the same direction, southward down the coast of Africa. It's possible he did so because no one had been out that way before; no European had ever sailed across the equator, nor even reached the tropics by ship. It's possible Henry established Sagres simply to satisfy his princely curiosity. But many historians believe Henry had surmised somehow that Africa had a bottom and that a ship from Europe could sail around it into the Indian Ocean. If so, his notion flew in the face of conventional fifteenth-century cosmology.

In the second century, Ptolemy, an Alexandrian Greek who liked symmetry, drew a map depicting the world as a single landmass consisting of Europe, Asia, and the northern (the known) part of Africa. For the sake of balance, Ptolemy connected the southern part of Africa to another huge landmass he made up from scratch. Terra Australis Incognito, the great (unknown) Southern Continent, spanned the bottom of the world and reached northward into the subtropics, turning the Indian Ocean into a very large landlocked lake. If that were the case, then of course you couldn't sail into the

Indian Ocean from Europe. No one questioned Ptolemy's map, until Henry, if that's what he was doing. In any case, Henry's voyagers went looking in that direction.

None got very far, none reached the equator, though they discovered the Azores and Canary Islands. However, Henry's concept and methods were far more important than his geographic accomplishments. At a time when common seamen suspected that necromancy controlled the compass and sea monsters ate Christians in the "Torrid Zone," Henry sought only observed, empirical facts. Henry wanted *data*. To get them to go and gather data, he berated, cajoled, threatened, and overpaid timid captains to swallow their fear and sail down the coast of Africa, see what they could see, and then come back and tell him about it. He conceived of exploration as a progressive, collaborative, federally funded endeavor in which no single expedition needed to reach the goal or answer all the questions. Each needed only to press a little farther south than the former and return with fresh knowledge to aid the ensuing expedition. That's what Boorstin meant by the prototype of modern exploration, and the concept of progressive discovery through accumulated data sounds rather like that underpinning today's oceanographic expeditions.

If the Sagres concept depended on data acquisition, then these captains needed to record it in a comprehensive and systematic form. At first they were bringing back sloppy, incomplete records, or worse no record, which was tantamount to not returning at all. Henry therefore mandated that his captains write down in standardized form everything they had observed about prevailing winds, currents, potential harbors, rivers, watering sites, wildlife, natives, *everything*. Henry thus invented the logbook, a giant step in the advance of ocean knowledge. Some historians caution us not to get carried away viewing Sagres from too modern a perspective. Not much is known for certain, and Henry's voice is nowhere to be found. Maybe it's stretching the point to see in Sagres the germ of the contemporary oceanographic institute, but it's not baseless.

However, the concept did not develop, and Sagres died with Henry. He had been gone twenty-eight years when, in 1487, Bartolomeu Diaz dropped his hook in Lisbon harbor mud and proclaimed the triumphant news that Africa did, indeed, have a bottom offering free, open passage into the Indian Ocean to any man with the nerve to make the trip. Diaz would have been that man, except that his crew threatened to throw him over the side if he tried to take them any farther. He named the bottom of Africa the Cape of Storms, objectively reflecting his experience, but the crown, disapproving from a morale standpoint, renamed it the Cape of Good Hope.

Now there was no question about the objective and motivation of exploration. This new generation of explorers would be of a different stripe than Henry. Vasco da Gama, who actually reached India using Diaz's route, Columbus, Magellan, and the rest were men in a rush, hard, practical, ruthless, ambitious, unrelenting, and they didn't give a damn about data. Crossing oceans in the 1400 and 1500s was a dirty, dangerous business; living conditions were execrable, the food worse; sanitation was nonexistent; and it took forever. Fatal disease was so rampant that ships were customarily overcrewed by fifty percent to compensate for the inevitable loss; and, of course, the overcrowding nurtured the diseases that killed sailors. Money was the only rational reason to brook that level of misery. To bring a shipment of cloves, pepper, nutmeg, or cinnamon—just one little shipload—back to Europe from the Indian Ocean or the East Indies (present Indonesia) would make a lowborn captain famous and fortunate, this in a society that had never before offered legal upward mobility to his sort.

On the very day Diaz returned to Lisbon, an odd, ambitious, red-headed Genoese named Christopher Columbus happened to be in town on business, trying to raise royal backing for his "Enterprise of the Indies." Upon hearing Diaz's news, Columbus knew it was hopeless. The king of Portugal wasn't going to back a speculative voyage by an Italian now that a Portuguese captain had discovered a sure thing. But Columbus's idea to reach the East by sailing west, across the Sea of Darkness made sound geographic sense in contemporary cosmology—that is to say, Ptolemy's "island earth." If the world consisted of a single landmass, essentially the Eurasian continent, then there could be only one ocean. And if you crossed it in westerly direction from Europe, you would eventually fetch up in eastern Asia. Furthermore, by Ptolemy's reckoning, the Western Sea was only about two thousand miles wide. Daniel Boorstin called Ptolemy's "the most influential error in Western history." But Marco Polo had confused matters as well. He reported that when he reached the eastern shore of Asia, he looked out on a vast ocean. Believing Ptolemy, Polo took it for the Atlantic Ocean. There was no room in men's minds for two new continents and an extra, huge ocean.

Columbus sold the idea to Ferdinand and Isabella, who had just finished running the Moors (and the Jews) out of Spain, and they were ready for a piece of the action out East before their Portuguese rivals cornered the market. As everyone knows, Columbus did not reach Asia, bumping instead against a New World that no one had imagined or wanted. In all, he made four voyages, brilliant feats of navigation, across the Atlantic, exploring most of the Caribbean basin, believing all the while that he had reached the spice islands. Columbus could never face the enormity of his failure, despite the weight of evidence, and he died in 1505 still insisting that he had reached Asia. School boards, at least in my time, couldn't brook the truth, either. They wanted textbooks that said Columbus *discovered America*, a fine thing to have done, and it couldn't have happened by accident and certainly not by a weird, geographically confused quasi-mystic who was in it strictly for the gold.

While there's little to admire in his terrestrial work, Columbus deserves immortality for his maritime accomplishments. Not by Henry's method, not by trial and error, but in a single swoop, Columbus found the best sailing routes across the Atlantic in both directions, and they remain today the best routes. Since we're talking about sailing ships, this is to say he found the best wind. Wind is crucial here, both to exploration and to oceanography.

Columbus knew that he could not sail directly west from Spain because the prevailing winds in those latitudes blow directly onto the Iberian Peninsula. (Wind is identified by the direction from which it blows; these, then, were west winds.) Ships in his day could make no progress to windward, but even in today's far more weatherly sailboats, no sensible navigator would pick a course that required beating to windward across the Atlantic. Bound from Europe to the Caribbean, he would do exactly what Columbus did in 1492, for the first time in history: Sail south from Spain to around 28 degrees North latitude. There he would find that gift of nature to sailors—the Northeast Trade Winds.

The Trade Winds, which gird the globe in two tropical belts on either side of the equator, are among the most stable meteorological systems on Earth. In the Northern Hemisphere, they blow from northeast to southwest at twenty to thirty knots, right across the Atlantic. The Trade Winds in the Southern Hemisphere blow southeast to northwest in a slightly thinner belt. The edges of both wobble somewhat north and south, and their velocities vary seasonally, but they never quit entirely. Slightly south of the Canary Islands, just as he had expected, Columbus felt the warm wind over his left shoulder, and only then did he turn right. Though he did not discover the Northeast Trades—Henry's captains had done that—Columbus was the first human ever to ride them across the Atlantic. Twenty days later, right on his chosen latitude, cruelly near the distance he'd expected to reach the East Indies, he sighted land. He had fetched up in the eastern Bahamas, either San Salvador or Samana Cay, where, he wrote, "The natives were poor in everything."

Since favorable wind outbound meant foul wind homebound, Columbus needed a totally different route back to Spain. From the west wind blowing onto the Iberian Peninsula, he had extrapolated a west-wind system originating on the unknown side of the Atlantic that would blow him home. All he had to do was sail north to about 35 degrees North (about the latitude of Charleston, South Carolina) until he met the prevailing westerlies, and then turn right. He arrived in triumph, right back where he'd started, after a rough passage, in March of 1492. On subsequent voyages, he found and named most of the Caribbean islands after saints, and he named the locals for the place he'd meant to go, the Indies, but geography had trapped him in the wrong ocean. However, this was the Sea of Darkness no more. The routes back and forth had been blazed. As historian J. H. Hale put it, Columbus "set bounds to the Atlantic. It became finite."

The Spanish asked themselves, if Columbus had bumped into some New World where Asia was supposed to be, where was Asia? It could only be farther west. Spanish explorers began to search for a way around or through the New World to the *East* Indies. They couldn't be far. Maybe there was a passage or a strait of some sort, and maybe you could see right through it, like Gibraltar. Meanwhile, resignedly, the Spanish poked around their New World Empire, which in 1500 consisted only of the Caribbean Basin, to see what it offered in the way of profit. There were no spices; there was almost no gold; but there was a lot of free land for a man willing to leave everything behind in Spain and move to this essentially lawless outpost. Conditions tended to attract those who had nothing to lose in Spain. Desperate but determined fellows comfortable with killing and enslaving—that was the sort you needed to make something of the New World, the king and the pope readily agreed, since they were going to get a hefty cut of everything. Among these was Ponce de Leon, in many ways typical of the men we now call conquistadors.

You used to hear a lot about Ponce at an impressionable age growing up in south Florida. He frightened me as a kid. A mural painted by a WPA artist on an inside wall of the little Lake Worth Public Library, where I first discovered books, pictured Ponce astride a shiny black warhorse. He seemed to be angry, glaring out across what appeared to be the Everglades, brown, wind-bent saw grass dotted with sable-palm hammocks in the middle distance, a flock of snowy egrets hanging in the air. In the far distance, up where the wall met the ceiling, beyond a sliver of beach, the Atlantic Ocean glimmered in the sun. Black-eyed, hawk-faced, Ponce seemed to menace the nonfiction stacks. Why was he so angry? He had just discovered Florida. Yet he looked hostile, not happy. Maybe he was frustrated that he hadn't found the Fountain of Youth.

Born to impoverished nobility in backwater Spain, Ponce had sailed away with Columbus on the Second Voyage to seek his fortune and stayed on, settling in Santo Domingo. Ponce was skilled at running down recalcitrant natives who had taken to the hills to avoid enslavement in the sugarcane fields. He "had a dog," wrote the contemporary historian Antonio de Herrera, "called Bexerillo, that made wonderful havoc among these people . . . for which reason the Indians were more afraid of ten Spaniards with the dog, than 100 without him, and therefore [Bexerillo] had one share and a half of all that was taken." For those good offices, Ponce was awarded permission to cross the Mona Passage and conquer Puerto Rico. This he did with brutal dispatch and was appointed governor in 1509. There, he and his dog founded colonies and plantations with plenty of slaves to do the real work. He sent for his wife and daughters, and they lived the good life for several years, until Columbus's son Diego removed Ponce from office under prior claim based on his father's original contract with Ferdinand and Isabella. Pushing fifty with nothing to show for his efforts, Ponce petitioned Seville for permission to sail in search of the fabled island of Beniny (Bimini), said to be rich in gold, lying somewhere to the north. (In her delightful classic *The Everglades, River of Grass*, Marjory Stoneman Douglas points out that the finely detailed contract between Emperor Charles V and Ponce, granting him control for life over the island and its treasure, minus the crown's cut, does not mention any fountain or spring or magic waters of any kind. The Fountain of Youth, she writes, is "the first and most deathless of all American myths.")

Ponce's three-ship fleet—with Anton de Alaminos, another veteran of the Second Voyage, doing the piloting—picked its way deftly through the Bahamas, then called "Lucayos." Holding its northeast heading, the fleet passed out of the island chain and crossed about seventy miles of open water. Then, on March 27, 1513, they sighted a long, unbroken beach backed by impassible vegetation. Ponce ceremoniously named it *Pascua Florida* for the Easter season. Historians differ as to where he actually landed or how far north he sailed, but it doesn't matter. What he found when he turned around and tried to sail back south down the Florida coast, however, matters a great deal.

Sails drawing nicely in a fresh breeze from astern, the ships were making bow waves and leaving foaming wakes, but getting nowhere. In fact, they were going backwards. Here's Herrera again, apparently quoting Ponce's log of April 22, 1513:

Sailing south and entering . . . the broad waters of the sea, all the three ships . . . saw a current which, although they had a good wind they could not stem. It seemed that they advanced, but they soon recognized that they . . . were driven back, and that the current was more powerful than the wind. Two ships, which were somewhat nearer the coast, came to anchor, but the currents were so strong that they made the cable tremble. The third vessel, being a little more towards the sea, could find no bottom. She was carried away by the current, and they lost sight of her, though it was a clear and calm day.

This is the first-ever record of the Gulf Stream.

Ponce sailed to Havana to announce his discovery of Florida, for which he was knighted and appointed governor. In February 1521, he sailed back to Florida to establish a colony on the west coast in the vicinity of Sanibel Island. Six months later, after repeated attacks by natives, he abandoned his new realm and returned to Havana with a festering arrow wound in his thigh. (Some historians have held up this continuous hostility by Florida natives as evidence that other Spanish slavers had preceded Ponce to those shores.) In any case, Florida was useless to the Spanish, hot as hell, the air dense with bloodsucking insects and arrows. None of that would have forestalled invasion if Florida had contained any sign of gold. The Spanish were generally disappointed with their empire. The sugar plantations were better than nothing, but the Spanish weren't there for the agricultural opportunities. Disappointment turned to joy suddenly in 1519.

Hernando Cortez landed near Vera Cruz on Mexico's Gulf Coast, burned his boats to signal his all-or-nothing resolve, and marched inland. At the future site of Mexico City, Cortez happened upon the Aztec capital of Tenochtitlan, the residents of which were festooned with gold. Instead of hacking him to pieces, the Aztecs welcomed Cortez, mistaking him for their god Quetzalcoatl, whose prophesied return Cortez seemed to fulfill. That was bad luck for the Aztecs.

Cortez and his tiny band of killers essentially destroyed Aztec culture to get at their gold. Gold, looted first from these Aztec and later from the Inca in Peru, would change the direction of history in both the New and Old Worlds. In the New World, ancient cultures would vanish. In the Old World, Spain and Portugal rose to superpowers. By 1530, the two Iberian nations, their rapid expansion, had shifted the locus of Western Civilization from Mediterranean to Atlantic shores, but that's getting a little ahead of the story.

Cortez had a problem back on the beach near Vera Cruz. He still had to get the goods back to Spain. As always, any benefits the conquistadors looted from the locals, especially gold, belonged to the king, who owned the New World in partnership with the Catholic Church. Cortez would receive his cut and his new titles only after the gold had safely crossed the Atlantic. A transatlantic passage was not work for steely conquistadors on armored horses; war dogs were useless at sea. Cortez needed a real mariner, an experienced professional, and he chose wisely: Anton de Alaminos. Having made his name piloting Ponce's fleet to and from Florida, discovering the Gulf Stream, Alaminos had gone on to explore the Gulf of Mexico and the Yucatan Peninsula. And he knew exactly how to get the gold to Spain. It would be a modification of Columbus's route, using the Gulf Stream to speed his advance. Gaining two to four free miles each hour, the first gold fleet swept up the coast of Florida in fair wind. When he felt the prevailing westerlies fill in, Alaminos turned his stern to the wind and headed northeast, straight for Spain. This would be the homebound route by which the Spanish transferred the wealth of the New World back to the Old World for the next 150 years.

It's interesting to note that the Spanish treasure fleets consistently pulled out of the Stream too far south to take advantage of the favorable current as it turns seaward at Cape Hatteras. Besides losing the current's boost, cutting the corner like that sent them into the

Sargasso Sea—into the convergence zone between the Trade Winds and the westerlies—where there is little wind. This belt of fluky, variable wind gained the name "horse latitudes," because becalmed Spanish crews drove their warhorses, expendable on the home-bound passage, over the side to save water, but this may be a myth.

The most logical explanation for pulling out of the favorable current where they did is that they didn't know where the current went or when they were in it. Alaminos had discovered the Florida Current, that part of the system running close to land between Florida and the Bahamas; he knew nothing of the current's "downstream" course. It's difficult, however, to glean just what Spanish navigators knew and did not know due to the stultifying level of secrecy that prevailed during the Great Age of Discovery. The Spanish did collect logs and other reports in the Institute of the Indies, which still stands in Seville, but the flood of the new was overwhelming, and the authorities weren't all that interested anyway. There was no such thing as a sixteenth-century version of Sagres as a clearing-house of maritime knowledge. We don't even know who named the Gulf Stream. He must have been Spanish, and he must have assumed on the evidence of his eyes that it issued from the Gulf of Mexico. The story of the Spanish Conquest was an every-man-for-himself gold rush. In that atmosphere, hard-earned knowledge of the ocean that facilitated crossing it was not something to be shared, even with conquistador colleagues.

Possibly, the treasure fleets kept to the south for fear of pirates in the north. England and France, armed with new ships, advanced naval gunnery, old animosities, and fresh jealousies, were dispatching pirates (Francis Drake, most famously) to pick at the fringes of Spanish power. There was good money in piracy, but it couldn't change the geopolitical facts. The Portuguese had sewn up the east-about route around Africa to the Spice Islands, while the Spanish kept an iron grasp on the New World, leaving France and England, as they saw it, to wither in the North Atlantic. Surely God, who made the world, had not made it so that only Iberian Catholics could pillage and loot its far-flung regions. Soon the Dutch got into the act with the same sentiments. But for now, while they nurtured their naval power for the inevitable war to come, Northern European nations concocted a new geographic feature born of wishful thinking and their northern location: the Northwest Passage.

Just as there was an ocean passage around the bottom of Africa, perhaps there was a passage over the top of North America that led straight to Cathay (China). If they could only find the opening, this route to the riches could prove to be a fortuitous geographic advantage since east–west distances are shorter in the higher latitudes than nearer the equator. Henry Hudson, Jacques Cartier, John and Sebastian Cabot, Martin Frobisher, Raleigh, Gilbert, and John Davis—they were all searching for the Northwest Passage. Chesapeake and Delaware proved to be dead-end bays. The Hudson River looked likely for a time, but no, it turned completely fresh not far upstream of the little Dutch settlement they called New Amsterdam. Cartier thought he had it as he sailed into the wide mouth of the St. Lawrence River, but hopes began to fade as the waterway narrowed and then ended upstream of present Montreal at a set of rapids he sarcastically named La Chine. By process of elimination, the search moved farther and farther north into ever more dangerous water in the High Arctic. None of these men was exploring America as they told us in school. Each was looking for a way over or through the damn thing. The quest for the passage took on existential meaning adjusted periodically to fit the tenor of the times, but generally about nationalism and (Western) man's attainment of geographical goals as a symbol of his triumph over brute nature. The long, fantastic saga—which began four years after Columbus "discovered America," proceeded through layers of tragedy, rank foolishness, great heroic acts, and desperate acts of murder, mutiny, and cannibalism—did not close until 1907, when the brilliant Roald Amundsen sailed through the Northwest Passage, taking three years to do so. You can't make up stuff like the search for the Northwest Passage. (I like Pierre Burton's definitive history *The Arctic Grail*.)

Meanwhile, the Spanish had not given up their ambitions to reach the East from the west. Explorers were conducting their own search for a route westward, leapfrogging their way down the east coast of South America. The New World was not making it easy. The distances were unbelievably long. Maybe *El Paso* did not exist. Then in 1520, Ferdinand Magellan, a granitic, relentless Portuguese sailing for Spain, found a way through the New World: the Strait of Magellan. That it actually existed was spectacular news. That it existed 4,300 miles south of Havana was not so good. Also, it was a nasty piece of work, a 250-mile-long twisting crack in the crust of the Earth prone to vicious ten-knot tides and savage storms. When, finally, Magellan had picked his way through the strait, he came upon open water as far as he could see. It couldn't be a very large body of water, he surmised. Just a few days to reach the islands where riches grew on trees.

That there was open water on the west side of the New World was not entirely unexpected, and Magellan was not the first European to lay eyes on *El Mar Pacifico*, as Magellan named it. Marco Polo had seen the other side of the Pacific, but he didn't know what he was looking at. And in 1513, the same year Ponce discovered the Gulf Stream, a conquistador psychopath named Vasco Balboa had sighted it from a peak on the Isthmus of Panama. Like everyone at the time, he assumed it was a sound or a big bay. As one historian put it, in the Western imagination the world was never very large, and the East was just a little farther west. There was never room for another ocean.

Magellan sailed confidently northwest from his strait toward the East Indies. Nothing appeared. Soon, though. Still nothing. When he turned west, the staggering enormity of the thing began painfully to reveal itself. Never lucky, Magellan happened to sail the only track across this island-spattered ocean that lacked land. His eighty-nine-day passage was arguably the greatest single sail in human history— it certainly was if hideous, prolonged, scurvy-ridden misery is a measure of greatness. Best to let Magellan's loyal chronicler, one of the only people during the Great Age who went to sea out of curiosity, tell a piece of the story. Antonio Pigafetta wrote: "We ate only biscuit turned to powder all full of worms and stinking of urine which the rats had made on it. And we drank water impure and yellow . . . And of the rats, which were sold for half an ecu apiece, some of us could not get enough." A truly poignant figure, Magellan, after finding *El Paso* and surviving the first crossing of the Pacific Ocean, was killed on a beach in Mectan, the Philippines, after senselessly involving himself in a local squabble between war lords.

The Portuguese expanded eastward around Africa, while the Spanish pressed westward—and Magellan closed the circle. Then in 1579, Francis Drake added a final piece to the chart of Western expansion when he found quite by accident a wide, open-water passage south of Magellan's untenable strait at the very bottom of South America, at a place that would come to be called Cape Horn. Now there was no impediment (except the weather) to ambitious men from Europe who wanted to make their fortunes on the other side of the Pacific. When the Great Age of Discovery was complete, certainly by the time Drake completed his circumnavigation, the second in history, 1580, Europeans had discovered that the world was far larger than anyone had imagined a century earlier, containing two new continents as well as that other ocean. In fact, it was covered by far more water than anyone had ever imagined.

The future clearly belonged to sailors. But there was more: Europeans had learned that all those oceans were connected one to the other. A ship from anywhere could reach any other place on the face of the Earth that had a coastline. This meant that, in effect, there was only one ocean, a *world ocean*. Centuries later, with time and technology, ocean scientists would repeat this great discovery in a new context and change, still again, our view of the world.

Chapter 3

NOTES IN A BOTTLE

In 1768, when England and her American colonies were still speaking, Benjamin Franklin visited London in his official capacity as postmaster general. There he heard a curious complaint lodged by the Colonial Board of Customs: Why did it take the British mail ships (called packets) *two weeks* longer to reach New York from England than it took the average merchantman to reach Newport, Rhode Island? Further, the merchants, leaving from London, had to sail down the Thames, then the length of the English Channel before they even began their Atlantic crossing, while the mail packets left from Falmouth in Cornwall on the ocean's doorstep. Still the merchants reached Newport a fortnight ahead of New York–bound packets. There was no appreciable difference between the ships; both were equally slow. Why, then? Was there some difference between the two destinations? Should the mail be sent to Newport instead of New York? Franklin had no idea, but he had sources.

He hailed from a long line of seamen, notably the Folgers, among the original settlers of Nantucket and now rising stars of American whaling. One of the brightest, his cousin Captain Timothy Folger, happened to be in London at that very time. Franklin invited Captain Folger to dinner and put the question: "Why does it take two weeks longer to sail from London to New York than to Newport?"

It doesn't, said Folger. The difference had nothing whatever to do with the respective destinations—and everything to do with the captains. Merchant skippers routinely avoided the Gulf Stream when crossing from England. The mail-packet captains, on the other hand, sailed dead into its foul easterly set, passage after passage. As Folger explained, when American whalers, who had been finding rich pickings on the northern fringes of the Gulf Stream, encountered westbound ships at sea, they informed the captains "that they were stemming a current . . . to the value of three miles an hour: and advised them to cross it and get out of it." Appreciating the tip, merchant captains had adjusted their course. But the bullheaded packet captains did not. "They were too wise to be counseled by simple American fishermen," said Folger.

As some versions of the story have it, Franklin replied, "Gulf Stream? What, sir, is the Gulf Stream?" It's a better story that way, but Franklin already knew about the current's spectacular sprint up the Eastern Seaboard, and he'd already proposed, in writing, a theory of why it flowed so fast. He knew, too, that the Gulf Stream turned seaward at Cape Hatteras, but as to its course after that, he knew next to nothing. He asked his cousin then and there to sketch a chart of the Gulf Stream's course.

His latent interest in the sea revived, Franklin spent the return passage to Philadelphia hauling up water samples in buckets, computing and comparing their temperatures, jotting notes, pondering. Ashore, he pursued the study by interviewing whalers and merchant captains. Honored, they told him all they knew and put their logbooks at his disposal. Franklin was not the first natural scientist to seek knowledge of the sea from those who made their livings crossing it—the Royal Society had circulated their *Directions for Seamen, Bound for Far Voyages* in 1666, and Henry the Navigator's entire concept was founded on captains' logs as a source of data. But Franklin was the first American natural scientist to systematize mariners' logs in a dedicated study of the Gulf Stream. Out of it came his famous Gulf Stream Chart, published initially in 1770, in

England, where it was completely ignored. Subsequent versions were printed in France in 1778 and the United States in 1786. In the 1786 version, Franklin's favorite, engraver James Poupard sketched in the bottom right corner the familiar figure of a portly fellow in tails and a tricornered hat standing dry-shod on a rock engaged in a lively discussion with King Neptune.

The British edition of the chart, the original, had been so thoroughly ignored that everyone thought it lost forever—until 1979, when Woods Hole oceanographer and Gulf Stream expert Phil Richardson found it in the Bibliothèque Nationale in Paris. "That was one of the most exciting discoveries of my life," he told me, "and it was almost too easy." With time to kill one September afternoon, he decided to have a look in the library. He had a French government grant "with some fancy writing on it" that he waved around to gain entry to the Map Room and to a very private portfolio containing early charts of the North Atlantic. Apparently it was so private no one had looked inside until Richardson arrived. There they were, not one but two copies of the British version, plus a French version. Trying to appear calm, Richardson returned the treasures to the portfolio, said *merci*, walked straight back to his apartment ("I couldn't sleep all night"), and outlined an essay that appeared in *Science* magazine. Richardson, of course, loved being the American oceanographer who found the "lost" English chart in the French library. His discovery evoked much hoopla at home, including front-page coverage in the *New York Times*. This, he said, stood him in good stead with his mother-in-law.

An aging Franklin poured out his findings in "Maritime Observations," published by the Philosophical Society's *Transactions* in 1786. "As I may never have another occasion of writing on this subject, I think I may as well, once and for all, empty my nautical bucket." It brimmed with ideas—for sea anchors, catamaran hulls, shipboard lightning rods, watertight compartments, and a soup bowl designed to stay put in heavy weather—all far in advance of their time. Franklin also poured out his Gulf Stream research, including the final version of the chart. He contended that the distinguishing characteristic of the current was heat, that its water "is always warmer than the sea on each side," and "[T]hose tornados and waterspouts frequently met with" in the Stream were the result of cold air swooping in to replace warm air rising from the hot current. In the cold northern reaches near Newfoundland, that warm, moist air condensed into the thick fog "for which those parts are so remarkable." There's a story that during the Revolutionary War Franklin kicked around the idea of using the Stream as a terror weapon. If somehow it could be deflected, as with a dike, England would be plunged into a new ice age.

It would make for a pleasing story to tell that the great polymath nailed the Gulf Stream first time out, that his chart stands the test of time as the first true depiction of the Gulf Stream. It was an enormous early contribution, transferring esoteric nautical knowledge about the behavior of the ocean to public consciousness. Franklin had measured sea surface temperatures, recorded and analyzed his raw observations, combined them with shipboard reports, and then drew a conclusion that explained his data. These were acts of oceanography. So, too, was his impulse to publish, to pour out the bucket of data for anyone to read. Further, he recognized a causal relationship between Gulf Stream warmth and England's moderate maritime climate. However, it's worth pointing out for our purposes that the chart is accurate in the way of a caricature.

His Gulf Stream flows through the North Atlantic like a giant, docile river, keeping cooperatively, permanently to its banks. He meant for his chart to aid the mariner, and it did. Once an ocean current was revealed, only damn fools and mail-packet captains continued to stem it. But the chart also misled mariners. If the edge of the Stream was indeed as distinct as a river's, and if it was "always warmer than the sea on each side of it," then navigators could use a simple thermometer to find the flow—and because that edge, as drawn, was stable, they could also approximate their position. The logic was sound, if only the real Gulf Stream behaved as drawn and the "cold wall" stayed put, as good walls should. The "thermonavigator" might find hot water, but that didn't tell him whether he was in the main flow or not. He couldn't even be certain, based on temperature alone, that the current was setting in the charted direction. The important point here is not to show that Franklin was wrong, but that he could not have been right.

Franklin didn't even have access to that most basic of oceanographic necessities: a research vessel. He crossed the North Atlantic four times, as a passenger, on merchant ships whose captains would have hooted at the idea of diverging from their best course so someone, even Ben Franklin, could take temperatures in a different strip of ocean. In modern language, his study suffered from "instrument error" (inaccurate thermometer) and "sampling error" (too few). No private person or entity in his day could afford to buy, fit out, man, and provision an oceangoing ship that offered no return on investment except enhanced knowledge, and so it remains true today. That left the science dependent on governments. The navy was the only arm of government that had ships, but most of its officers up and down the ranks saw no career advantage in ferrying *civilian* scientists around the ocean. Naval officers would have done just that had they been so ordered, but their civilian authorities in the war department and in Congress generally shared the navy's disinterest in and distrust of science.

Some notables in the eighteenth century—Robert Boyle, Edmund Halley, Robert Hook, Luigi Marsigli, and Jacob Bernoulli—had been thinking about the sea in theoretical and mathematical terms, investigating whatever aspects of it could be carried into a laboratory. But theory feeds on fresh observational data, and almost no one was collecting data. This was partly a matter of practicality, as well as the dearth of ships that could be spared for nonmilitary purposes. Even if you had a ship or two, what would you do with it? What tools do you need to study the sea? How do you learn anything useful about something so vast as the Atlantic Ocean? Never mind the Pacific Ocean. And it was partly a matter of attitude. If you meant to go out to sound and survey the approaches to a harbor in the interest of safe navigation, well, that was one thing. It was quite another to go out and collect data to learn how the ocean worked. What was the practical point of that?

No one went to sea as common sailors except the lower orders, wastrels, shirkers, fugitives, and failures at respectable pursuits. There was no such thing as desirable oceanfront property between the American Revolution and the Civil War. Harbors were ramshackle, dirty, and dangerous places where good boys were led astray in brothels and reprobate bars. No one messed about in boats for recreation, and no one went to the beach on holiday until well after the Civil War. Most people in and out of government viewed the open Atlantic as a hostile wasteland where civilized rules were suspended, terrifying if you thought about it, but there wasn't much reason to think about it absent a marine disaster or naval war. Before anything like oceanographic research could happen, there had to be a general shift in ocean attitude.

The first such shift—from an absolute barrier to human ambition to a pathway to everywhere—had defined the Great Age of Discovery during the Renaissance. Conquest or monopoly, or both, were the purposes of exploration, and the oceans were the routes to riches, deadly but worth it. A second paradigmatic shift began during

Franklin's lifetime, during the Enlightenment, with the advent of the "scientific expedition." The three voyages of Captain Cook between 1768 and 1780 stand among the earliest and purest expressions of the new attitude. During Cook's Second Voyage, which overlapped the Revolutionary War, the American Navy issued orders that, should they encounter Cook's ships at sea, American captains were to leave them alone, since Cook was engaged in work for the common good and peaceful edification of all nations.

After Cook, the goal of marine exploration was to acquire scientific and geographic knowledge about the world, not enslave its far-flung natives and take their treasure or to convert them to Catholicism and take their treasure. The new focus of exploration shifted to the vast reaches of the Pacific and the Polar seas, and its objective was to learn the true shape of the world, chart new lands, gather unknown plants, animals, and in some instances willing human specimens—and, crucially, to bring back these maps, records, and specimens to avail others in understanding the processes of nature. The historian William Goetzmann called this period the Second Great Age of Discovery.

Louis de Bougainville, James Clark Ross, Robert FitzRoy, Dumont d'Urville, La Perouse, Lewis and Clark (on land), and the model and hero of them all, James Cook—those of us whose childhood idols were explorers tended to idealize their exploits, an attractive melding of sea-story adventure and refreshing high purpose. Maturing, we recognized that they were all military-backed expeditions connected thereby to national interests and international competition. To fund and outfit a scientific circumnavigation was seen by 1800 as a measure of a nation's level of enlightenment, a matter of patriotic pride. (Members of Congress in the United States, which came late to scientific exploration, actually argued that we had to put an expedition out there, even if we didn't give a damn about what it found, lest we look like know-nothing rubes in European eyes.) *Endeavor, Resolution, Erebus*, and *Terror, Astrolabe, Beagle*, and a handful of other immortal vessels were freighted with the usual suppositions about Western entitlement and superiority. Sadly, also, the discovery of new and exotic places opened them to the missionaries, exploiters, and colonists who inevitably followed in explorers' wakes. That said, science was not merely a smokescreen for conquest. These were real scientific expeditions, and they were indeed refreshing combinations of adventure and intellectual purpose.

The onboard presence of a naturalist, or a team of them on the larger ships, was essential to the concept of the scientific expedition. His role was to recognize, collect, and describe all that was new. Equally essential were artists to record it all with photonaturalistic precision, and in their best work, you can feel their excitement at the new reflected in the attention to minute detail in this leaf or that fish's fins, despite miserable shipboard conditions. Among the better-known naturalist "savants" who launched their careers on scientific voyages were Joseph Banks (with Cook), Thomas Huxley (Ross), and Charles Darwin (FitzRoy). However, all of these expeditions aimed to find new lands on the far side of the ocean, not specifically to understand the ocean itself. Edmond Halley (of comet fame) led the first recognizable oceanographic voyage aboard the leaky little sloop *Paramore* in 1700 to study tides and geomagnetism, but he was well ahead of his time. Nothing similar was launched from U.S. shores until the 1850s when Matthew Fontaine Maury and Alexander Dallas Bache, Franklin's grandson, organized government sponsored expeditions devoted mainly to sounding the deep ocean. The purest early expression of the oceanographic cruise was the British *Challenger* expedition in the 1870s, but despite brillian accomplishments, it contributed relatively little to knowledge about the ocean's physical dynamics. Even if, due to some upsurge of interest in the workings of the ocean, an entire fleet of research vessels had been funded and dispatched in the 1870s to study currents it could not have produced a product much more finely granulated than Franklin's chart. There would have been no tools more sophisticated than a sounding lead, an unreliable thermometer, and a bucket. The measurement of ocean motion required tools unavailable for another two centuries after Cook's death.

Broadly, there are two ways to measure a current in the open ocean. You can set an object(s) adrift and somehow follow it (them). In the parlance, this is known as the Lagrangian method, or the float method. By the other means, the Eulerian method, you measure with some sort of meter the current's flow past a fixed point. It's rather like cinematography. You can follow the action with the camera, or fix the camera and let the action flow past.

In the spring of 1990, en route to Seattle from North Korea, the container ship *Hansa Carrier* battled her way across the International Dateline in a ferocious typhoon-strength storm to become an accidental footnote in the annals of Lagrangian research. Among the most soulless of vessels ever to ply the sea, container ships are essentially long, thin warehouses without roofs (decks). Cargo is packed in standardized containers about half the size of a railroad freight car and stacked into the ship, layer upon layer, sometimes reaching fifty feet above the bulwarks. Profit motivates shippers to pile on just as many containers as the mathematics of stability allow, and then some. Most of the time, they get away with it, but the *Hansa Carrier* did not. Rolling heavily, she flipped *twenty-one* containers over the side. They broke up and sank, while some of their contents—30,910 pairs of Nike athletic shoes—remained afloat.

Six months later, shoes by the hundreds began washing up in wearable condition on west-facing beaches from British Columbia to Oregon. The trouble was that right-feet shoes had never been attached to their left-foot mates. As shoes continued to wash ashore, beachcombers placed ads in local newspapers for matches, and swap meets were held up and down the coast. Oceanographers, noticing the footwear furor, placed ads of their own requesting finders to notify research organizations where and when they came by their shoes.

In 1992, another ship in the North Pacific lost a container full of bathtub toys, twenty-nine thousand rubber duckies, to serve ocean science. There must have been a dreadful lot of bathtub jokes kicking around the West Coast oceanographic community at the time, but several serious papers were published in technical journals on duck drift. There have been other recent unintentional Lagrangian experiments—when in 1997, five million Lego pieces went over the side near Cornwall, England, and again, in 2001, with the loss of 262,500 plastic soap dispensers in the North Atlantic. Lost hockey gloves, computer monitors, and cans of noodle soup have done their part to reveal surface circulation.

Perhaps the most revelatory no-tech Lagrangian experiment was performed in the late nineteenth century by Prince Albert of Monaco. A bored young gentleman of twenty-five, Albert had no pressing princely duties and, with his marriage recently annulled, no personal shoreside obligations. He did, however, have a solid education in marine engineering and navigation, and he had money. To his royal father's chagrin, he spent a princely sum of it on a small schooner, the *Hirondelle*, and in 1873, went yachting for twelve seasons. Then in 1885, he turned his attention and his schooner away from nautical leisure toward physical oceanography.

As Susan Schlee points out in her excellent history of oceanography, *The Edge of an Unfamiliar World*, "In 1885 no one really knew where the Gulf Stream water went once it left the more familiar coastal zone off New England and Canada." Some previous investigators had "maintained that the current never crossed the Atlantic, while others insisted that it did, dividing somewhere in the North Atlantic, to send one arm north along the British Isles and another south toward the Iberian Peninsula." Among the proponents of the latter view was a remarkable amateur ocean scientist of the sort turned out periodically by the Royal Navy, which James Rennell joined at the ripe old age of fourteen. He began his career as a surveyor, producing masterful charts of Indonesian harbors for the navy and, later, maps of India. Badly wounded in 1776, he was invalided back to England where he turned his mind to ocean matters, specifically to the Gulf Stream. Based on ship's logs from seventeen passages between Halifax and Bermuda, he concluded that the Gulf Stream curved seaward from the North American continent toward England, but the Stream itself never reached England, recirculating instead into the Sargasso Sea or melding into south-setting currents off the coast of Spain. However, a segment of its water, driven by the wind, "drifted" along a broad front, and it was this water England has to thank for its moderate climate. He called it the North Atlantic Drift. Today we call it the North Atlantic Current, but in the 1880s, there was no real evidence of its existence. This was one of the questions Prince Albert meant to answer.

During three voyages, the prince and his professor friend, Georges Pouchet, from the Museum of Natural History in Paris set adrift 1,675 casks, glass spheres, and bottles, each containing a message in ten languages asking beachcombers to report where and when they found the floats. They dropped them in the Bay of Biscay, in the open ocean northwest of the Azores, and, lastly, near the Grand Banks southeast of Newfoundland. Though only 227 of the floats were ever recovered, their landfall locations—in the British Isles *and* the West Indies—seemed to indicate that Rennell was right. The Gulf Stream did recirculate southward on the east side of what seemed to be a circular flow around the boundary of the North Atlantic, and a slow, wide drift of warm water diverged northeastward from the main flow.

But Albert's bottles and that stuff lost overboard illustrate the weakness of pre- or non-technical drift experiments. Floating objects retrieved by beachcombers may reveal the general set (direction) of a current if the point where they were lost was known, as in the case of the *Hansa Carrier*, but they cannot reveal the route they followed to reach shore. Nor can they reveal the current's velocity (drift), since there is no way to learn exactly when the objects came ashore, only when they were found. To be useful, Lagrangian float objects must contain an electronic or acoustic means of reporting their locations as they drift along.

Among the most memorable early Eulerian experiments (those measuring flow past a fixed point) was conducted between 1884 and 1890 by U.S. Navy Lieutenant John Elliot Pillsbury. He figured out a way to anchor his small steamship *Blake* in the teeth of the Gulf Stream in fifteen hundred feet of rushing ocean water. Using a mechanical current meter of his own design, he measured "sections," that is, separate points in a picket-fence line, across the Florida Straits and off Cape Hatteras, as well as flow between the Windward Islands in the Caribbean. His work was incredibly meticulous, devoting eleven hundred hours to measuring ("occupying") just the section between Key Largo, Florida, and Gun Cay in the Bahamas. The James Cook of oceanography, Henry Stommel, wrote that Pillsbury's "investigations stand out during the entire history of the exploration of the Gulf Stream as examples of what a conscientious oceanographic survey should be." And during his painstaking work, he fell in love with his subject: "In a vessel floating on the Gulf Stream one sees nothing of the current . . . but anchored in its depths far out of sight of land, and to see the mighty torrent rushing past as a speed of miles per hour, day after day . . . one begins to think that all the wonders of the earth combined can not equal this one river in the ocean." However, with all possible respect for his diligence and seamanship, this was not a practical application of the Eulerian method. For each point in a section, Pillsbury had to anchor the ship, take his measurements, then retrieve about a mile of anchor cable, proceed to the next point and repeat the grueling and dangerous procedure.

Like its Lagrangian counterpart, a practical application of the Eulerian method requires an electronic current meter that can be left behind to do its work, not only measuring the current passing, but also recording and storing that data for later retrieval. Today's sleek, miniaturized current meters can be left in the water almost permanently if the research vessel retrieves them once a year to download their data and replace their batteries. If a single current meter can measure the current's velocity at a single point, then an array of them strung on a mooring cable anchored to the bottom and held vertically by a floatation device at or near the surface can provide a full-depth profile of the ocean's dynamic structure at that particular location. Likewise, a string of moorings festooned with current meters set athwart the current under consideration can deliver extensive knowledge about that section of ocean across both the horizontal and vertical fields.

Electronic current meters capable of recording and storing data over long periods of time speak to one of the inherent problems faced by the ocean scientist: that currents vary both in velocity and direction over all scales of time and space. MIT oceanographer Carl Wunsch put the problem this way:

Measurements made from a ship cannot be made as fast as the ocean changes . . . [A] modern oceanographic vessel moves no faster than a rather sluggish bicyclist (10 to 14 knots). At this pace, it takes a ship two or more months to cross the Pacific Ocean, stopping along the way to observe, and the ocean system changes many times during that time. Furthermore, with this strategy only one line across the ocean is measured, leaving oceanographers with little or no idea what was happening even 50 kilometers from where they made their observations. (*Oceanus*, Spring, 1992)

Fluctuations in the forces acting on oceans such as winds, tides, air temperatures, even slight oscillations in Earth's orbit reverberate across the surface and in the interior of the ocean, some immediately and others in delayed response. Scientists can't measure any aspect of ocean motion just once and expect to have nailed it for all time, since a week later it will likely be behaving differently. Are we observing the mean flow or a temporal variation? Is there such a thing, really, as mean flow, or only a range of chaotic variations? Only constant measurement can tell.

Also, scientists in many other fields have the luxury of *seeing* their subjects, if with optical aid, but oceanographers can see only the surface of theirs, literally and figuratively. Saltwater covers 70.8 percent of the globe, over 500 million square miles, and over half of that lies below 10,000 feet. The *average* depth of the Atlantic is 12,612 feet, while the average height of dry land is only 2,756 feet. Mount Everest could disappear in the deepest water, the Mariana Trench, leaving 7,126 feet between the mountain peak and the surface. Clearly, the identity of the ocean could not be gleaned by remaining on the surface. Yet, utterly opaque, the deep ocean cannot be observed directly.

Oceanography is a young science because it could not mature, given "the brute difficulty of observing the oceans," until the advent of modern solid-state electronics applied to both Lagrangian and Eulerian devices, surrogates for human senses. None was available before World War II, and many, including fast computers and Earth-observing satellites, did not come into their own until the 1980s. I'm not sure we can legitimately say that oceanography is the most technology-dependent of sciences, but I would hazard to say that it could not have become a science in the modern understanding of the word without the advanced technology first available to the generation of oceanographers only now approaching retirement age. Here is a brief sample:

New Eulerian devices such as the Acoustic Doppler Current Profiler and the Inverted Echo Sounder use pulses of sound to calculate water temperature and current velocity. Various kinds of "autonomous Lagrangian drifters" (designated SOFAR, RAFOS, and S-PALACE) can be ballasted to "float" at any depth and at fixed intervals to climb to the surface and report their data and their precise positions to satellites that then transmit the data back to shoreside scientists' computers in near real time. Satellites also solved the old navigation problem in a single swoop with the Global Positioning System. Not long ago I bought a handheld GPS receiver about the size of a cell phone powered by two AA batteries for $149, and it can tell me where it is anywhere on the globe with a range of accuracy about the size of a tennis court. I took its accuracy and its price entirely for granted. But the technology, one of the most important developments in the history of ocean science, has only been around since the early 1980s.

Chemical oceanographers have found their own variations on the Lagrangian method. By analyzing, for instance, the dissolved oxygen content of water samples taken from a known location and depth, chemists can deduce the "age" of a water mass. *Age* refers to the length of time since the water was last on the surface, that is, when it was last exposed to the atmosphere, the only source of oxygen. I met chemists aboard the research vessels *Oceanus* and *Ronald Brown* who were sampling chlorofluorocarbons (CFCs) not to understand the destructive extent of our pollution, but to use it as a "tracer" to follow the water. CFCs are useful tracers because they don't exist in nature, and since the 1992 amendments to the Montreal Protocol banning production, no new CFCs have been produced, but the old finite quantity still circles the globe with ocean chemists following its course. Also, unlike oxygen, CFCs are not used by marine organisms such as plankton and fish, and can therefore be more accurately isolated as tracers. Similarly, tritium blasted into the atmosphere during the H-bomb tests of the 1960s serves as an effective ocean-current tracer.

The "glider," among the newest and perhaps sexiest ocean-measuring device is a member of the genre of instruments called Autonomous Underwater Vehicles. Another device to carry oceanographic sensors into the depths, the glider, which looks like a double-ended torpedo with tail fins and a set of wings, is different from the others in that it's self-propelled. It "flies" forward through the water not by means of a motor and propeller or any other conventional means, but by exploiting with elegant simplicity the principle of buoyancy. Changes in its buoyancy, accomplished by pumping about four cups of mineral oil back and forth between two bladders, one inside the aluminum hull and the other outside, causes it to dive, swoop, and glide through the water. A glider named *Spray*, manufactured by the Webb Research Company and designed by Breck Owens (WHOI), Russ Davis, and Jeff Sherman (Scripps) has recently made an historic submerged passage through the Gulf Stream. Launched on September 11, 2004, in the waters south of Nantucket, *Spray* covered about twelve miles a day on a rollercoaster course between the surface and 3,300 feet, collecting temperature, salinity, and pressure data along the way. Every seven hours during the trip, *Spray* came to the surface, cocked one wing to the sky, and transmitted its position via Iridium phone to shore. Then, according to programmed instructions, it rolled and presented its other wingtip containing the ocean sensors and transmitted that data. Though *Spray* had been overwhelmed by the Gulf Stream current and swept north of the desired course, this didn't damage the trip. When next she came to the surface, Owens and associates simply reprogrammed her course and sent her on her way again. This ability to talk to the vehicle en route, collect the data in near real time, and change course if desired constitutes an enormous stride forward.

The march of technology, so essential to measuring the ocean, has changed both the practice and the culture of oceanography. "Henry Melson Stommel, the most original and important physical oceanographer of all time," wrote his friend and former graduate student Carl Wunsch, "entered oceanography [1944] when the field still had . . . the atmosphere of an avocation for wealthy amateurs who used their own yachts for research; he left it at a time [1992] when it had been transformed into a modern branch of science, often driven by the perceived needs of national security, and of global, organized, highly expensive programs requiring massive government funding. . . . He sometimes recognized, but often did not, that his intellect was driving him and the study of the ocean in one direction—toward the use of modern sophisticated instrumentation and computers and to the organization of giant field programs—while his heart clearly lay with the science of his youth, which involved intense work at sea with gifted amateurs and crusty old fishermen using primitive instruments made by clever local machinists and craftsmen." During the span of that single, great career, oceanography attained maturity, as we shall see.

One might be excused for thinking that, given all their gee-whiz technology capable of measuring the ocean from so many directions, both Lagrangian and Eulerian, oceanographers have answered all the important questions about where the water goes and how the ocean works. They've learned a lot since Stommel arrived at WHOI, and more since his death. But every oceanographer I speak with said the same thing: We need more measurements over a longer period of time. The gear is brilliant, so are the people crafting and using it, but the ocean is so vast in space and time, so variable, that their best efforts have left gaps that only time and money will fill.

Chapter 4

THE GEOGRAPHY OF MOTION

M otion is as intrinsic to oceans as wetness. Perpetual motion is the fundamental difference between life on land and life at sea. Waves are the most readily apparent form of ocean motion, defining the quality of life at sea (from a cradle endlessly rocking to bestial upheaval), but of course you don't have to leave the land to observe waves. They can be seen (if not experienced) by those Melville called "water gazers," who find peace and perspective watching trains of breakers come ashore. Except for tsunamis, ocean waves are caused by wind; when the wind stops, the waves relax, and, after a time, disappear.

Tides are another form of ocean motion observable from land. In the rhythmic rise and fall of the tides, poets have posited metaphorical reflections of mortality—death comes typically on the ebb tide, rebirth with the flood. No doubt in Neolithic times coastal cultures, now gone, noticed that when the Moon was full and when it was new, the high tide was higher and the low tide lower than during other phases of the Moon. No one pegged the causal relationship between the Moon and tides until Isaac Newton (born 1624, the year Galileo died) came along to displace the old Aristotelian world order with a new organizing principle: "universal gravitation." Tides, he demonstrated, are caused by the gravitational attraction of the Sun and the Moon, mostly the Moon.

But when Otis Redding sang "Sittin' on the dock of the bay/ Watchin' the tide roll away," he was observing the *apparent* motion of water in the bay. Tides don't exactly roll in and roll out. Nor do they literally rise and fall. Instead, the Moon draws up two bulges of water, one extending toward the Moon, the other, on the opposite side of Earth, away from the Moon. Alternating tides result not from the movement of the bulges themselves—they remain stationary—but from the movement of Earth rotating beneath them. Contrary also to popular belief, there are tides in those "tideless" seas such as the Mediterranean and the Baltic. There are "tides" in lakes and ponds and in fishbowls. Tides undulate in long waves through the depths of the oceans. The tug of the Moon even affects dry land, the so-called solid-body tide, which produces a slight but measurable bulge in the very rocks of Earth's crust.

If Otis Redding hung around on the dock for a few hours, he observed that the ebb turned around and rolled back in. That's why the apparent horizontal movements of water associated with tides are called periodic currents. And the reason those newspaper tide tables can be so precise about their periods—high tide in Portland at 12:23—is that astronomers know precisely the orbits of the celestial bodies tugging at the water. However, alert mariners keep a weather eye on local conditions. A stiff breeze blowing against the flood will retard its arrival and vice versa.

Out beyond the horizon where only mariners and oceanographers go, another sort of current flows through the surface of the sea. Descriptively, it's called an *ocean current*, but that's also a technical term. Ocean currents transport massive quantities of water over great distances in a single direction—permanently. Because they're permanent, ocean currents have acquired names that take capital letters. Of these, the Gulf Stream is the most thoroughly studied and the only one most everyone can name. But there are many others, including, randomly: North Equatorial, Kuroshio, Agulhas, East Australian, Antilles, Canaries, and North Atlantic. All are surface currents, though some, like the Gulf Stream, exert themselves thousands of meters down. Some ocean currents transport warm water, others cold. Ocean currents exert an influence on regional climate disproportionate to their depth because, at the surface, they are in contact with the atmosphere. To put it only slightly unscientifically, warm currents warm the air, and cold currents chill it. Air—in the form of wind—influences local climate by carrying the warmth (or the chill) it received from the water onto the land.

There is no such thing in any ocean as a singleton current flowing from here to there and ending, the way a river ends at its mouth. All ocean currents are melded components of large, basin-wide circulatory systems called *gyres*. In plain English, gyre refers to a circle in either form or motion. In that sense, those capitalized names don't indicate separate currents with distinct origins and endings, but arcs of a unified circle. Among the first things the neophyte notices after a short dip into geophysics is that nature loves things that spiral, rotate, whorl, orbit, and gyre. Circles have no beginning, no end, and circles don't use up mass or energy, but conserve both, and that's what nature likes about them. The oceans are full of circles, scientists learned in the 1970s, energetic swirls and eddies of all sizes from tens to hundreds of miles in diameter. Some are short lived, lasting for weeks or months, while others spin on for years. Strictly speaking, the currents that comprise the gyres temporarily waver and vary in direction and velocity, but we can still call them permanent features in all oceans.

The Gulf Stream is an influential member of the North Atlantic Subtropical Gyre. There is a subtropical gyre in the South Atlantic as well, another in the Indian Ocean, two more in the North Pacific and South Pacific. "Subtropical" refers to their locations, in the midlatitudes, twin belts (between about 25 and 45 degrees) around the midsection of both hemispheres where most of the world's population lives. Recognizing their universality, let's use the North Atlantic

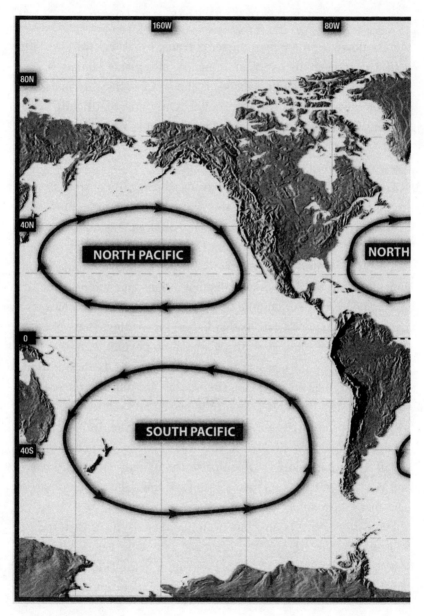

Subtropical Gyres of the world

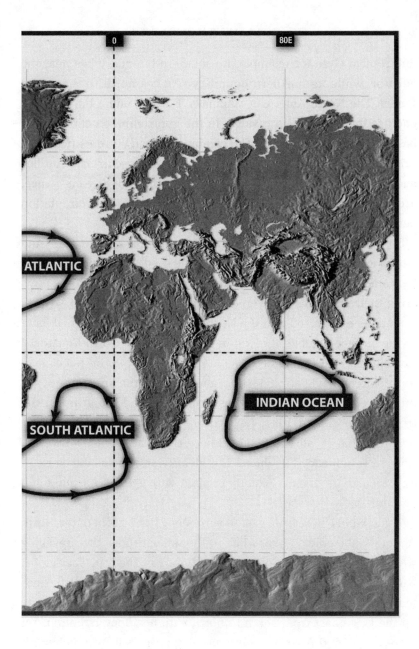

Subtropical Gyre for example. Its southern boundary lies near the equator, while its northern boundary reaches north to the Grand Banks. The North American landmass, Europe, and a bit of Africa enclose its basin on both sides. In the approximate center of the basin lies the Sargasso Sea. The combined ocean currents that comprise the gyre—the North Equatorial and Canary currents, Antilles and North Atlantic Currents, and of course the Gulf Stream—wheel around the Sargasso Sea in a clockwise motion. The circulation never stops. The gyre has attained a "steady state."

So what fuels all this motion? And why is it rotary motion? And why is it steady? Centuries before anyone used *ocean* and *science* in the same sentence, sailors had concluded that wind, the force powering their ships, also powered the currents. On his Third Voyage, Columbus recognized that the Northeast Trade Wind attached itself to the surface, hauling it along in the form of the North Equatorial Current (though the name came along later). Explorer, buccaneer, fourth circumnavigator in history, and arguably the originator of sea literature, William Dampier, observed the same thing out in the tropical Pacific. In 1691, he wrote, "Tis generally observed by Seamen, that in all the Places where the Trade-winds blow, the Current is influenced by them." But identifying wind as the cause of ocean currents doesn't exactly explain why gyres go around and around.

Trade Winds blow from east to west along the bottom of the North Atlantic Subtropical Gyre, while in the mid-latitudes the prevailing westerlies blow in the opposite direction over the top. That global wind pattern induces a certain clockwise torque or twist to the system. But what about the Gulf Stream? Ostentatiously blue, it blasts up the U.S. coast from south to north with headlong intention. Yet there is no wind from the south; nothing propels it from behind. If wind causes ocean currents, then is the Gulf Stream somehow an exception to the rule?

The discovery of the sea has taken the formal path of scientific inquiry—gather data and then, when the data seem sufficient, explain it in theory form. But the very vastness of the sea, the difficulty and expense of collecting data invited early scientists to skip right to the theory part. Some were better than others, but none was complete. Only two years after Ponce discovered the Gulf Stream, the chronicler Peter Martyr thought he had an explanation. What happened was that the Trade Winds pushed the North Equatorial Current westward across the Atlantic where it bumped into solid land. This deflected the current northward as the Gulf Stream. At a certain point, coming under the jurisdiction of the west-wind belt, it turned eastward toward Europe. But if the Gulf Stream was a deflection of the North Equatorial Current, why did the Gulf Stream flow more than twice as fast as the North Equatorial Current? Martyr had nothing to say about that, but he had included a solid principle—that the course of an ocean current is shaped by the continents that bound its ocean.

Benjamin Franklin tried his hand at explaining the Gulf Stream in a 1765 letter to a French scientist, proposing that when the wind-driven North Equatorial Current collided with North America, a pile of water stacked up. Therefore, the water level on the Florida coast was higher than that at Cape Hatteras, and the Gulf Stream flowed so fast because it was going downhill. That, too, proved incorrect. If wind didn't force it to flow so fast and narrow up the coast, then there had to be some other estimable force acting on the ocean. Not even the great polymath could have figured that out given the level of ocean knowledge available in the eighteenth century.

It turned out to be *Earth*, more specifically Earth's ceaseless rotation. We've all known since childhood that night turns to day and back again because Earth rotates as it orbits the sun, but we still talk in terms of sunrise and sunset, not rotation. The fact is we're going around and around Earth's axis at spectacular velocity. However, we're not all going around at the *same* velocity due to the physics of rotating spheres. A person standing anywhere along the latitude of Cape Farewell at the southern tip of Greenland, about 60 degrees North, is hurtling eastward at five hundred miles per hour. At 30 degrees North latitude (that of St. Augustine, Florida, on this side of the Atlantic—Agadir, Morocco, on the other side), people and things are spinning at 866 mph. Those standing on the equator are hurtling eastward at a solid one thousand miles per hour. To put it unscientifically, since Earth is fatter at the equator, it has to go around faster in order to keep up with the skinnier parts to the north and south.

Only subterranean burrowers could survive on a planet blasted constantly by one-thousand-mile-an-hour winds, but we don't feel the speed, as when we stick our hand out the window of a moving car, because we're not passing *through* the air as Earth rotates. The atmosphere is moving right along with us. For things coupled solidly to Earth's crust such as mountains and things coupled firmly to the ground by gravity, rotation is largely irrelevant. But upon things less solidly attached, such as air and water moving over its surface, the effect of this massive body in swift rotation is dramatic.

In 1836, the French mathematician Gaspard Coriolis calculated mathematically the influence of Earth's rotation on objects moving over its surface. This whole business of the "Coriolis effect" is dizzyingly complex, if you do it justice, requiring lofty math and a grasp of abstruse principles such as the conservation of angular momentum, but we don't need to get into that. This, suffice it to say for our ocean purposes, was Coriolis's great contribution: When objects move either toward the equator or away from the equator, their paths are apparently bent to the right in the Northern Hemisphere and to the left in the Southern Hemisphere due to Earth's rotation. Coriolis, talking about objects moving above the surface of Earth such as artillery shells, had little to say about the effect on winds and ocean currents, but the implications were clear to William Ferrell, a painfully shy West Virginia schoolteacher who happened to be a mathematical genius.

In 1856, he applied Coriolis's principles to ocean motion for the first time, and the results would have propelled this retiring fellow to stardom, but the work was little noticed at the time. The crux of his theory held that, when a fluid—air or water—flows great distances over Earth's surface, Coriolis becomes an actual force that tugs the flow to the right (looking downstream) in the Northern Hemisphere, and to the left in the Southern Hemisphere. A flow of water bent constantly to the right will eventually form a circle and rotate clockwise: the North Atlantic Subtropical Gyre. Again, the same principle obtains in the other hemisphere, where currents bending leftward produce gyres rotating counterclockwise.

At-sea investigators began to notice a peculiar thing about this gyre. It wasn't a symmetrical circle. On the Europe side, the south-flowing Canary Current was so broad and sluggish you could hardly find it. But on the west side, the Gulf Stream sprinted north in a narrow jet no one could miss. If the gyre was a unified system of currents driven by wind and shaped by the Coriolis effect, why was the west side so different from the east side? Gradually, observers noticed that this peculiarity is shared by subtropical gyres in every ocean. All have a western boundary current, an eastern boundary current, and two transverse currents, north and south, linking the circle. And in each the eastern boundary currents are broad, diffuse, and sluggish, while their counterparts in the west, such as the Gulf Stream in the North Atlantic and the Kuroshio Current in the North Pacific, are narrow, tightly packed, and very fast. But, as always, there is a big difference between observing the characteristics of a thing and understanding what caused those characteristics.

"The coldest winter I ever spent was one summer in San Francisco," quipped Mark Twain. The city isn't that far north, on the same latitude as Washington, D.C., where no one ever shivered in summertime. Washington's climate is determined by continental conditions and to a lesser extent by its heritage as a swamp. Situated on the east side of the North Pacific Subtropical Gyre, San Francisco's climate is determined by the ocean. That gyre, like its kin in the North Atlantic—both circulating clockwise—carries warm water northward up the western boundary and over the top of the gyre. It then brings cool water down the eastern boundary. The California Current, flowing down from higher latitudes, conducts cold water south along the coast for hundreds of miles.

I knew a guy who, having spent a decade commercial fishing out of Sitka in Southeast Alaska, used to entertain us with stories about the increasingly deleterious effects of incessant rain (and alcohol) seeping into the psyches of the locals as winter wore on. Some who couldn't take it fled to the lower forty-eight, while others who couldn't take it stayed on anyway, turning surly, tense, too dangerous to associate with. But look at Sitka's position up there at 58 degrees North latitude. By geographic rights, the whole region should be choked half to death by ice from Halloween to Memorial Day. Sitka's precipitation remains in liquid form for the same reason that palm trees survive in Cornwall, and that Norway remains ice-free in winter: The Kuroshio Current is doing for Southeast Alaska what the Gulf Stream system is doing for Western Europe, shipping heat over the top of the gyre and in the process making human habitation possible, if soggy, along six hundred miles of coast between Vancouver Island and Yakutat. But it is not warm water per se that warms and moistens the British Isles and Southeast Alaska. Instead, the North Atlantic Current offshoot and a rough counterpart (the Kuroshio extension) in the North Pacific gives up its heat to the atmosphere, and the west winds carry it onto the respective continents, bringing warm, moist maritime climates instead of the ice-choked winters typical to other places at the same latitudes.

In a 1993 paper published by the American Geophysical Union, William Schmitz and Michael McCartney from Woods Hole Oceanographic Institution wrote, "Where does the water come from, where does it go, and what happens along its path? Those seemingly simple questions about the oceans' (semi-) permanent circulations are at the heart of physical oceanography." The esoteric-sounding principles of ocean science "come ashore" in the form of weather and climate, as we'll see.

Chapter 5

WIND ON THE WATER

Winds—moving air—provoke ocean currents. Wind attaches itself to the surface and causes water to move. In fact, the fancy technical term for wind is *atmospheric forcing*. But as my oceanographer friends are wont to remind me, in nature, wind and the rest of the elemental forces aren't so simple once they get together and start moving. So it'll be useful later to go back a step now and look at what causes wind: the Sun.

Incoming solar radiation heats Earth's surface without significantly warming the air on the way down. Our atmosphere receives its warmth indirectly as both the solid and watery parts of Earth's surface reradiate heat back upward. Technically this is because of the difference between the short wavelengths of the Sun's direct rays and the long wavelengths of its reflected rays. The former pass straight through the air, but the longer reflected rays cannot escape the atmosphere, and this of course is the famous "greenhouse effect," a perfectly natural and desirable result—in moderation. Wind exists not exactly because the Sun heats the Earth, but because it does so *unevenly*. Oceans, for instance, retain vast quantities of heat, while land heats up and cools off very quickly, as anyone who has gone camping in a desert quickly notices. So we can say that the quantity of solar energy reaching Earth varies routinely on a daily basis simply because Earth rotates on its axis.

Solar energy also varies annually because Earth's axis of rotation is skewed 23.5 degrees off the vertical. During the northern summer, Earth tilts its Northern Hemisphere toward the Sun, and during the summer solstice, around June 21, the Sun reaches its most northerly point in the sky, directly overhead at noon along the Tropic of Cancer, 23.5 degrees North latitude. In northern winter, Earth tilts away from the Sun, and at the winter solstice, about December 22, the Sun reaches its southernmost point over the Tropic of Capricorn, 23.5 degrees South latitude. And this of course is why, from our northern perspective, the seasons are "reversed" in the Southern Hemisphere.

Since in nature's physical systems, heat and pressure are siblings, any disparity in temperature, daily or seasonal, local or global, creates a commensurate disparity in pressure. All wind, from soft afternoon zephyrs at the beach to category-five hurricanes, originates with the "downhill" flow of air from zones of high pressure toward zones of low pressure. To meteorologists, the slope down which air flows is known as the *horizontal pressure gradient*.

Oceanographers later borrowed the phrase once they recognized that water and air behave the same way—they flow—when pressure gradients are present in the system, but let's stick with wind in order to get to water. When the Sun heats a portion of Earth's surface, hot air rises, leaving behind a region of low pressure, a sort of vacuum. Rankled, nature seeks to fill the vacuum to redress the atmospheric imbalance by drawing in cooler air from wherever it's available. The process goes on constantly. We call it weather.

I do most of my sailboat racing on Long Island Sound, like a lot of others along its populous shores, and we're to be pitied for that, at least a little bit. A stable mass of air, the Bermuda High, parks over us in summer, and this brings depressing stability, from a sailor's viewpoint, to the atmosphere. There is little or no disparity in pressure, no gradient, so there can be no breeze. Sailboats drift, rolling inelegantly in wakes from passing powerboats. Morale plummets. Our only hope for motive power on a typical day in August lies to the south, with Long Island itself. By mid-afternoon, the pavements, twelve-lane expressways, mega-malls and Cineplex parking lots baking in the sun have generated a thermal hole in the atmosphere. The heated air surges skyward, leaving behind low pressure, and cooler air is drawn in to redress the imbalance. In this case, the most readily available cool air is situated over the ocean, lying to the south of Long Island, and the resulting flow of air is, therefore, referred to as the "sea breeze." Old salts on the Sound say that the sea breeze was never so powerful when they were young as it is today, which they attribute to all the development on Long Island. They reckon that on a summer afternoon the endless concrete creates an unnaturally deep pressure gradient, resulting in heavier wind.

The same sort of process happens on a global scale. Earth is girded along the equator and out several hundred miles in either direction by a belt of windlessness, the famous doldrums, or technically the Intertropical Convergence Zone. The reason there is no wind in the doldrums is not for lack of movement in the atmosphere, but for the direction of the movement—straight up. That was not a useful wind to the explorers who, centuries before anyone understood nature's mechanics, named the doldrums after bad sailing experiences (the root of the word means "dull"). As every school kid knows, hot air rises, and from that homely principle, a giant, stable, global wind system results.

All that hot air rising from the equatorial regions does not bleed off into space due to its own gravity; if it did, our Earth would be nothing but a dead rock in orbit. Our atmosphere is a "stratified fluid," layered, that is, by temperature and pressure. For instance, half of all the atmosphere's water lies below three kilometers, while half its total mass lies below eight kilometers above Earth's surface. We can say for our purposes that the atmosphere has a "ceiling," about ten kilometers high at the top of the troposphere layer that, in effect, halts the rising equatorial air. (Technically, the troposphere exists because, among other reasons, ozone absorbs sunlight, which warms the air directly, creating an inversion, the tropopause, but we can still think of this as a ceiling.) Since the laws of nature require unequivocally that mass must be conserved, the rising column of hot equatorial air has to go somewhere else when it bumps up against the "ceiling." It splits and spreads off in opposite directions, to the north in the Northern Hemisphere, southward in the other hemisphere. Flowing horizontally at high altitude along the ceiling, the air masses cool, grow dense, literally heavier. The hot, low-pressure air that ascended over the equator, having been cooled at altitude, subsides back toward Earth's surface somewhere around 30 degrees latitude, creating vast zones of high pressure. Now only one thing can happen: High-pressure air rushes back, down a very steep horizontal pressure gradient, toward the equator. And since the equator never cools off, since hot air constantly rises, spreads, cools, sinks, and speeds back *on the surface* toward the equator, the circle remains unbroken. Mass is conserved. The surface component of that vertical circle is wind, but of a very special sort: the Trade Winds.

Sailors named them Trade Winds, though no one knows just when, probably because, by blowing unceasingly, they facilitated the movement of goods across oceans, making a lot of (mostly European) merchants and pirates very wealthy. There are two Trade Wind belts, one in either hemisphere, the result of that rising equatorial air splitting when it encounters the ceiling and spreading north and south. The difference is that in the Northern Hemisphere, the Trade Winds blow from the northeast, and in the Southern Hemisphere from the southeast. Here again, maybe especially here, Monsieur Coriolis and his effect re-enter the scene:

One would think that if wind blows from high-pressure regions back to the low-pressure zone at the equator, then in the Northern Hemisphere, the Trade Winds should come from the north and vice versa in the Southern Hemisphere. They would do just that—if Earth

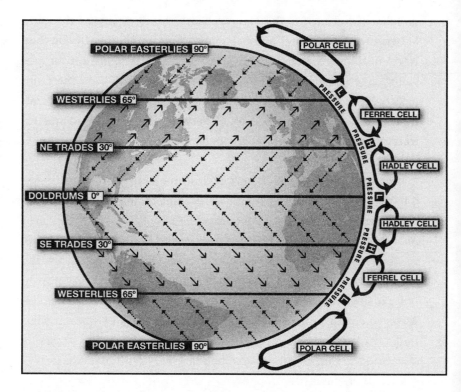

Air Pressure Distribution and Resulting Global Wind Problems

did not rotate. Because it does rotate, the flow of wind is bent to the right in the Northern Hemisphere. A north wind when bent to the right becomes a northeast wind, the Northeast Trade Winds; and again the mirror image appears in the Southern Hemisphere where south winds bent to the left become southeast winds.

This circulatory system as a whole, the rising air at the equator and the return flow in form of Trade Winds, is known as the Hadley cell. But the Hadley cell accounts only for the circulation in the lower latitudes, about 1,800 miles on either side of the equator. The rest of Earth's broad atmospheric circulation happens in a similar cellular structure for the same reason, the disparity of pressure between one place and another due to uneven heating by the Sun. North of Hadley's there is the Ferrel cell, which accounts for the prevailing west winds up in the mid latitudes. North of that, the Polar cells behave the same way, producing east winds in the very high latitudes. And the convergence zones between the cells are characterized by fluky light and variable winds, the sort of places sailors still avoid.

It can be made to sound very neat, three closed circulatory systems producing wind belts with intervening zones of calms. But in the real world, the three-cell model of the atmosphere is neither neat nor closed. Each cell constantly interacts with, influences, and melds with its neighbor so thoroughly that meteorologists view the model as an idealization. Still we can make this generalization without causing the pros to wince: Wind results when the atmosphere seeks to equalize disparities in pressure provoked by uneven solar radiation. But balance can never be sustained because air is unstable stuff and the Sun continues to shine unevenly on Earth. That's why our weather changes so rapidly.

Getting back to seawater, scientists talk about the atmosphere and the ocean as a "coupled system." The interaction happens on multiple, complex levels not entirely understood, but one type of coupling occurs when wind blows over the ocean. A small portion of wind energy, about three percent, is imparted via friction to the water. This is technically called "wind stress." Even a light breeze that barely riffles the surface moves water, but not much. Friction between wind and water—"viscosity"—is happening in that case on a molecule-to-molecule level, not nearly enough to set an ocean current in motion. To transport whole parcels of water, the wind needs to blow hard enough and long enough to set up waves. Waves act as a gear-like mechanism projecting the wind's friction hundreds of meters beneath the surface. Oceanographers call this "eddy viscosity."

The power to produce waves depends on three aspects of wind: its velocity, its duration, and the distance it blows over open water—its "fetch." If it blows across hundreds of miles of water and if its duration is nearly constant, then the wind doesn't need to blow all that hard to drag large quantities of water along with it. The Trade Winds in both hemispheres, with a mean velocity of around 25 knots, have been blowing since the infant Earth cooled and settled into its present orbit. The Northeast Trades, for instance, have been "pushing" the North Equatorial Current westward across the North Atlantic since the drifting tectonic plates assumed their present positions about 150 million years ago. So we can say that when wind blows across oceans, friction couples with the water and pushes it downwind, right? Well, no, it's not quite that simple.

A theme quickly emerged in conversations ashore and at sea with my generous oceanographer friends. I remember "it's not that simple" stated on the rolling transom of the NOAA ship *Ronald H. Brown* by Jochem Marotzke, another time in rougher weather by Molly Baringer, and before that, on an earlier trip by Chris Meinen and Lisa Beal. It recurred in late-night talks with Carlos Fonseca in the *Brown*'s computer lab, and the next day in the main lab with Stuart Cunningham. Tony Sturges wrote it in various iterations in response to my technical questions. *It's Not That Simple* came to stand as a sort of motto of physical oceanography. Nothing in the dynamics of the ocean is simple, not in the deep nor at the surface. And wind does not push water in the same direction as the wind. This fact was not firmly understood until the early years of the twentieth century. A Norwegian named Fridtjof Nansen took the first step toward explaining what really happens to water when wind blows over it.

Chapter 6

THE HILL IN THE OCEAN

M y heroes have always been marine explorers. Perhaps no more than aficionados of any activity, students of exploration tend to build pantheons. Who was the greatest of them all? Everyone would agree on that. James Cook. He's in a pantheon of one. Among mortals, Roald Amundsen has to come next. He was the first to navigate the Northwest Passage and to reach the South Pole. Cook then Amundsen—we all pretty much agree on that. In my view, Amundsen's role model Fridtjof Nansen comes next.

By 1890, Nansen, not yet thirty, was growing melancholy, brooding that his greatest accomplishments were already behind him. A pioneer in marine biology, in skiing, and in Arctic exploration, Nansen embodied a refreshed Nordic ideal: the intellectual as a man of action in wild nature, the scientific Viking—and he was already world famous for his first-ever crossing of the Greenland Ice Cap, on skis, a feat judged impossible at the time. Tall and handsome, blond, blue-eyed, not only did Nansen look and act the part of the romantic explorer-hero, his timing was ideal. Not much of international note had happened in Norway since Viking times, but now with a list of world-class artists including Ibsen and Grieg, and with Nansen as the symbol of her accomplishments and her potential, Norway meant to take her place as a modern European nation. Furthermore, talk of Norwegian independence (from Sweden) was in the crisp air. Though Nansen was keenly aware of his symbolic importance and responsibility to the new nationalism, he wanted more for himself.

The ice cap crossing three years behind him, he fixed his melancholic gaze (Nansen and Ingmar Bergman would have understood each other) on the North Pole.

There was a stubborn myth still kicking around geographical circles in the late 1800s of an ice-free Polar Sea containing significant land, perhaps even another continent. No one had been up there, and as the history of exploration had shown time and again, blanks on the map inevitably filled with myth. Nansen didn't buy it. There was no land in the Arctic Ocean, only water, and it was perpetually frozen. Further, like any other ocean, the Arctic contained currents, and the floating ice flowed along with them. There was empirical evidence to support Nansen's view of a frozen yet dynamic Polar Sea. Drift objects—a native kayak, tree trunks, and supposedly a corpse—from Siberia turning up in Scandinavian waters suggested the existence of an east-setting current. But the best evidence of a trans-Arctic current was wreckage of the American exploration vessel *Jeanette*, which had been trapped in the ice near the Bering Strait (between Alaska and Russia) and crushed during an 1879 attempt to reach the North Pole. Almost everyone on this ill-equipped, poorly planned, and fecklessly executed expedition starved to death on the Siberian coast after abandoning the *Jeanette*, but her bones drifted on for three thousand miles across the Arctic Ocean and came to rest in the pack ice on the east coast of Greenland. Maybe, surmised Nansen, she had drifted right over the Pole. And that's what he decided to do.

Nansen explained his idea in a letter to Baron Oscar Dickson, a wealthy Swede who had bankrolled the Greenland expedition: "My plan is to build a ship as small and strong as possible . . . and of such a construction that it could not easily be crushed by the ice . . . With this vessel, we go through the Bering Strait . . . sail in ice-free water as far as possible, then go into the ice until we are beset [and] drift towards the Pole." Rather than frontally assault the ice as if it were Napoleon's fleet as the British Navy had been doing—and dying in droves—Nansen meant to travel in tune with the ice, enlisting assistance from the pack. Uncomfortable with a Swede funding their hero, the Norwegian government paid for the design (by Colin Archer) and construction of Nansen's ship, the immortal *Fram*, "Forward" in Norwegian. She was a steam-assisted, heavily timbered schooner, 128 feet overall, with a radically shallow draft and round bottom, and she's still alive. To see her in her own museum in downtown Oslo was, for me, a sort of pilgrimage.

Fram sailed from Vardo on June 24, 1893, bound east over the top of Siberia to her starting point near the Bering Strait. They had a rough trip of it—shallow draft and a round bottom don't make for stable sea boats—but these fourteen Norwegians didn't feel pain like normal explorers. *Fram*, captained by Otto Sverdrup, entered the ice on September 21, 683 straight-line miles from the Pole. That Nansen is a boyhood hero of mine and that the details of his expedition are fantastic may not be enough reason to digress very far from the point—the effect of wind on oceans. But that Scandinavians, beginning with Nansen, would soon revolutionize the science of the sea, and that so much crucial to ocean dynamics and climate stability happens in northern seas might justify a short sail off course.

The *Fram* concept worked brilliantly; she rode the ice almost as if it were a dry dock. But when he recognized that *Fram* would not drift over the Pole as he'd hoped, Nansen, the scientist, gave way to Nansen, the ambitious fame-driven explorer. He decided to leave the ship, knowing he could never regain her, and make a dash for the Pole. Along with a hard case named Hijlmar Johnassen and fifteen dogs, he headed north toward immortality or a miserable death. Though they bested the record for "Farthest North" (86 degrees, 10 minutes North) of any human before them, they were brought to a halt 230 miles from the Pole. The dogs were fading, some of the weakest had already been killed to feed their fellows; and the ice conditions were dreadful: "Open leads . . . endless upheaval—and

this interminable lifting of the sledges over every single unevenness
. . . We are undeniably worn out" (Nansen's journal). Recognizing
that to press on would be suicidal, they retreated southward, heading for a little-known string of rocks called Franz Josef Land, that
"cold, congealed, frozen land," as its discoverer, Julius Payer had described it a few years earlier.

On the 132nd day after leaving *Fram*: "At last we have seen land!
Land! Oh wonderful word! After nearly two years, we can see something raise itself once more over that everlasting white line out there
on the horizon." But it took another miserable week to reach the
land. They dug a depression in the ice and gravel, roofed it over with
driftwood and polar bear hides, and there they hunkered for the winter gnawing on polar bear meat and anything else they could kill.
Elsewhere, Nansen once remarked that in Arctic exploration
Norwegians had a temperamental advantage over explorers from
elsewhere in that they could sit in silence on the same block of
ice for six months and be perfectly content. Still the winter went
hard on both men's psyches. Come spring, they headed south down
the chain of rocky islands. On June 17, 1896, Nansen heard dogs
barking—all of his own dogs were dead by then—and he ran toward
the sound. "Soon I heard a shout, saw a dark shape moving between
the hummocks. It was a dog, but further off there was another form.
It was a human being . . . We quickly approached each other, I waved
my hat, he did the same . . . I came closer, and then I . . . recognized
Mr. Jackson."

"Aren't you Nansen?" Jackson asked.

"Yes, I am Nansen."

"By Jove, I am devilish glad to see you." And as Jackson recorded,
"We shook hands again very heartily."

The history of Polar exploration is rich with moments of coincidence and irony; if it were fiction, we might roll our eyes at the bla-
tant implausibility. And here in this meeting in the frozen middle of

nowhere, we have one of those moments. Frederick George Jackson, as Roland Huntford, Nansen's definitive biographer put it, "was the quintessential Victorian adventurer." He had avidly applied to be part of the *Fram* crew, and when Nansen politely turned him down on the grounds that he was not Norwegian, Jackson funded his own expedition. His purpose was to prove the existence of the ice-free Polar Sea, the very myth that the *Fram* expedition had exploded, and so the only reason we remember Jackson's name is for his rescue of Fridtjof Nansen.

Nansen and the *Fram* arrived almost simultaneously back at Trondheim. Then on September 9, the reunited crew, with Nansen's wife Eva aboard, sailed up the fjord to Christiania (now Oslo) and a hysterical welcome, a "tumult of applause," he wrote. "In short," as his biographer put it, "Nansen mania had broken out, not only in Norway, but also worldwide." After the confetti had settled and the international paeans subsided, Nansen, as was his wont, fell into a funk. The fresh fame he'd longed for didn't really suit his temperament, and he was troubled by this other irony: *Fram* had drifted just nineteen miles short of Nansen's Farthest North. Had he stayed aboard, sparing himself the pain and the mortal risk of his trek, he still would have broken the record. Not only that, as Nansen saw it, he had squandered time and opportunity on the attempt at the Pole.

Nansen had never claimed that this was to be a scientific expedition, but now, ashore, he regretted that he'd not done more science, specifically oceanography. But he and his people had done quite a lot, actually. They had sounded the Arctic Ocean for the first time and discovered it to be much deeper than anyone had expected. They took hundreds of water samples using the latest device, and finding it wanting, Nansen and his engineer redesigned it onboard, coming up with the "Nansen Bottle," the forerunner of today's Niskin bottle. They also improved the thermometer in use at the time and with it produced the first full-depth temperature measurements in the Arctic. But perhaps most significantly, *Fram* and Nansen brought back to Norway the intellectual seeds of an ocean-science revolution.

The "trans-Arctic current" Nansen had theorized turned out to be weak. Wind, not current, had ushered *Fram* across the frozen ocean. Nansen had soon noticed that the ship was not drifting dead downwind. Instead, she was constantly diverging to the right of the wind direction. Nansen understood exactly what was going on: It was the Coriolis factor. As the estimable Roland Huntford writes in *Nansen*, not only did Nansen understand the deflective force exerted by Earth's rotation, he went further, into the theoretical, concluding that, as "the depth increased, each successive layer of water moving over the next . . . would produce increasing deviation until at a certain depth, the movement would be *against* the current on the surface." However, aware that he lacked the math to prove this creative hypothesis, he carried his raw observations to a professor at the University of Oslo, Vilhelm Bjerknes, who was then initiating the famous "Bergen School" of meteorology. Nansen probably knew about Bjerknes's 1898 paper "On Fundamental Hydrodynamical Principles and Special Application to the Mechanics of the Atmosphere and the Oceans." The professor dropped the matter on the desk of a bright young mathematician at the University of Lund called Vagn Walfrid Ekman (1874–1954) and said in effect, "Here, solve this."

It's remarkable that for a time on either side of 1900 the leading edge of oceanographic thinking issued from Scandinavia. On the face of it, this isn't totally surprising, these being sea-adapted people. Vikings, after all, settled briefly in the "New World" almost five hundred years before Columbus was born. And dependency for protein on fish would naturally encourage Danes, Swedes, and Norwegians to learn a thing or two about the ocean. But this Nordic burgeoning had as much to do with ocean theory as with ocean experience. Arguably for the first time, scientists were ready to figure out how in broad form oceans worked. And for the first time they had the intellectual tools to approach the question, a new combination of physics, mathematics, a dab of meteorology, and a new science called fluid dynamics.

The Scandinavian theorists started from the assumption that all oceans were alike in certain fundamental ways. Water is a fluid. What's more, it's a *stratified* fluid. A thin layer of warm water floats atop a much larger layer of cold, dense water to put it simply. (To put it less simply, we'd just add the other layers, but it would still be a stratified fluid.) Second, all oceans are subject to winds blowing over their surfaces. And third, all oceans are situated on a rapidly rotating Earth. It must follow, then, that all oceans behave in similar ways due to the laws of physics applied to water, wind, and rotation. That was part of the new point, to distill all ocean behavior down to the simplest actions expressible in simple equations without relinquishing too much of its reality. Ekman had the math and then some, yet he was no dry-shod academician. He went regularly to sea to collect his own data, notably on the *Armaur Hansen* expedition of 1930, when he credibly measured surface currents in the Arctic seas. But he'll be remembered forever for producing the first satisfactory theory of wind-driven surface currents and, for our purposes, the most relevant part of the theory is the *Ekman transport.*

To remove the variables that make oceans so complicated, Ekman conceived an abstract ocean intentionally different from the actual ocean. His ocean was infinitely wide; there were no continents to complicate the flow; and no bottom features influenced it. Then he blew an abstract wind over his pure ocean. What he meant to learn from this, what he hoped to describe mathematically, was how the water behaved under the influence of wind and nothing else. When his calculations were complete, Ekman demonstrated that water in a wind-driven surface current does not flow downwind. Instead, the net transport of water is directed *90 degrees to the right of the wind direction* in the Northern Hemisphere. This was consistent with Nansen's observations, but now it had numbers attached to it. It had been pinned down.

Another Norwegian, Harald Sverdrup (no relation to Nansen's Captain Otto) expanded the Ekman transport concept out to ocean-basin scale—out to the gyre. Sverdrup is best known as the director of the Scripps Institute of Oceanography. His tenure there, which began in 1936, was supposed to have been limited to three years, but the war interceded, his homeland was occupied by Nazis, and as it turned out he stayed on for a dozen years, guiding Scripps to its modern form as a premier ocean-science institute. He made seminal contributions to the development of oceanography during and after the war both at Scripps and back in Norway, where he returned in 1948, until his sudden death in 1957. But Sverdrup had attained his place as one of the founding fathers of physical oceanography before he left Norway.

To isolate his intended subject, the effect of wind and Coriolis on ocean currents, Ekman had removed everything from his ocean model except wind and water. Sverdrup reinserted continents, which "closed" the ocean basins. When a wind-driven current such as the North Equatorial Current encounters the continental land-mass, it must be deflected in one direction or another. In the North Atlantic, of course, it bends northward in the form of the Gulf Stream, but the same general fact applies to all the oceans, giving rise to gyres in all oceans. That was step one in the Sverdrup model; step two had to do with the effect of Ekman's rightward deflection.

In the North Atlantic Subtropical Gyre, for instance, the east wind at the bottom of the gyre transports water to the right, that is, north-ward. Meanwhile, the west wind blowing over the top of the gyre transports water 90 degrees to the right, or southward. The result of this, Sverdrup determined, is that water piles up in the center of the gyre—*creating a literal hill in the ocean*. Since the crest of the hill is only about three feet high, a sailor wouldn't notice in the vastness of oceanic scale that he was sailing uphill, but it had to be there, this literal bulge of water covering hundreds of square miles. The physics required it.

Meteorologists grasped the implications immediately. This hill was the equivalent of a high-pressure region in the atmosphere, and it cued the same kind of dynamics, the downhill flow from high pressure to low pressure. Any kind of hill implies slopes—gradients—and wherever there is a gradient there has to be flow. Now, in the hill, instead of wind, it was water that wanted to flow down the gradient slope. All things being equal, water would flow outward from the crest of the hill straight down the slopes, describing a wagon-wheel pattern. But things are not equal. Earth rotates. Rotation changes the path of the flow, whether of wind or water, by bending it to the right in the Northern Hemisphere. Therefore, the water flows *around* the hill in a spiral pattern turning the gyre clockwise. The Ekman transport feeds water into the hill, while gravity takes it away. Equilibrium is attained, a steady state. Meteorologists already had a term for this equilibrium—*geostrophy*, that balance between the pressure-gradient flow and Coriolis. Seeing the gyre as a huge oceanic high-pressure system causing (in the Northern Hemisphere) clockwise rotation was one of Sverdrup's great contributions.

It's worth repeating the significance of this, since it comes up all the time in oceanography. All oceans are stratified fluids on a rapidly rotating sphere, and all (except one, as we'll see) are contained in separate basins by continental land. Therefore, all oceans respond in the same way to the forces acting on their surfaces—by dragging up a hump of water about three feet high near the center of their basins. Because the forces of wind and Coriolis never cease, the hills are permanent features in all oceans. They are said to be in "geostrophic balance."

In 1905, Nansen and Bjorn Helland-Hansen, who contributed something of the higher math, composed the "geostrophic equation" to represent that balance between the horizontal pressure gradient and Coriolis. And what made this theory and the equations to describe it so liberating both intellectually and in practice is that it could be used to calculate the velocity of the resulting current without measuring it directly. It was called the "dynamic method," or more commonly the "geostrophic method." Still today every single oceanographic research expedition stops at regular intervals to measure the ocean's temperature, pressure, and salinity, for these are the raw-data observations necessary to calculate differences in water density from which the "geostrophic velocity" is calculated. The discovery of geostrophy, as fundamental to oceanography as plot to the novel, and the broader application of fluid mechanics filled a gaping hole in ocean thinking, the absence of which had prevented Franklin and investigators during the nineteenth century (Matthew Fontaine Maury and Alexander Bache, for instance) from understanding the Gulf Stream's behavior. Armed now with the principle of geostrophy, scientists could begin to explain how the ocean works.

The burgeoning of ocean science around 1900 in Scandinavia was not limited to physical oceanography. Michael Sars (Nansen's father-in-law), his son George Ossian Sars, and another Ekman named Gustav were pioneering modern marine biology, viewing for the first time the ocean and its living inhabitants from an ecological standpoint. But despite the brilliance of the Scandinavians, there remained still other holes in the fabric of ocean knowledge. Most glowingly, ignorance about the deep ocean was almost total. But, then, Ekman, Sverdrup, Helland-Hansen, and others never presumed to address anything but surface circulation. And there were still certain limitations to their explanation of surface circulation. To say that the geostrophic balance is a steady state should not imply that all gyres are always the same, that the ocean currents comprising the gyres all wheel around one direction or the other without variation in velocity or direction. Further, the new theories left unexplained that shared oddity of the gyres we mentioned earlier—they flow fast and narrow on the west, broadly and sluggishly on the east sides. Speaking of the North Atlantic, while remembering that similar western boundary currents flow in all gyres, the new theories could not explain why there was a Gulf Stream. The answer to that quandary had to wait another forty-eight years after the turn of the century during another flowering of ocean minds in a sleepy little Cape Cod town called Woods Hole. It had to wait for a giant by the name of Henry Stommel.

Chapter 7

HENRY STOMMEL

H enry Melson Stommel died on January 17, 1992, at age seventy-two. He had arrived at WHOI in 1944, as a conscientious objector to World War II, and except for a brief stint at Harvard, which he hated, and a longer, happier teaching experience at MIT, he spent the bulk of his forty-eight-year career at the Woods Hole Oceanographic Institution. Upon his death, WHOI published in a special issue of its house organ, *Oceanus* magazine, a memorial to Stommel by his friends and colleagues. Among them was Tony Sturges, professor emeritus of physical oceanography ("fizzo," he calls it) from Florida State University to whom Stommel was "a father figure." I was honored that Tony loaned me his personal copy of that memorial issue, and reading it, I felt moved and a tad envious of the writers who said that knowing Stommel had made their lives better. Most of the finest minds in modern fizzo wrote tributes, and all said generally the same thing in different words and anecdotes. Not only was Stommel a towering ocean genius in a pantheon by himself, but he was also a generous, humorous, modest, and altogether delightful human being. Henry Stommel was universally admired and universally loved, not a typical combination in our species. His should be a household name; yet to most of us who are not ocean scientists he is virtually unknown.

Born in Wilmington, Delaware, Stommel was raised in New York by his mother and two matronly aunts. He wrote this about his childhood: "It was a bedlam of hot-tempered, argumentative three generations of contentious women. There was no peace among them.

I know from whence the fierce demon within me that never lets me
rest comes from, and why I had to seek a private refuge in my own
mind and science" (*Autobiography*). He graduated from Yale in
1942, considered a career in the ministry, did a bit of graduate work
in astronomy, but lacked any experience at all in oceanography
when he arrived at WHOI. The field was different in those days before big science found its way to oceanography, or vice versa, as the
case may be. Maturing rapidly, oceanography was no longer a loose
amalgam of meteorology, physics, and mathematics, but a particular
branch of Earth science, and the technological side had taken giant
steps during World War II. Yet the ordering principles of the science
were still being invented or expanded by Stommel and many of the
people who wrote tributes to him. In the flexible atmosphere at
WHOI, without big money or intrusive bureaucracy, iconoclasts
flourished. None of its first-generation scientists had any formal
training in oceanography, essentially because there was no such
thing. Columbus Iselin, the first director, was a wealthy yachtsman
and adventurer, and in the earliest years, some people dismissed
WHOI as the "Harvard Yacht Club." Frederick "Fritz" Fuglister was a
musician and painter who had been doing Orosco-style murals on
public buildings for the WPA before turning to oceanography. Val
Worthington had lately flunked out of Princeton for lack of interest
when, thinking to give oceanography a try, he showed up on the
WHOI docks. Throughout the 1930s and '40s, these guys were performing open-ocean science from the deck of a sailboat, the legendary ketch *Atlantis*. They were improvising, learning as they went
along, ingeniously adapting old technologies to measure the ocean
and inventing new technology when nothing else would suffice. With
some nostalgia, Carl Wunsch called this "the string-and-sealing-wax
school of oceanography." If it's too romantic to compare WHOI in
those early years to Paris between the wars, or to New York in the

1950s, as settings for a wealth of original ideas and acts that would reverberate for decades, I'm not the first to romanticize the place.

One gathers also from the tribute issue and elsewhere that this first generation at WHOI had a lot of fun being oceanographers. Several of those who wrote tributes to Stommel mention "peels of laughter" echoing through the halls of WHOI when he was around. Referencing their lack of advanced degrees, Stommel, Fritz Fuglister, and Val Worthington formed the Society of Subprofessional Oceanographers. As the first president of "SOSO," Stommel established the William Leighton Jordan Esq. Award to be presented "to the oceanographer who makes the most misleading contribution to his field." The announcement of the award read, "Ignorance and utter incompetence do not automatically qualify. The work cited must be distinguished not only by being in error, but it must be outstandingly bad: wrong both in principle and fact, and revealing the most mistaken intuition and faulty insight. It should be . . . willfully artful, well and plausibly presented, and totally misleading." When Stommel traveled to California, in 1964, to receive the Sverdrup Medal of the American Meteorological Society, Fuglister, "in a bold coup d'état," as he put it, seized the presidency of SOSO.

Suddenly in 1948, with only four years of experience beginning from scratch, Henry Stommel published a short paper in *Transactions of the American Geophysical Union* called "The Westward Intensification of Wind-driven Ocean Currents." It came out of nowhere, and it stunned the professional community, propelling Stommel to the forefront of the science, and he never left. As the story goes, Stommel and a more senior scientist at WHOI, Raymond Montgomery, stopped at a diner en route from Woods Hole to a professional conference in Providence. Over coffee, young Stommel asked Montgomery what he should be studying, what questions needed answering. Well, said Montgomery, there is still that old

question of "western intensification" in the gyre, that asymmetrical-
ity we've been talking about by which western boundary currents
flow fast and narrow, while eastern boundaries laze along on a broad
front—or, in other words, why there is a Gulf Stream. It's not entirely clear that Stommel had ever heard of western intensification,
but even if he had, the more likely case, there remained that big difference between knowing that the gyre was "western intensified"
and explaining why. As Montgomery later wrote, Stommel solved the
old problem *qualitatively* in twenty minutes on a paper place mat.

Time and again friends and admirers wrote in the tribute issue
about Stommel's unique ability to thrust straight to the heart of a
problem by distilling ocean complexity and variability to a graspable
essence no one had ever thought of before. This was to be the first
of many dazzling applications of that talent. After his talk with
Montgomery, Stommel went home and began building analytical
models of the ocean to replicate certain combinations of wind and
Coriolis, the two forces that drive the gyres, and by process of elimination, find the one that best matched the real-world gyre with an intensified western boundary—with a Gulf Stream in it. Essentially,
these models were visualizations, acts of imagination expressed in
the concrete language of physics. Today, such analytical modeling is
performed by powerful computers; Stommel used a pencil.

In each model, Stommel decided, there would be one "real-world"
constant: the winds. Everyone knew by 1948 that wind powered the
ocean currents in the gyre, and the "torque" the wind caused the
gyre itself to rotate, so he set about duplicating the North Atlantic
wind pattern, trades blowing one direction at the bottom of the gyre
and the westerlies blowing the other way at the top. Eliminating
variables, he placed his first model ocean on a stationary Earth, thus
excluding Coriolis from consideration. Only wind acted on this
ocean, which we'll call model "number one." When his calculations

were complete, he had a "picture" of this gyre. Its streamlines formed concentric circles, a symmetrical gyre. This did not match reality. There was no strong, narrow Gulf Stream (or Kuroshio) in this model.

In model "number two," he retained the same wind pattern, but he added Coriolis into the mix. However, he intentionally modeled an unrealistic version of the Coriolis parameter—one that remained constant from the equator to the pole. Calculations revealed the resulting streamlines: they were also concentric. This gyre was still symmetrical, no western intensification, no Gulf Stream. Stommel was not surprised. He knew the answer back in that roadside coffee shop. This modeling, this creative manipulation of the physics was all about proving his penetrating insight. Now in his "third model," he had to figure out how to replicate the actual Coriolis parameter. Coriolis was key.

By 1948, everyone to whom it mattered knew that the Coriolis effect was not constant. They knew that its influence *increased with latitude*. This stems from the fact that Earth, as mentioned earlier, spins at different velocities depending on latitude, fastest near the equator and progressively slower as we move toward the higher latitudes north and south of the equator. Coriolis is nonexistent at the equator, stronger in the mid-latitudes, and strongest at the poles. Therefore, as a parcel of water (the Gulf Stream, for instance) moves from the tropics north toward the higher latitudes, Coriolis exerts a progressively more powerful influence.

What we're getting to is the principle oceanographers call *vorticity*. Vorticity means nothing to most of us in our daily lives, yet it's fundamental to ocean behavior, another way in which the ocean can seem something out there beyond our ken. Vorticity is the tendency of seawater to rotate in response to wind or to Earth's rotation. That tendency is everywhere present in the ocean on scales ranging from basin-wide subtropical gyres to the little swirls and eddies you see when tidal current flows around rocks or dock pilings. To be called "rotational" the motion does not need to complete actual circles; it needs only to bend, to curl or torque. Ekman's transport, for instance, is a rotational motion in that the flow is bent either left or right of the wind direction.

There are two kinds of vorticity—called *planetary* and *relative* vorticity—and a third, *potential* vorticity, which is a combination of the first two. Wind imparts relative vorticity to a parcel of water, while Earth's rotation imparts planetary vorticity. Since we're speaking here of horizontal rotation, the parcel of water must be rotating in either a clockwise or counterclockwise direction. And to accommodate their equations oceanographers have arbitrarily designated clockwise rotation as "negative" vorticity and counterclockwise rotation as "positive" vorticity. A water parcel may acquire positive vorticity from one force and negative vorticity from another such to cancel out all rotary motion.

To understand why the planetary vorticity increases with latitude, the principle crucial to Stommel's third model, please imagine a carousel of water rotating horizontally on the surface. Like a real carousel, that water has a vertical axis of rotation (like an axle), and the axis points toward the center of Earth (because the carousel is rotating horizontally). Before we fold planetary vorticity into the mix, let's imagine that our parcel of relative vorticity is perched right on the equator. Now, Earth itself has its own axis of rotation—which in this case is perpendicular to our water parcel's axis of rotation. Our circle of water will continue to rotate as it goes around and around with Earth's rotation. But in that case, planetary vorticity contributes nothing to the relative vorticity—because the axes of rotation are perpendicular to one another. Now picture what happens if we move the parcel of spinning water and its axis of rotation northward away from the equator toward the Pole. The angle between Earth's axis and the carousel's is decreasing because they are no longer perpendicular to each other. Now the two kinds of spin, relative and planetary, are beginning to align, to complement each other, and their sum—their potential vorticity—is increasing. The further north the gyre proceeds, the closer its axis comes into alignment with Earth's. If the gyre made it all the way to the Pole, its axis and Earth's would align completely, and their package of vorticity would be at its greatest. (The figure skater who spins faster when she draws in her arms is often used as an illustration of vorticity increasing with latitude.) Since oceanographers want not only to observe these deterministic factors, but also to quantify them, vorticity in its various forms are measurements. So, for instance, we can say that relative vorticity is a measure of the degree to which a parcel of water is spinning around its own axis. Planetary vorticity is a measure of the extent to which Earth's rotation coincides with the vertical axis of that spinning parcel of water.

Apparently, the proof, the composition of the analytical models came easily to Stommel. He essentially dashed off the famous 1948 paper, and it's amusing to hear that he was always self-conscious about, as he saw it, the shallow state of his higher math. (After the splash of this particular paper, he wondered aloud whether he should go get a graduate degree to which Fuglister, I believe, responded, "Who's going to teach you?") The paper is dense with abstruse equations, but we don't need to parse the math to recognize his intuitive leap. Into his third model he factored the wind pattern and the realistic Coriolis parameter that increases with latitude. Unlike the first two models, this did not produce concentric streamlines. As he wrote, "The most striking feature of this figure is the intense crowding of the streamlines toward the western border of the ocean."

There it was, for the very first time, an explanation of why the Gulf Stream flows so fast and narrow. But part of the brilliance of the paper, lost somewhat in the shadow of subsequent discoveries, was that he did not set out to explain the Gulf Stream. As Joseph Pedlosky wrote in a introduction to Volume Two of Stommel's collected works, "Once the problem is viewed as a global structural problem in which the Gulf Stream is a limb of a strongly asymmetric circulation cell the problem changes permanently and profoundly. The Gulf Stream is now part of the general circulation of the ocean and not a geographic curiosity."

Like an artist, Stommel viewed the same objective reality as everyone else, but he perceived in it essences of meaning unrecognized by others. Everyone in the field knew that Coriolis increased with latitude; it is basic Newtonian physics. Yet none of those fine minds had thought to apply the principle to an ocean current. Stommel called it the *beta curl*, and the 1948 paper signaled to the still-small community of oceanographers that someone very special had joined their ranks.

What in effect happened, to simplify Stommel's conclusions, was that as the currents on the west side of the gyre flowed north and "gained" planetary vorticity they steepened the gradient slope on the west side of the hill in the ocean. (The hill is no more symmetrical than the gyre, and indeed both are asymmetrical for the same reason.) As we established earlier, if the gradient steepens, then the flow down the gradient must accelerate. And we've also established that the water can't flow straight down the slope, because Coriolis bends it to right such that it spirals around the hill in a clockwise direction (in the northern hemisphere). And since the Coriolis term increases as the water heads north on the west side of the gyre, the spiral tightens on that side. On the east side of the gyre, the opposite occurs. With apologies to my patient fizzo friends, I'm going to corrupt their precise terminology for the sake of merciful simplicity, and say that if water "gains" planetary vorticity as it flows away from the equator toward the pole, it must "lose" planetary vorticity as it flows back southward toward the equator. The twist softens; the streamlines spread out and relax. The gradient slope, which steepened on the west side due to all that enhanced vorticity, flattens over here on the east side for want of it. If the gradient flattens, the flow decreases, and the current spreads out, slows. In the real world, the Gulf Stream, the North Atlantic's western boundary current, is barely seventy miles wide, and it flows northward at three or four knots. The North Atlantic's eastern boundary current, the Canary Current, is more than one thousand miles wide and flows south at about one half a knot. The same phenomenon takes place in the North Pacific where the Kuroshio Current forms the fast and narrow western boundary current, while the broad and sluggish California Current forms the eastern boundary.

Combined, those progressive steps from Ekman through Sverdrup to Stommel paint a comprehensive theoretical picture of wind-driven surface circulation applicable to all oceans—and a batch of equations to describe them for all time. Yet there was a lingering question, answered in the 1950s by yet another pioneering giant most of us have never heard of by the name of Walter Munk. With all that vorticity going down on the western boundary of the gyres, why didn't the Gulf Stream and its cousin currents just continue to accelerate? Never mind four knots, why didn't the Gulf Stream top ten knots, or more? What kept it "under control" at its observed velocity?

When Walter Munk turned fourteen, in 1932, his prominent Austrian family dispatched him to New York to learn banking. He stuck it out for three years, hating every minute, before announcing that he was off to the California Institute of Technology to study physics. With a master's degree in hand, he traveled down to La Jolla to try oceanography, and there met Harald Sverdrup, who agreed to take him on as a doctoral candidate with the warning that the employment outlook was not prosperous; he probably wouldn't find a real job in oceanography for the next decade. But Sverdrup had not reckoned World War II into the bleak job picture.

The war had a far greater impact on the status and practice of oceanography than any other event before or after. Suddenly the nation needed ocean science. Among a long list of other contributions, Sverdrup and Munk calculated a method of predicting surf conditions on invasion beaches from North Africa to Normandy, saving countless lives. During the halcyon days of the Cold War, Munk helped lead the transformation of oceanography from its single-ship expedition status to something much broader and more efficacious involving remote measuring devices such as acoustics, radar, seismology, satellites, and intricate multi-ship research projects—the modern age of oceanography. As the American military geared up to test its atomic bombs in the Bikini Atoll, it occurred to someone that this activity might evoke a tsunami, and just ten days before the first explosion, the brass sent Munk and William von Arx to Bikini to answer that question. The peaceful upshot was the first-ever tsunami-warning system. Perhaps more than Sverdrup and even Stommel, Munk, one of the several greatest geophysicists of his time, was interested in all Earth systems, not solely the ocean's. But in the early 1950s, he was applying himself to the circulation in subtropical gyres.

Expanding Stommel's work, Munk built a series of more realistic models, enlarging the focus beyond the subtropical regions to include the high latitudes, with their subpolar gyres, as well as the equatorial zones. When he was finished, we had for the first time a realistic whole-ocean model of wind-driven circulation generally applicable to all oceans. And to the question of why the Gulf Stream remained in a steady state of velocity rather than accelerating off the chart, Munk answered *friction*. Stommel had not ignored friction in the 1948 paper, but Munk took it much further.

In unscientific language, the wheeling gyre currents "rub" against their continental boundaries, against land, and against adjoining water masses. But Munk wrote it in the language of vorticity. As the Gulf

Stream speeds north gaining all that so-called "negative" vorticity, friction along the boundaries induces relative vorticity in the opposite, "positive," direction. Friction-induced vorticity isn't strong enough to drag the Gulf Stream to a halt, but it's rather like trying to run through shin-deep water. You can do it, but your speed, compared to dry-land running, will be much reduced. Further, Munk demonstrated that the faster a current flows, the greater the friction it induces. There is a lot of friction on the western boundaries, less on the eastern boundaries, and the result is equilibrium in the gyre— the vorticity package was balanced, and a steady state was the result.

One step at a time, that famous quartet found a means of unifying the surface behavior of all the world's oceans. For us, the brilliance of their work can be obscured by the (necessary) technical language to express it, but we might remember that before Ekman and Sverdrup, before Stommel and Munk, the common characteristics of ocean motion were only dimly perceived, buried in disparate sets of temperature and salinity data. Oceanographers and the explorers before them had recognized that some kind of gyre activity took place in the oceans, but this perception was not useful in practice because it was merely perception, what scientists call "empirical" knowledge. The gyres were observed, but they had not been *explained*. By the mid 1950s, a new, comprehensive, and useful theory of ocean behavior had been formulated. By distilling ocean motion to its fundamentals that could be pinned down in simple equations—and therefore proven—this quartet of giants, it seems safe to say, turned oceanography from a pursuit akin to exploration into a science.

However, we need to add that this work alone could not explain the actual behavior of the ocean, nor was it ever meant to. Stommel put the matter this way in the last three sentences of the 1948 "westward intensification" paper: "The artificial nature of this theoretical model should be emphasized . . . The writer thinks of this work as suggestive, certainly not conclusive. The many features of actual ocean structure omitted in the model should be evident." And he put the same principle in slightly different terms in his *Autobiography*: "The mental pictures of the ocean which I hope to share with you are views of the ocean's circulation on the grand scale—views not so much of what it is, but of how it works."

If the oceans never changed, if the gyres went round and round in geostrophic balance just as the theories said, then, to exaggerate only slightly, you wouldn't need all those expensive instruments and ships and smart people who go out there and get seasick trying to measure the damn thing. On the broadest of timescales, oceans behave as the theories stipulate. On every other timescale they vary constantly. In ocean-science language, this is the difference between "basin-scale" and "meso-scale" motion. The former is an intellectual generalization, the latter an actual, on-site measurement. Both are essential.

Chapter 8

RINGS AND "MESO" THINGS

When Stommel published his 1948 milestone, observational oceanographers were beginning to acquire the technical tools capable of measuring the actual ocean, and that is the difference between these postwar years and all that came before. If the opening phase in the history of the science described the broad basin-scale picture of ocean dynamics, the wind-driven gyres and their geostrophic balance, culminating in the early work by Stommel and Munk, then this second phase was about measuring the ocean directly. How did it actually behave in nature?

Oceanographers couldn't claim a complete understanding of the whole if they didn't know the configuration of its parts. Now was their chance. There was still ample romance attached to the image of the tough, intrepid sailing scientist, and some cultivated it actively, but now they had, in rudimentary form at least, gear capable of observing meso-scale motion. Maybe these were the good old days of physical oceanography. The science was too new to have acquired bureaucracy or other impediments to individuality. Best of all, ocean scientists had solid support in the form of money and clout from the Office of Naval Research. Physical oceanographers had proven themselves essential, especially to submarine warfare, during the late war. And since submarines lurking in the ocean loaded with ICBMs were to be linchpins in the new Cold War concept of "Mutually Assured Destruction," the future looked bright for fizzo, if not for civilization. What's more, navy brass weren't telling ocean scientists what to study or how. No, they were handing out money with barely a string attached on the surprisingly rational assumption that oceanographers knew best how to study the ocean, but also because the navy wanted to keep a range of scientists on retainer ready to handle whatever came up. As Spencer Weart noted in his book *The Discovery of Global Warming*, the navy bought answers to questions they never asked.

Submariners particularly appreciated a new device invented by Carl-Gustav Rossby in 1934 and improved by his friend, the South African scientist Athelstan Spilhaus, who named it the "bathythermograph." The BT could record in real time and with reasonable accuracy water temperature and depth as it was towed behind the submarine. Submarine warfare had also fueled huge advances in acoustics, allowing scientists to "see" into the lightless depths with sound waves. The *Titanic* disaster had prompted the first experiments with sound projection in the ocean, when the idea was to sonically probe the water ahead of the ship in search of icebergs. This didn't work too well, but the idea was solid, and a device that could look forward could also look down and map the bottom of the sea. During World War II, with far more sophisticated gear, Maurice Ewing, Roger Revelle, Allyn Vine, and other new acoustic experts taught the navy that in specific layers of the ocean certain combinations of temperature and density so thoroughly distorted sound waves that submarines could lurk there undetected by sonar. BTs and sonar helped submariners find those thermal hiding places, and likewise sub chasers could use the gear to search out enemy subs availing themselves of those same hiding places. After the war, the scientists used these and other technological legacies of style to measure ocean behavior for its own sake, for the sake of knowing.

The Gulf Stream drew some of the earliest and most concerted attention by newly armed and determined fizzos. It is of course a magnificent piece of nature, no less than the great terrestrial treasures Yosemite, the Grand Canyon, or Niagara, harder to appreciate, but a lot more influential in our lives. No question it warranted study, but so did the Agulhas and the Antarctic Circumpolar Current and the Equatorial Counter Currents. What brought the Gulf Stream to prominence was its position within a two-day steam from Woods Hole, Massachusetts. WHOI was twenty years old in 1950, venerable by oceanographic standards. WHOI had ships, facilities, all the newest gear, serious navy clout, and experienced scientists itching to get under way. And with this "American" ocean current that everyone had heard of, sexy, as ocean currents go, right on their front door, there was no need to sail farther afield. (Tony Sturges tells me that West Coast oceanographers are a bit bemused by what they see as an East Coast obsession with the Gulf Stream. I mentioned that to a fizzo aboard the *Ronald Brown*, and he said, "Well, they're just jealous. They don't have a Gulf Stream over there on the east side of the gyre.")

Oceanographers, not all from WHOI, learned new aspects of the current and clarified some old conjectures. No, the Stream did not go to Europe, Fuglister and Worthington proved, but it dispatched a branch of its water, the North Atlantic Current, into Nordic seas. They determined also that east of about 60 degrees West longitude, which cuts through the Grand Banks near a prominent hill on the bottom called Scotch Caps, the Gulf Stream—as a stream—ended, unraveling into fingers and filaments of uneven velocity. Scientists, who already knew, thanks to Captain Pillsbury, that the Florida Current section of the Stream projected its flow all the way to the bottom, now learned that it also reached the far deeper bottom east of Cape Hatteras. This, in turn, started people thinking about what part, if any, bottom topography, seamounts and canyons and things played in redirecting the flow. Seagoing scientists also found the sharp temperature gradient between its own hot water and the cold inshore waters of New England, the old "north wall" that Franklin had drawn, but in nature the wall shifted positions regularly. There is no such sharp shear in temperature on the south side of the main flow in the Sargasso Sea, and sometimes the temperature gradient slid so gently from the Stream to the Sargasso, you couldn't find the border.

Temperature and salinity profiles of the Gulf Stream—notably those obtained by the six-ship fleet from WHOI and the Canadian Coast Guard called Operation Cabot, in 1950—turned up a curious phenomenon. The main flow seemed periodically to shed great masses of water, and after departing they seemed to form up into eddies of some sort, wheels of water rather like miniature versions of the gyres. Operation Cabot had found indications of an eddy-like structure departing the main body of the Stream, but, unable to follow it due to technical limitations, they couldn't tell what it did after separating from the main flow. Only more sea time and improved measuring devices could nail this down.

Because the quantity of water transported in the Gulf Stream and other ocean currents is so great, scientists needed a new unit of measurement. The volumetric flow through the Florida Straits runs at about thirty-six million cubic meters per second. Approaching Hatteras, the Stream is packing sixty million cubic meters per second. Those kinds of numbers quickly grow unwieldy, so scientists settled on the "Sverdrup" in honor of Harald Sverdrup. One Sverdrup (Sv.) equals a volumetric flow of one million cubic meters of water per second. Someone calculated that two Sv. was enough to fill indoor sports stadiums such as the New Orleans Superdome from field to ceiling in two seconds. After the Gulf Stream bends east at Hatteras, the transport grows to around 150 Sv., enough to fill the combined basins of the Great Lakes in two days. Yet neither the Stream itself nor the offshoot North Atlantic Current carries that much water beyond the Grand Banks. Since the water had to go somewhere, scientists concluded that it had to be recirculating. Those eddies might be responsible for the recirculation, if they were big enough; and if so, then they were playing a far greater role in mixing and moving heat around the North Atlantic than anyone had suspected. But there was no way to know until someone managed to follow one from birth to, well, whatever happened afterwards. That took a long time, since it required equipment much more advanced than the BT.

In 1977, Phil Richardson and his WHOI colleagues received word via satellites tracking the new free-floating buoys they had set down in the Gulf Stream that a large eddy had just broken away from the main flow on the south side. Naming it "Ring Bob," Richardson and other members of the newly established "Ring Group" sped toward the position aboard the research vessel *Knorr*. Technology had informed them of Bob's existence, but they didn't need machines to tell them when they had arrived. "Immediately on entering the central part," Richardson wrote, "we noticed a seaweed smell, similar to that of a seashore on a summer day. The water was obviously green and turbid as compared to the clear and deep blue of the nearby Gulf Stream and the Sargasso Sea. The temperature of the surface water in the center was 39 degrees F., and 9 degrees F. colder than the surrounding water." Tracking Bob by satellite, then repeatedly catching up with it by ship, Richardson and his colleagues managed, for the first time, to learn the biography of a Gulf Stream eddy from birth to death.

Eddies, or more accurately "core rings," originate when meanders in the main flow grow too long to sustain themselves. Picture, please, a U-shaped meander to the south. In that case, cold water from over the continental shelf will be entrained between the warm arms of the "U." When the upper arms sag toward each other and touch, the parcel of water separates to become a "cold-core ring" shaped rather like an inner tube with a core of cold water in the center while warm water rotates around the core. This happens on average about fifteen times a year. An equal number of rings propagate on the north side of the flow, when meanders head that way

and separate from the flow. In that case, since they will have entrained warm Sargasso Sea water, they are called warm-core rings.
The other difference is that warm-core rings rotate clockwise, while
cold-core rings rotate in the opposite direction.

Ring Bob began life as a meander in February, and by March, it had
wheeled away from the Stream and headed southeast in the Sargasso
Sea at about three knots parallel to the main flow, but in the opposite
direction. Briefly during May, the thing jinked away from the Stream
on a more southerly course. Throughout the summer it continued to
rotate in geostrophic balance, a narrow ring of warm water surrounding a still-distinct cold core. In early September, after turning eastward toward Cape Hatteras, Bob's life ended when it merged with
the parent current that then carried Bob's water back northward toward the place of its birth. Meanwhile, the Ring Group was monitoring by satellite about six other rings orbiting both north and south of
the Gulf Stream's axis.

Richardson and colleagues determined that the rings contributed
to the circulation about six times as much volume as that normally
contained in the axis of the Stream. Like their parent current, rings
projected their flow all the way to the bottom. Cold-core rings,
which spend their lives spinning in the vast Sargasso Sea, are somewhat larger, two hundred miles in diameter, and longer-lived than
their counterpart warm-core rings in the cold continental slope water between the northern edge of the Stream and the coast of New
England. Warm-core rings also head back southeastward, but their
habitat constricts in the region near Hatteras as land closes in, and
they usually meld with the Stream sooner than cold-core rings. As
much as fifteen percent of the Sargasso Sea may be aswirl at any
one time with cold eddies and forty percent of the continental shelf
water by warm eddies. That means that a great deal of water is mixing with water of different temperatures and salinities, "crossing
thermal boundaries," as the pros put it, and whenever that happens,

things change. The system pulses with energy. You can feel it, as Richardson described.

The richness of all ecosystems, marine and terrestrial, depends of course on the availability of food. In the ocean, the food chain begins with nutrients—phosphorous, iron, and nitrates, the same stuff found in farm fertilizer—little bits of continents washed into the ocean from rivers and rainwater runoff. That's why continental-shelf waters are generally richer than offshore waters; and cold water is richer than warm because it naturally contains more nutrients. Those minute plants called phytoplankton photosynthesize the nutrients in the upper, sunlit layer of the sea, combining carbon dioxide with water to produce proteins and fats, the base of the food chain on which the other kind of plankton, the animal version, phytoplankton, feed. Some are herbivores, grazers on the zooplankton, while others, such as copepods, are predators. But all plankton species share one fact of life—they drift on currents; the word itself means "drifter." And further enriching this drifting soup are the egg and larval forms of fish, crabs, squid, almost every animal that lives in the oceans. To this foundation of the ocean food chain finfish—herring, mackerel, striped bass, swordfish, and cod—are attracted, big ones eating smaller ones, link by link right up the chain to whales and the master predator, humans. As meanders evolve into warm- and cold-core rings that cross those thermal boundaries, they expand the ecosystem's productivity by reducing the temperature stresses of either environment and by spreading nutrients across a wider area of ocean, thus allowing for a broader range of species at the intersections of the currents.

I asked Phil about the contemporary thinking as to what causes the Stream to meander in the first place. "All currents that are not strongly constrained by topography (I'm thinking of the Florida Current in the Straits of Florida) are unstable, meander and shed eddies," he wrote in an e-mail. He used the word "turbulent," which in

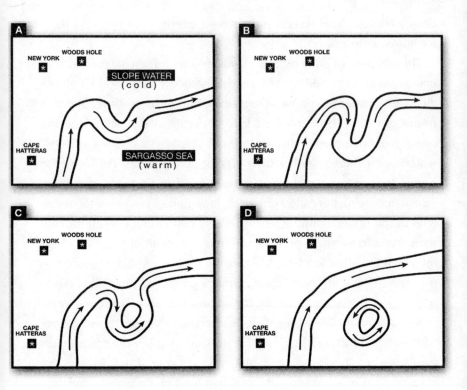

Typical Formation of a Cold Eddy

fizzo language means that it behaves unpredictably, without a consistent pattern, chaotically, though the Gulf Stream is also turbulent in the popular sense of rough as hell. Shortly after its departure from the continent, the deep reaches of the Gulf Stream encounter a run of submerged mountains strung picket-fence fashion athwart its flow. These, the New England Seamounts, are thought to disturb the flow, kicking it away from its "normal" easterly course and causing it to meander. Other "perturbations" include temporary changes in the wind field, older eddies interacting with the flow, and interactions with a remarkable ocean feature, the Deep Western Boundary Current, another of Stommel's great discoveries, which we'll get to shortly. Phil Richardson closed the e-mail saying, "Right after the ring study I began working in the equatorial region in large part to get away from the nasty conditions in and around the Gulf Stream in winter."

One might get the impression that the only ocean research of note during the two decades following Stommel's 1948 paper was going down in the North Atlantic, and a lot of that devoted to the Gulf Stream. To the extent this was true, it more reflected the political and practical than the purely oceanographic. Nobody was saying then or now that the North Atlantic is the "most important" ocean. But at the close of the war, the nations best able to foot the high cost of ocean research were the same nations that went exploring during and after the Great Age, those situated on either side of that ocean.

Also, one of the central lessons of the prewar Scandinavian theorists was that all oceans shared certain important traits of behavior due to shared forces, wind and Coriolis, that shape it. If in the basin-wide scale, the North Atlantic reflected the other oceans, then perhaps it did so more or less on the meso-scale as well. If as Richardson wrote, all fast ocean currents, when free of land, meander and cast off core rings, then we could expect to find ring structures elsewhere in the world as soon as scientists got around to looking, which is to say when some government was moved to pay for the trip. Time passing, technology advancing, scientists did indeed find other energetic rings, and they found that, as well as mixing different water types, the rings helped currents transport water around "difficult corners." The classic example of this is the Agulhas Current in the Indian Ocean.

Since most of the Indian Ocean lies in the Southern Hemisphere, its subtropical gyre circulates counterclockwise, in the opposite direction from the North Atlantic subtropical gyre. So, though it flows southwestward down the east coast of Africa, the Agulhas Current is the Indian Ocean counterpart to the Gulf Stream. (Rather than thinking of these fast, warm, narrow boundary currents as flowing north in the Northern Hemisphere and vice versa in the Southern Hemisphere, we might think of both as flowing from the equator toward their respective poles.) Near the tip of Africa, the Agulhas takes a sharp left-hand turn, sharper than ninety degrees, and flows eastward across the Indian Ocean toward Australia. The turn is called a "retroflection," and it isn't common. The Agulhas is forced to retroflect at the bottom of Africa when confronted by the heavy westerlies that prevail in those latitudes. These winds, having attained legendary status in seafaring history for their deadly power and velocity, gained a proper name, the Roaring Forties (referring to their latitude belt), while their vicious, colder cousins to the south are known as the Screaming Fifties. Unimpeded by the presence of land, these stormy westerlies circle Antarctica in a clockwise direction northward to the latitude to Cape of Good Hope. The water across which they blow (the southern reaches of the Pacific, Atlantic, and Indian oceans) is called the great Southern Ocean, the only one on Earth not constrained between continents.

There was no way, everyone assumed, that Indian Ocean water contained in the Agulhas Current could round Good Hope against the heavy west winds and the current they produce, the Antarctic

Circumpolar Current, volumetrically the largest in the world. Yet oceanographers found water identical in temperature and salinity to that in the Agulhas Current "around the corner" in the South Atlantic. It was later discovered that the Agulhas had been casting off eddies that sort of wheeled their way around South Africa into the Atlantic.

⌐

Now, it's important to notice that everything we've been talking about, gyre structures, Stommel's western intensification, geostrophy, and all those small-scale features, are limited to surface circulation. Despite the new technologies and the infusion of cash, fifteeen years after Stommel's famous 1948 paper, oceanographers knew next to nothing about the dynamics of the deep ocean, or whether, in fact, there were any dynamics in the deep. You couldn't claim to understand an ocean five kilometers deep if you'd only looked at its surface behavior, the upper twenty to thirty percent, and everyone knew that.

Chapter 9

DEEP

In 1751, Captain Henry Ellis, an English slaver with a scientific turn of mind, found himself becalmed as usual off the coast of Sierra Leone. Calms were a fact of life for slavers, and death for their cargoes, since their rotten business required them to sail beneath the bulge of Africa into the Gulf of Guinea, dead in the doldrums. But Ellis is probably the only slaver whose name still appears in any science textbook. As the *Earl of Halifax* wallowed on a long, endless swell and the equatorial sun baked the pitch from her deck seams, the captain wondered what the ocean was like down there beneath the lake-still surface. He cobbled together a mile of line, lowered a weighted bucket on the end of it, and then retrieved his water sample. It was cold. Ellis wrote delightedly in his log that ensuing bucketfuls afforded cool baths and chilled wine "vastly agreeable in this burning climate." But he was also curious: Just how cold was it? And furthermore *why* was it cold?

He rigged the bucket with a thermometer and a closable flap, a "bucket sea-gauge," he called it, probably the first-ever device designed expressly to sample the deep. His findings: a chilly 54 degrees F. It had to be colder than that, Ellis reasoned, since he had pulled the bucket up through warmer water. To measure the true temperature (about 40 degrees F.), Ellis would have had to capture in situ water and seal it somehow against "thermal corruption." But never mind the precise numbers—it was too early for precision—that water was *cold*. Whether or not Ellis figured out for himself why it was cold isn't exactly clear to me, but he took that all-important next

105

step for explorers and ocean scientists alike—he reported his findings ashore. Other mariners, time on their hands, took deepwater samples and showers, and after a while it became clear that the sun didn't drive its warmth very far beneath the surface. The deeper ocean seemed to be uniformly cold.

In 1797, Benjamin Thompson, a.k.a. Count von Rumford, a roguish but farsighted fellow, published his seminal paper proposing that the cold water underlying the tropical ocean originated in the polar regions. Others no doubt had concluded as much, but Thompson went further: The fact that cold water had projected all the way to the equator had to mean that there was some kind of flow in the abyss. Twenty-three years before that publication, in 1774, Benjamin Thompson was fleeing a tar-and-feathering by his neighbors, citizens of Rumford (today's Concord), New Hampshire, under the impression that Thompson was a British spy. He beat it out the back way in the nick of time, abandoning his wife, whom he'd married for her money, and infant daughter. If he wasn't a spy at the time, only a Tory sympathizer, he became one soon thereafter, but apparently he wasn't wildly talented. His cover blown again, the Royal Navy spirited him off to England, where he ingratiated himself to the court of George III and the British military establishment.

Then, in 1784, during the waning days of the Holy Roman Empire, the Duke of Bavaria hired him as minister of war. The gig came with a title, and sticking it to the locals back home, he chose Count von Rumford. In his official capacity, he invented the crouton to add heft to soldiers' watery soup, and he popularized the potato in Europe by serving it to the troops. In his spare time, he invented a drip coffeemaker and a kitchen range. But what really interested the count was heat, a study he pursued seriously, the story goes, after burning his mouth on a bite of apple pie, though that might have been his own smirking riff on the Newtonian apple incident.

He built a huge alcohol thermometer with a softball-sized bulb, and when, after some experiment, he placed it on the windowsill to cool, he noticed that dust particles in the alcohol were streaming energetically up the center of the tube, splitting at the top and streaming back down the sides: *convection.* My glossary of oceanography defines convection as "mass motions within a fluid resulting in transport and mixing of the properties of that fluid." Convection, it says, is "a principle means of energy transport." Rumford had not discovered convection, nor was he anywhere near the first to observe it. The Franklin stove worked on the same principle, and cooks since the dawn of pots would have noticed convective activity in boiling soup. (Some of us are old enough to remember those vile lava lamps that worked on the same principle.) But his next step, applying it to the ocean, was entirely original. In 1779, he wrote:

> If the water of the ocean, which, on being deprived of a great part of its Heat by cold winds, descends to the bottom of the sea it will immediately begin to spread on the bottom of the sea, and to flow towards the equator, and this must necessarily produce a current at the surface in an opposite direction; and there are the most indubitable proofs of the existence of both these currents.

The count was proposing a comprehensive theory of ocean circulation consisting of two neat convective circles, one in either hemisphere, with water sinking at the poles, then flowing along the bottom toward the equator, where, warmed, it rises to the surface and flows back toward the poles to repeat the cycle, like those Hadley cells in the atmosphere. Later, other scientists, notably Alexander von Humboldt and Joseph Prestwick, offered alternative hypotheses as to the shape of convective circulation, but these were variations on the theme, and none was better than the next. None could be tested against the data, because there were no deep-ocean data and no way to obtain any beyond that drawn up in a bucket sea-guage.

However, all this "convective" thinking was predicated on the assumption that each winter, water on the surface of the polar seas grew relatively denser than the water around it, and sank. It followed, then, since water can sink no deeper than the bottom, it must spread horizontally toward the equator, a thick layer of cold water wedging its way under the less dense layers above, driving those less dense layers upward into warmer layers. Thoroughly warmed, the water mass came to the surface, and then it flowed back north again in the Gulf Stream system. This made sense; it conserved mass, and it wasn't entirely speculation. There was some physical evidence that the sinking actually happened. Chemists were finding plenty of dissolved oxygen in deep-water samples. Seawater can obtain oxygen only when in contact with air at the surface. That the oxygen seemed always present in seawater, despite the ocean creatures that "breathed" it off, indicated that oxygen was being replenished as "new" water sank.

A parcel of water (or air) sinks because it is denser—heavier—than the water parcels beneath it. Cold water is heavier than warm water. Salty water is heavier than freshwater. While Rumford had demonstrated that temperature, which caused variations in density, was the prime mover behind the sinking, he recognized that salinity also contributed to the density mix. Here were the earliest glimmers of the complex deep-ocean dynamics now known as *thermohaline circulation* (THC). A thorny sounding term, it's simply a conflation of heat (*thermo*) and salt (*haline*). My glossary defines thermohaline circulation as "vertical circulation induced by surface cooling, which causes convective overturning and consequent mixing." Precise usage of the term has not been completely sorted out yet. Sometimes oceanographers use it to refer to the sinking itself, and other times to refer to the vast global system of ocean circulation.

But in either usage, THC is a process that "begins" with the sinking. John Toole, senior scientist at WHOI, described it in simple language: "Global thermohaline circulation is a wholesale vertical overturning of the sea, driven by heating and cooling, precipitation and evaporation."

Precipitation, which dilutes salinity, is greatest in the high latitudes close to the poles and in the low latitudes close to the equator. Precipitation is lowest in the mid-latitudes. Therefore, Arctic waters, though very cold, are low in salinity. Warm tropical waters, on the other hand, baked by the sun and churned by the Trade Winds, are high in salinity due to heavy evaporation, which "takes away" water but leaves salt behind. If only the coldest and saltiest water grows dense enough to sink, yet the two are naturally segregated into separate, distant zones of latitude, then somehow saline tropical water must be transported to the Arctic. The Gulf Stream system delivers it. The Gulf Stream itself sprints through the mid-latitudes and arrives at the top of the gyre with its freight of salt largely intact. The North Atlantic Current carries on northeastward, becoming the Norwegian Current flowing northward into the Seas between Scotland and Iceland. Around 70 degrees North latitude, in the vicinity of the Svalbad Islands, remnants of the Norwegian Current (the Irminger and Greenland Currents) bend back southward between Iceland and the east coast of Greenland. Winter sets in. Now the water, both cold and saline, grows heavy enough to sink through less-dense water to the bottom.

The bottom up there is not very deep, only about two thousand meters in a trench-like feature blocked to the south by a high sill climbing, in some places, to within several hundred meters of the surface. The sinking cannot begin in earnest until the dense water pooling in the trench overtops the sill and spills into the deeper North Atlantic. However, *spill* may be too tame a verb to describe the event. Water avalanches, plunges, cascades, a submarine Niagara, down the cliff into the abyss. The very violence of its churning plunge causes mixing with the surrounding water, forming a new, less-dense water mass. The Labrador Sea on the west side of Greenland contributes its share of water to the sinking by a similar process. The resulting water mass is denser than most, but not all, other water masses, and it has a name: North Atlantic Deep Water. Naming it makes sense because it has a distinct identity distinguishable from other water masses by its temperature-and-salinity fingerprint, which it conserves even after it spreads south. If a water mass can be identified, then theoretically it can be followed.

Meanwhile, in Antarctica's Weddell Sea, the densest water in the world is being formed. The Antarctic Ice Sheet projecting itself far out over the Southern Ocean accounts for both the low temperature and the high salinity. When seawater freezes, its salt content leaches out in a briny solution that increases the water density quite sufficiently to sink all the way to the bottom without any input from something like the Gulf Stream. This water mass also has a name: Antarctic Bottom Water (AABW). Once it sinks all the way to the bottom, two or three miles down, AABW spreads northward to the equator.

Indian Ocean water never grows cold enough to sink. And no such sinking occurs in the Pacific for a couple of reasons. The simple fact that the Pacific is so much wider than any other ocean leaves a vast area of it exposed to the heavy rains of the equatorial/tropical belt that dilute salinity. Also, the North Pacific never grows as cold as the North Atlantic because the Kuroshio Extension does not flow as far north as its counterpart, the North Atlantic Current. It's rare indeed to find those two components of density—temperature and salinity—in such combination to trigger sinking. It happens only in these two places on the globe: in the seas on either side of Greenland at the north end of the North Atlantic and in the Weddell Sea on the South Atlantic side of Antarctica.

The fact that water sank at either end of the Atlantic was established far earlier than any idea of what happened after it sank. Commonsense and basic physics required that it spread south from Greenland (and north from Antarctica) in the abyss. The physics also required it to upwell somewhere else in order for it to flow poleward again on the surface. But that's where knowledge ended. There was no way to learn where, specifically, the water went after it sank without directly measuring the flow in deep water, and this required more than common sense and basic physics. It required a machine, a deep-submersible current meter or some sort of Lagrangian device, but no such thing existed in the nineteenth century, and at the close of World War II it was still impossible to measure deep currents directly. Maybe, conveniently, there was no measurable flow. There had to be some kind of movement, yes, but you couldn't call it flow in the sense of a current. Maybe you could call it *seepage*. Anyway, it was too slow to be to be measured in human timescales.

Years passing, this concept hardened, and the layers in the deep ocean came to be seen as nearly stationary. Besides, there was a lot of fresh excitement about surface circulation, and that, after all, was where the important dynamics took place, in the ocean gyres and the air-sea interaction. That's where practical discoveries about fisheries and improved navigation, so important to the funding bodies, would be found. Ekman, Sverdrup, and the rest of those Scandinavians with their geostrophic method, had laid down a firm intellectual base, and new technologies were opening doors to fresh surface-research opportunities. But oceanographers were naturally unsatisfied by their state of abyssal ignorance. "It's difficult to imagine just how little was known from direct measurements about the deep ocean in the 1950s," wrote John Gould, the Scripps Institute oceanographer, adding that "K. F. Bowden in 1954 could summarize all the previous measurements in a single paper in the journal *Deep-Sea Research*, and the total duration of all those records was counted in hours rather than days."

By the mid–1950s, however, big changes were afoot. Two oceanographers on opposite sides of the Atlantic, fellow travelers then unknown to each other, were going at the question from different directions, preparing work that would radically alter everyone's thinking about the deep ocean. On the east side of the Atlantic there was John Swallow, and on the west side, Henry Stommel.

Brilliant as it was, Stommel's theory of western intensification was essentially conventional oceanography in practice. He had taken a set of known data and explained it in a new way. But there were no data on deep-ocean flow. Stommel was about to describe a major feature of the ocean that could not be observed and could not be proved. He and his collaborator Albert Arons approached the question of deep circulation by composing a set of analytical models to replicate the physical forces acting upon the deep ocean. This time, wind didn't figure into the mix, since no wind ruffled the abyss, that is, the eighty percent of the ocean lying below one thousand meters. But Earth still rotated. Abyssal water couldn't evade the influence of the old "rapidly rotating sphere." Vorticity still mattered. Stommel and Arons tried this way and that to replicate the physics of deep ocean circulation, gradually narrowing the problem to its essence. And in 1960, they published "On the Abyssal Circulation of the World Ocean" in *Deep-Sea Research*, a recondite journal perused only by other physical oceanographers.

No, Stommel and Arons concluded, the water sinking in the seas around Greenland couldn't be seeping barely perceptibly southward across a broad, basin-wide front as conventional wisdom had long held. The laws of vorticity prohibited that model. Instead, after it sinks, this so-called North Atlantic Deep Water must form up into a narrow, relatively fast current that flows at depth back toward Cape

Hatteras *under* the Gulf Stream! Obviously, flowing at an average depth of 2,800 meters, this current could be nowhere near as fast as the Gulf Stream, but it would be shaped like the Stream—like a western boundary current. It would then proceed southward near the continental shelf, maintaining its narrow, compact character as it flows under the equator into the South Atlantic. Stommel called it the *Deep Western Boundary Current.* The very idea of a deep current behaving like a western boundary current, like the Gulf Stream, for God's sake, was stunning. The fact that Stommel and Arons had predicted its existence based on no hard data at all was awesome, almost unbelievable. But this was Henry Stommel talking; you had to take it seriously. Yet that didn't mean any Deep Western Boundary Current actually existed in nature. The Stommel–Arons paper was essentially a manipulation of abstruse physics combined with clever modeling. Sure, the math was solid; that was Albert Arons's contribution. But until the Deep Western Boundary Current could be observed in nature, actually measured, it would have to remain a current on paper.

Stommel knew that, of course, and he proposed a means of measuring it. What you could do was fabricate some kind of float that could be ballasted to match the density of the water at a predetermined depth in order to make it stay at the depth and go wherever that water went. You could follow its drift acoustically from a nearby ship or, ideally, from shoreside listening stations, if the float could be programmed to emit some kind of sound pulse. Stommel suggested small bombs contained in the floats and set off at fixed intervals to serve as the sound pulse. (Though he loved mechanical toys, models, and gadgets, hands-on oceanographic engineering was not his forte.) Meanwhile, a British oceanographer named John Swallow, with superb engineering skills, was working on the very thing. The history and present practice of oceanography tend to unfold incrementally rather than dramatically, but in the collaboration between Henry Stommel and John Swallow, an abstract idea whose time had come was about to meld with technical practicality to produce a moment of drama.

Stommel, Walter Munk, Harald Sverdrup, minds capable of encompassing the vastness of oceans, shaped the root concepts of the science, but for the paradigm of the seagoing scientist embodying that attractive, romantic combination of intellect, practical problem-solving, and jury-rigging ingenuity, we might look to John Crossley Swallow. He's gone now, and I've only seen black-and-white shipboard photographs of a burly, bearded man with decades of salt wind and ocean sun etched into the folds of his face. In tribute to Swallow, after his death in 1992, his friend and colleague John Gould wrote that he "was a physical oceanographer of outstanding international stature, known and revered around the world as a man of great integrity and gentleness." All of his colleagues refer, in one way or another, to that gentleness, to his human warmth and goodwill. Swallow was the best kind of shipmate. "He was always happy," wrote Michele Fieux. "He tried to talk to everybody on board, from the captain to the youngest sailor. Even if they didn't speak English he made the effort to communicate with them and showed them how he respected their work." (I noticed that crews on research vessels, keenly aware of status and hierarchy, watch for any signs of snobbishness from the scientists and respond accordingly.) Swallow said that going to sea for at least a month at a time cleared his mind of the superfluous and shaped a fresh connection with shoreside life.

After World War II, with a fresh Ph.D. in geophysics from Cambridge, Swallow joined a project at the National Institute of Oceanography to measure deep currents directly using a variety of antisubmarine sonar. The idea was to track acoustically a sound-emitting device that was slowly sinking beneath a parachute, but

Swallow wasn't pleased with this method. When the device reached the bottom, its useful life was finished, and all you had was a measurement of a column of water at a single place and time. "Instead," wrote John Gould, "he had the elegant notion of building a neutrally buoyant float . . . The idea was that, as water is compressible, an instrument designed to be less compressible than seawater could be ballasted to sink to a depth at which its density equaled the density of the water around it. There it would stay, neutrally buoyant and moving with the water. It could then be tracked acoustically from an attendant ship." This, the "Swallow float," partook of the same principles Stommel was proposing (minus the bombs), but apparently the two knew little about each other's work at the time.

Swallow fabricated his floats from common aluminum scaffold tubing, and to attain the proper degree of compressibility with the fine tolerances required, he adjusted their wall thickness by bathing them in caustic soda. Bolted together, one tube was dedicated to flotation, while the other carried batteries and, as Gould described them, "primitive electronics and Navy reject transducers." Vibrating at ten thousand cycles per second, the pings could be heard by hydrophones hanging over the side of a ship several miles away. Scientists could then know to a fair degree of accuracy where the floats were located relative to the ship. However, in the 1950s, there was still no reliable way to know precisely where the ship was located.

Swallow tested and tinkered and improved his device in the Mediterranean Sea and Indian Ocean, while trying to solve the navigation problem, to mixed results. Inevitably, Stommel and Swallow got word of each other's work, and in March of 1957, they went to sea aboard the British research vessel *Discovery II* to search for the Deep Western Boundary Current. Choosing a spot about midway between Bermuda and Charleston, they addressed the nav problem by locating, with World War II sonar, a prominent, known bottom feature and marking it with a surface buoy. *Discovery* could then reckon her position in relation to the buoy using (World War II) radar, which could precisely measure the distance between the radar unit and its "target," cumbersome but accurate.

As Swallow described the cruise: "The weather was poor, and [the ship] was hove-to for two of eight days . . . Three neutrally buoyant floats were used but only one gave a useful measurement. The first one was abandoned after one fix, after *Discovery II* had collided with the anchored buoy and spent the night lying-to, with the buoy and its floats wrapped round the screw. . . . "

They managed to track a single float. It wandered off erratically, but definitely did not head south with any Deep Western Boundary Current. Maybe that was because it didn't exist. After extricating herself from the tangle, *Discovery* put in at Charleston to refuel, where, unfortunately, Stommel left the ship. Back out again, Swallow deployed eight floats, some to ride beneath the Gulf Stream, the rest in three kilometers of water east of the Stream. And then everyone waited to hear where they were heading. The signals were faint at first, and the float tracks seemed to wander randomly. But then the signals and the tracks resolved into a clear pattern. Seven of the eight Swallow floats headed distinctly southward in four thousand meters of water. That proved it. The Deep Western Boundary Current did, in fact, exist.

Henry Stommel wrote his autobiography, which was finally published in his *Collected Works* by the American Meteorological Society in 1995, after his commercial publisher had rejected the manuscript decades earlier. It's a peculiar work, a little frustrating in its seeming lack of personal insight, resulting perhaps from modesty, as if the autobiographical act made Stommel nervous. Of this triumphant moment in his magnificent career, he writes only: "The existence of the deep undercurrent flowing southward was quickly confirmed."

Surface and Deep Currents in the North Atlantic

Chapter 10

OCEAN WEATHER

The Deep Western Boundary Current rendered obsolete the old convenient notion of near quiescence in the deep ocean, but it also introduced a new set of questions without answers. In 1960, Swallow set out to fill in a few blanks by testing another piece of Stommel's physics that had led to the DWBC. Stommel and Arons had reasoned that the Deep Western Boundary Current, transporting a large, fast-flowing mass of water away from the pole toward the equator, could only exist if it were compensating for an equally large poleward flow of water. The law of the conservation of mass insisted that it be so. Stommel had postulated that a lot of the DWBC water was recirculating back toward the pole in the interior of the North Atlantic. The logic of the Stommel–Arons model essentially began with this northward flow. And since the northward flow, though slow, was so great, spanning the entire ocean, only a fast, narrow current could transport all that water back southward to obey the conservation of mass. Since almost all ocean motion takes circular form, the science contains numerous mind-bending chicken-or-egg questions. For Swallow, though, the problem was straightforward: If the real-world ocean was accurately reflected in the Stommel–Arons model, then in the interior of the North Atlantic, Swallow and his floats should find poleward flow.

Moving with his family to Bermuda to cut his commuting time to the middle of the ocean, Swallow launched a series of cruises aboard a 100-foot ketch named *Aries*, fully expecting to verify

Stommel's theory. However, the "*Aries* Experiment" found something startlingly different, and for those of us who like drama with our science, this may surpass Swallow's DWBC discovery. John Gould thinks so. He called it "arguably the most significant discovery about the nature of the ocean made in the twentieth century."

The experiment got off to a shaky start. Swallow was working almost alone from a sailboat deck, and his technology was still in its infancy, but the great tinkerer corrected glitches as they came up, and finally, his gear seemingly functional, he sunk the definitive batch of swallow floats into the deep. Apparently something was still wrong with the engineering. The floats were behaving erratically, unpredictably, definitely not drifting northward or, for that matter, in any other single direction. When he plotted their courses on a chart, the float patterns looked like a plate of spaghetti. He repeated the experiment again and again to exclude instrument error. His floats were doing what they were designed to do. It was the ocean that was behaving erratically, unpredictably. To his surprise and everyone else's, the *Aries* Experiment revealed that the deep ocean north of Bermuda was full of energetic activity. There was nothing like a single, broad, if sluggish current flowing north or consistently in any other direction, but a mishmash of currents with huge variability in time and direction. Further resolving his data, he found that the floats weren't exactly drifting off randomly. No, they seemed to be describing circles or arcs of circles. The interior of the ocean seemed to be alive with swirls and small-scale eddies, here today, gone tomorrow. Reporting his findings in journals and at professional conferences, Swallow always warned that his results could not be definitive. His sample area, a patch of the Sargasso Sea northeast of Bermuda, was probably too small; his acoustic tracking system was only semi-reliable; and *Aries* couldn't always keep up with the floats. But if his data were correct, if the deep ocean was as energetic as it seemed, then something entirely new to ocean science was going on down there. If his data were correct, then Swallow had discovered *weather* in the ocean.

A solid century of effort on the decks of such famous vessels as *Challenger*, *Meteor*, and *Blake* had produced volumes of data—maps of temperature, salinity, and chemical distributions—something akin to a "climatic" understanding of the deep ocean. But until Swallow invented his floats, no direct measurements of deep currents had ever been made. This had left scientists in a position rather like that of a meteorologist trying to predict tomorrow's weather in Boston, knowing nothing more than that it was summer in New England. If, as Swallow's preliminary work seemed to suggest, there were squalls, storms, even hurricanes present in the deep ocean, then previous models were quaint antiques. As Carl Wunsch pointed out in a 1976 essay, a similar rethinking had already occurred in meteorology. The old meteorological model held that weather was nature's mechanism to balance temporary differences in pressure within the overall atmospheric circulation. When the disparity in pressure (resulting from uneven heating by the Sun) grew too great, storms developed, and the "purpose" of storms was to vent excess energy and return a fresh balance. "But," wrote Wunsch,

> beginning in the early 1900s and culminating with observations made possible in the 1950s, meteorologists found that the system was much more complicated, and elegant, than they had thought. In many parts of the atmosphere, the smaller-scale storms (also called eddies) were feeding energy *into* the climatic circulation—driving it, instead of the reverse. Thus the notion of a climatic circulation that could be considered in any way independent of the storms or eddies also was quite wrong. (*Oceanus*, Spring 1976)

It wasn't that ocean scientists had failed to consider such a notion; they hadn't. But unlike their counterparts in atmospheric science armed with an accurate, inexpensive barometer to measure atmospheric pressure, oceanographers had lacked the tools necessary to measure or even discern the existence of ocean weather. The Swallow float was a significant first step, but only that. Wunsch recalls that oceanographers often discussed the question of ocean weather—"If one were looking for ocean weather for the first time, where should one go, what should one measure and for how long? How big were the 'storms'?"—agreeing that something concrete should be done to investigate it, but such conversations always concluded at the same impasse, the lack of tools.

If you meant to find and measure the deep-ocean equivalent of passing weather systems, you would need to maintain a constant presence in the deep ocean over an extended tour of duty. This would require more sophisticated versions of the Swallow float that could be tracked over the long term, at least a matter of months, and you'd need a lot of them, more than could be followed by research vessels. Therefore, the floats had to be trackable from land stations hundreds of miles away. Still, you couldn't cover the interior of an ocean with neutrally buoyant floats. Their work would need to be augmented with a new sort of current meter that could survive prolonged submersion while directly measuring deep flow, and in order to obtain full-depth profiles in real time, you'd need arrays of current meters on numerous fixed moorings. You'd need to do things that had never been done before with instruments that didn't yet exist.

Typically, as time passed, technology advanced, but not much happened during the 1960s. As the next decade opened, new Lagrangian floats and improved current meters began to excite fresh possibility. The topic of ocean weather was coming up in professional conventions as well as coffee klatches in the offices of WHOI and MIT. Everyone recognized that the scope and scale of the project put it far beyond the capabilities of any single institution. Five years before the *Aries* Experiment, in 1955, Henry Stommel had published another of his prescient papers envisioning a massive multi-ship cooperative expedition involving dozens of oceanographers from various countries and institutions all working in concert to understand the dynamics of the deep ocean. There had been other multiship expeditions before, notably Operation Cabot in 1950, but this ocean weather search would require a fleet. Planning began in the early 1970s. Soon the project had a name. It would be called the Mid-Ocean Dynamics Experiment, or MODE.

In addition to untried technology and techniques, MODE would require a tectonic shift in the culture as well as the practice of oceanography. Here were these uniquely individualistic, if not iconoclastic, oceanographers used to being chief scientists on single ships pursuing their own areas of interest however they saw fit, now trying to organize themselves into a complex structure requiring top-heavy layers of bureaucracy, reporting systems, and steering committees. "Big science," it sounded suspiciously corporate to many, but with so vast a problem to tackle, nothing less would work. MODE scientists—the final list read like an international who's who of physical oceanography—were willing to relinquish some freedom for the sake of new knowledge, as long as it didn't become a permanent thing. (One supposes also that there was a quantity of peer pressure as the list grew: "If guys like Swallow, Sturges, Munk, Rossby, Fofonoff, Knauss, Wunsch, Richardson, Rhines, and Stommel are going to participate, I can't be left on the beach.")

Among the first steps was to determine just what part of the "mid-ocean" they should and could attack. Their choice was at least partially dictated by practical, technical demands. They needed reasonably close access to U.S. ports, and they needed to remain within the tracking range of the new neutrally buoyant floats. So they settled on a circle of ocean 300 nautical miles in diameter between Bermuda and Florida, the center of which was situated 630 miles east of Cape Canaveral, Florida. That put the study area in the Sargasso Sea east of both the Gulf Stream and the Deep Western

Boundary Current (between 25 and 31 degrees N latitude, 67 and 72 degrees W longitude).

By 1973, with the funding in place, the planning complete, flowcharts drawn, bureaucracy established, people and equipment assembled, the fleet was ready for sea. Altogether, MODE engaged fifty physical oceanographers from fifteen different institutions, several hundred technicians, six ships, and two aircraft. Because of the "ignorance factor" and all the new untested instruments, the organizers had wanted a trial run to be called Pre-MODE, but the government funders nixed that idea; it had to be the real thing or forget it. Therefore, as Wunsch put it, they settled on the "cautious principle of children playing in a sandbox: nominally playing together, but each in fact building his own sandcastle. MODE was to consist of individual experiments conducted in the same area; but because of fears of instrumentation failures, no one element was to become so crucial that its failure or loss would jeopardize the others." But as Wunsch, one of the prime movers behind MODE, also pointed out, ignorance about open-ocean variability was so complete that despite technical snafus and possible planning errors the project would reveal something new. In that sense, it couldn't fail. And it didn't.

MODE confirmed the existence of an "open-ocean eddy field," that is to say, ocean weather. "The fact that eddies were found to be exceedingly energetic strengthened the hypothesis that they probably have some profound effects on the mean ocean circulation," and the old "notion of a slow, sluggish general ocean circulation by the climatological average winds and heating is gone forever" (Wunsch). MODE had provoked a number of questions it could not answer within its four-month life span: Was the MODE site typical of the rest of the North Atlantic? If so, was the North Atlantic typical of the other oceans? Were these eddies generic or were there, in Wunsch's phrase, a whole "zoo of eddies"?

In any case, there were a lot of eddies. Ocean weather didn't move with the alacrity of atmospheric weather, but by the standards of the thick ocean, weather was changing on all scales of time and space. And that had to mean something "profound" for ocean circulation. (As it turned out, MODE happened to have sited itself in an area of relatively *low* eddy activity.) But one thing was abundantly clear. MODE was the shape of the future. Despite the technical limitations and everyone's inexperience playing "in the sandbox," MODE had worked. Within its terms it had affirmed that, to put it simply, a lot more was going on in the deep ocean that anyone had expected. The sort of holistic multi-ship, multi-instrument approach involving complex collaborative, if top-heavy organizational structure, could be made to function smoothly with a little interpersonal flexibility. The results were worth it, and any other system could not have produced equal results. Those temperamentally unsuited to group play or anything even resembling a corporate structure didn't want to do it again, even if it was the wave of the future. And the majority who were willing to go again wanted a break to do some normal oceanography with one ship and one chief scientist. At least for a while.

Like it or not, everyone recognized MODE as a signal that "big science" had come to oceanography. Maybe it would blur the sheen of romance and the mystique of the grizzled seagoing intellectual, but through the efforts of those very people and their protégés, oceanography had outgrown the romantic "string-and-sealing wax" era and matured into a science capable of explaining the world ocean *and*, soon, its relationship to world climate. Absent war-inspired technology and the free flow of Cold War money to keep improving it, there could have been no appreciable development of ocean knowledge. Now, armed with ingenious technology, ingenious scientists had filled in the broad picture of ocean behavior painted by the Scandinavians, Stommel, and Munk to reveal much (but not all, never all) about the oceans' smaller-scale, real-world behavior. But it wasn't only a matter of attaining the capability to do big science—we can, so what hell, we might as well. No, oceanography was asking questions that only big science could answer. If MODE introduced oceanographers to the shape of the future, the next step would institutionalize it. It was called WOCE, the World Ocean Circulation Experiment.

The ambitious, audacious objective was contained in the name. What was the broad state of circulation in the world ocean? The scope of the question was far too vast to be served effectively by the MODE concept, a combined fleet aimed at a particular section of ocean for a finite period of time, hoping that the section was revelatory of the whole. WOCE would require a truly international cooperative effort consisting of a series of expeditions linked by common purpose. The unprecedented scope also dictated the project's limitations. WOCE could aspire to accommodate only a snapshot of world ocean circulation. Though everyone understood the importance and omnipresence of variability in the ocean's behavior, there was no way to repeat worldwide measurements in what fizzos call "time-series" projects.

And then there was the bureaucratic structure to be formulated. Organizationally, WOCE would make MODE seem like a high school car wash. International scientific oversight bodies needed to be established to decide which parts of the world ocean would be most revelatory of the whole, to decide which of the individual grant proposals would best address the whole, and to submit them to the funding agencies. Down the pyramid, steering committees and advisory panels from the various nations involved would need to be founded to help keep the research focused on the overall objective. The planning stages, which might have reminded the older scientists of wartime projects, took seven years to complete. Finally, in 1990, with the organizational structure in place, the technical "weapons" chosen and assembled—thanks in part to Carl Wunsch's tireless efforts—WOCE put to sea.

While shipboard measurements of temperature and salinity profiles were to be the mainstay of WOCE research, the project got a little help from outer space. Fueled by Cold War fear, satellite technology had burgeoned beyond purely military aims to serve Earth science with a new, overarching viewpoint on the subject. Arguably their most important contribution, GPS satellites had solved the age-old navigation problem. No more messing around with radar ranges to buoys marking a known position, as Swallow had been lumbered with, now the research vessel could fix her position within a ship length anywhere in the world. But satellites, particularly the U.S./French collaboration TOPEX/POSEIDON (another Wunsch-powered project), could also carry their own unique devices to measure the ocean as well as the atmosphere.

"Scatterometers," responding to microwaves "scattered" more energetically from a rough wind–roiled sea surface than when the wind was light, produced reasonably accurate basin-wide estimates of the surface wind field from which the velocity and direction of surface currents could be estimated. Satellite-mounted altimeters measured changes in sea-surface elevations—the hills in the ocean—that could then be used via the geostrophic method to calculate current velocity. However, satellites, then and now, share the same limitation: they cannot see beneath the surface. To learn about deep-ocean dynamics, WOCE scientists had to go to sea.

In all, WOCE ran about ten thousand hydrographic stations over some five hundred thousand miles of ocean. It focused initially on the western Pacific, that vast arc of seas and islands between New Guinea and Japan, which had for various reasons been oceanographically ignored. That done, WOCE turned its focus onto the Indian

Ocean and the high latitudes of the Pacific before returning to the North Atlantic, the science's "home ocean." Most of these hydrographic sections were one-shot measurements of temperature and salinity distributions, but the regions deemed most significant—critical chokepoints and passes such as the Drake Passage between Cape Horn and Antarctica and the overflow sills where thermohaline circulation happened, for instance—were remeasured.

Chemical oceanography stepped into greater prominence during WOCE. The device used to measure those temperature and salinity profiles, the so-called CTD, also collected in situ water samples from all depths, and chemists were able to follow the water in deep currents by measuring the "tracers" that flow right along with it. As mentioned earlier, tritium from the Pacific A-bomb tests, our own CFCs, freon, dissolved traces of oxygen, and various nutrients served to reveal abyssal circulation. And then there was the matter of carbon dioxide uptake by the world ocean. Everyone knew that the oceans are a worldwide sink for anthropogenic as well as natural carbon dioxide. To put it unscientifically, the ocean had been trying to save us from ourselves, but just how much of our effluvium could the ocean take before it gave up on us?

The WOCE field program was complete by 1997. Data analysis continues still. WOCE is an historical milestone in ocean knowledge for many more accomplishments than I've mentioned and also because it was a success. When the fieldwork was finished, analysis undertaken, WOCE, it became clear, had supplied the first-ever picture of the broad circulation of the world ocean. And as before, an understanding of the broad circulation implied the next questions: What are the variations? What went down on, say, a decadal timescale? And, most important, how did changes in ocean circulation signal changes in climate? WOCE didn't so much end as morph into the next big-science project. It's called CLIVAR for CLImate VARiation, and it's very much alive today.

CLIVAR might best be described as a set of internationally agreed-upon guidelines as to what aspect of the ocean-atmosphere system should be studied, a kind of aegis under which independent expeditions are funded and organized, but it is an emblem of the future realized. There are others, and we'll go to sea with a couple of them.

Chapter 11

OUT ON LINE W

In the pale light of dawn on April 27, 2005, the research vessel *Oceanus* was steaming south southeast through rude seas in a cold, gusty 30-knot wind. She was bound for a carefully chosen strip of ocean two hundred miles from Woods Hole designated "Line W" in honor of Val Worthington, a pioneer of Gulf Stream oceanography at WHOI. Line W, a string of moorings set down in the teeth of the Deep Western Boundary Current, which at this point (about 40 degrees N, 70 degrees W) flows along or just above the bottom slightly north of the Gulf Stream and in the opposite direction, was conceived to measure variations in the DWBC over the long haul. John Toole was chief scientist.

Passing through the main lab shortly before dawn, I found John still sitting in his place at a table near the after-end of the main lab. Leaning over his laptop, he typed for a while, paused, peered out, pondering, then resumed typing. I had no firm idea what, specifically, he was working on, and I refrained from asking, but he had been doing it with apparently unabated concentration since lunchtime yesterday. (He and I were sharing a cabin, but his berth had not been slept in, sheets, blankets, a towel still folded neatly at the foot.) There's a weight of pressure on the chief scientist that I hadn't fully appreciated when I came aboard on this my first oceanographic "cruise." Toole is in charge of *Oceanus*. He doesn't give orders—Captain Larry Bearse does that—but Toole's work is the reason we're out here. His research grant is footing the bill. That's how the system functions for scientists at the Woods Hole

Oceanographic Institution. WHOI is not a university with salaried faculty, though it participates in a joint program with MIT, offering one of the most highly prized Ph.D.'s. in physical oceanography. WHOI is a pure-science research foundation, and its scientists essentially live from grant to grant, on "soft money," as it's called, the lion's share coming from the National Science Foundation (NSF), which technically owns *Oceanus*. The Scripps Institution of Oceanography in La Jolla works the same way, and universities are depending increasingly on soft money to support their oceanography programs. Washington, Miami, Rhode Island, Maine, Florida State, and Oregon State, among other big-name ocean-science schools, all more or less expect their faculties to procure NSF or other federal grant dollars as a portion of their salary. At this writing, only the University of Rhode Island and Hawaii offer twelve-month salaries to their oceanography faculties, but even for these people, external grant money is necessary to pay for technicians, instruments, and ship time. The practice of physical oceanography is not nearly as expensive as manned space flight, but it's still costly, and there is no money in it, no fizzo equivalent of the oil-company geologists. People do physical oceanography for the love of scientific inquiry or for the love of the ocean. (I asked John why he became an oceanographer; he said, "I was good in math, and I liked to sail.")

Money is tight these days, and most scientists perceive that the present administration, mistrusting science and scientists, will sustain the squeeze. The National Science Foundation dispenses grants on the peer-review system by which scientists from the various disciplines evaluate proposals and then decide who among their colleagues will receive funding and who will not. Acceptance rates, I'm told, have been running about eight percent, a new low, over the last several years. To put it in scientific language, there is an inversely proportional relationship between a diminished pie and increased ferocity of competition over its slices. As one oceanographer told me, the peer-review system works great in the good times, but under the pressures of bad times, scientists tend to behave like everyone else.

The technicians at WHOI have no job security at all. When the project they're working on ends or the grant money otherwise dries up, they must find another scientist's project to work on, or leave the institution. Though the crew and officers aboard *Oceanus* are salaried employees of WHOI, their livelihood is also directly linked to soft-money uncertainty. Rumors were circulating back in the spring of 2005 that the NSF meant to slash WHOI's budget by thirty percent, and as a result this fine ship would languish at her dock for most of 2007. The older technicians, bridge officers, and crewman, whose pensions are keyed to the number of working days during their final years of employment, were discussing early retirement. (The cuts, as it turned out, were not quite so deep, but everyone was troubled to learn that more than twice as much money was being allotted to the manned space station as to all branches of ocean science combined.)

John Toole has developed, along with Ken Doherty, Dan Frye, and "a host of engineers and techs here at WHOI," in his words, an ingenious device called the Moored Profiler. It works like this: A cable is anchored to the bottom, and at the upper end, but still some fifty meters below the surface, the cable is shackled to a huge float, like a giant yacht-club mooring ball, made of syntactic foam weighing 2,200 pounds. The anchor and the float are there to keep the cable vertical in the water column. The profiler itself, an array of ocean sensors housed in a hard plastic pod with about the same internal volume as a family-sized picnic cooler, chugs up and down the cable by means of a tiny traction motor using only one or two watts of battery power. Back in the 1960s, investigators experimented with the concept, but for technical reasons, they couldn't make it work. What this device does that has not been done before with a single moored instrument is to produce a continuous picture, a "profile" of the entire water column over a long stretch of time, thereby addressing that old variability problem, present even down where the Deep Western Boundary Current flows, some 3,500 meters beneath the surface. And by placing a series of moorings with Profilers in a line astride the current, you can get full-depth coverage of a particular, pertinent area. (In April 2005, Toole and is colleagues were calling this Station W, but they changed it to Line W "in recognition that we were sampling a transect rather than a point," as John wrote in a personal e-mail.) The Moored Profiler's batteries will keep it running obediently up and down the water column for a full year on its own. If Toole and *Oceanus* come out here to replace the battery pack and retrieve the findings, stored internally on CD, then he can keep his profilers working indefinitely. Or as long as the money holds out.

It sounds easy said that way—cram a bevy of instruments into a container and make it run up and down on a long line—but that's a disservice to the ingenuity and foresight required to overcome the problems posed by this most hostile of environments to the works of man. Saltwater, enemy of all things electrical, is among the most corrosive substances in nature. Then there is the crushing pressure. The deepest of the five Moored Profilers need to function at some nine thousand feet, far deeper than the most advanced nuclear submarine can survive. The shallower moorings are prone to fouling by marine growth. If barnacles or other organisms obstruct its vertical shuttling, the profiler has been programmed to back off and gently try again five times. If it can't break through the obstruction, it gives up before damaging itself and continues its work between the obstruction and the other end of the cable. Also, the currents exert enormous drag on the instruments, their cables, and the hardware connecting the anchor and the float to the wire. Another specialty item, modern oceanographic cable, is woven to a diameter no thicker than a pencil, including its plastic jacket, in order to decrease drag

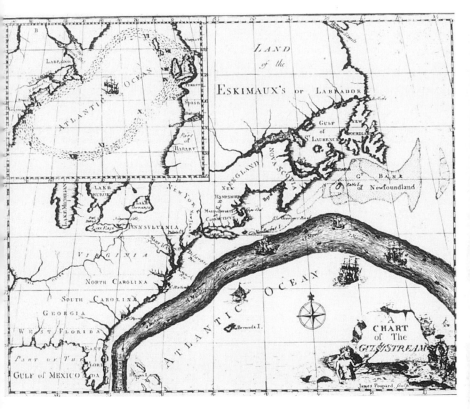

Benjamin Franklin's Chart of the Gulf Stream , c. 1786. (Courtesy NOAA archives)

The ketch *Atlantis* in heavy weather. Photo taken from the Canadian Coast Guard cutter during Operation Cabot, 1950. (Courtesy Woods Hole Oceanographic Institution archives)

Working on a dredge boom aboard *Atlantis*, c. 1930. Captain Fred McMurray faces the camera. (Courtesy WHOI archives)

Deck work aboard *Atlantis*, c. 1949. That is Maurice Ewing forward with plank. (Courtesy WHOI archives)

WHOI research vessel *Oceanus* in the waters near Woods Hole, Massachusetts. (Photo by Doug Weisman, WHOI)

Deck work aboard *Oceanus* on "Line W." (Photo by Marisa Hudspeth, WHOI)

Chief Scientist John Toole aboard *Oceanus* on "Line W." (Photo by Marisa Hudspeth, WHOI)

Henry Stommel in his office at WHOI, 1979. (Courtesy WHOI archives)

British oceanographer
John Swallow, who discovered
"ocean weather." (Courtesy
WHOI archives)

"WHOI Bob," an oceanographer from
the good old days, 1957. (Illustration
by Conrad Neumann, WHOI)

NOAA ship *Ronald H. Brown* in Puerto Rico, 2007. (Photo by Christopher Meinen)

RAPID Mooring Team at work aboard *Ronald H. Brown*, RAPID/MOCHA cruise, March 2006. (Photo by Mick Beal)

RAPID mooring team spooling oceanographic cable aboard *Ronald H. Brown* during RAPID/MOCHA cruise, March 2006. (Photo by Mick Beal)

Preparing the CTD for deployment during the Western Boundary Time Series cruise, September 2005. (Photo by Lisa Beal)

Launching the CTD from the *Ronald H. Brown* during the Western Boundary Time Series cruise, September 2005. (Photo by Lisa Beal)

Launching the *Ronald H. Brown's* boat during a man-overboard drill to "rescue" a dummy named Oscar. (Photo by Dallas Murphy)

A quiet night in the main lab aboard *Ronald H. Brown*. (Photo by RAPID/ MOC Team)

Physical Oceanography jokes in the main lab aboard *Ronald H. Brown*. From left: Chief Scientist Chris Meinen; the author, Dallas Murphy; Carlos Fonseca; and Guilherme Castelão. (Photo by Chris Meinen)

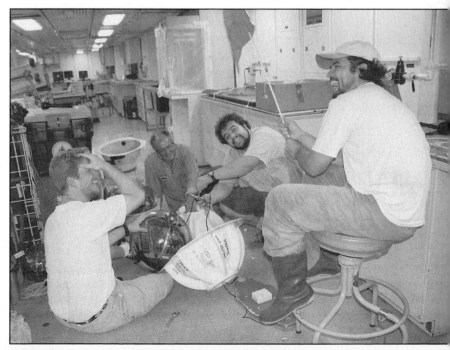

A quiet night in the mess room aboard *Ronald H. Brown.* (Photo by Chris Meinen)

A CTD operator records serenity samples during the Western Boundary Time Series cruise aboard the *Ronald H. Brown.* (Photo by Lisa Beal)

that would otherwise sweep a thicker wire and its instruments away from the vertical profile they were set to measure. That's called "blow-down." Sometimes the wire simply snaps. If the pieces can't be recovered, then scientists can never learn why. Some broken wire, when recovered, shows signs of damage from fish bites. And the inevitable result of all these stresses is loss. "When you put an expensive device in the ocean, you no longer own it," as one oceanographer put it. "Maybe the ocean will give it back, maybe not." John is justifiably proud of his recovery rate, a solid eighty percent, credit for which he ascribes to the skill of WHOI technicians, but that might be overly modest. His Profiler works; if it didn't, the high recovery rate would not be widely remarked on.

Away to windward encouraging patches of scattered blue sky peeked through black, agitated clouds, but First Mate Diego Mello told me earlier that a cold front was heading our way packing 35 knots with higher gusts from the southwest. (May is a transition month in the North Atlantic between the fast-moving fronts and depressions typical of winter and the stable Bermuda High settling in by late June, with the usual exceptions.) The ship's motion was pretty sharp in these moderate conditions, it seemed to me, but having never been to sea on a research vessel, I lacked context. I had had enough experience in boats, however, to know that a heavy southwester would really confuse the waves, particularly on the fringes of the Gulf Stream. As open-ocean research vessels go, *Oceanus*, 177 feet overall, thirty-three feet wide, is on the small side, and John had warned me back at the dock about her eccentric motion in a seaway. When she came up for refit in 1994—she was built in 1975—the Coast Guard determined that, according to their calculations, she lacked sufficient stability. Shipwrights were therefore ordered to lay some significant tonnage of lead deep in her belly along her keel, but nobody liked the result. She still rolled, but now instead of rolling back upright as beam seas passed beneath her, she snapped back sharply. In fact, it's called "snap rolling" in nautical parlance. Nonetheless, I was feeling very romantic about the vessel, a unique amalgam of floating lab and heavy industry, of delicate measurements and brute-force lifting capacity. This was what I wanted to experience, *real* oceanography having nothing to do with sheltered science in controlled laboratory conditions, keep the sea, take the measurements no matter the weather, right up to the point where the deck becomes untenable for human activity. And I was ready, having swallowed a few Dramamine in lieu of blueberry pancakes and breakfast meats.

Three siren blasts reverberated sharply through the ship, interrupting ocean musings, and a bullhorn voice said, "Fire in the engine room, fire in the engine room. All hands report to your abandon-ship stations. This is only a drill. Repeat: This is only a drill."

I hustled below to collect my survival suit and life jacket, edging along the corridor walls to avoid the firefighters in flameproof suits, helmets, and air tanks stringing hoses along the floor. When I returned with my gear, I paused to watch them charge into the engine room to attack the "fire," before reporting with the science staff to our abandon-ship station on the fantail. Diego was in charge. He picked me, the new guy, to demonstrate how to don the survival suit, generally called the Gumby suit. I almost got it right. "Put on the hood," he said gently, "before you put your arms in." It was hot in there, and, growing queasy, I was happy to hear him tell me, okay, I could remove it.

Diego led us up to the 02 deck. This, he said, is where we would gather if worse came to worst. Our inflatable lifeboat was mounted on the rail in a plastic housing that also contained water, tools, fishing gear, signaling devices, and an EPIRP, the emergency beacon that sends a distress message and position information to orbiting satellites, thence to Coast Guard stations onshore. Another EPIRB mounted in a rack nearby would go with us in the raft. Finally, Diego warned us to be constantly alert, since there were a lot of ways to get hurt in this "industrial" environment. And, above all else, he said, *stay on the ship*. "Remember, the nearest land is two miles straight down."

After the intercom order, "Secure from drill," we re-stowed our Gumby suits and life jackets, and then it was time for lunch. (Chris Moody's cooking was the best I would experience on any research vessel, but as one crewman replied when I mentioned Chris's prowess, "We deserve it.") For meals, three giants a day, crew, officers, technicians, and scientists gather unsegregated in the mess room, and contact with the broad mix of backgrounds, cultures, and nationalities is among the pleasures of shipboard life. For the duration of the cruise, at least, everyone is in the same boat.

Shortly after lunch, word came down from the bridge: "Ten minutes from station." *Oceanus* slowed gradually to a stop, and her motion, boisterous underway, turned nasty in the messy sea state. We moved as though moving were new to us, from handhold to handhold. The air seemed colder now, and the low clouds glowered. The fantail, built low to the water on research vessels to facilitate deploying and retrieving heavy objects, was almost constantly awash. The technicians (called "sci-techs" aboard this vessel) and deck crew, led by bosun Jeff Stolp, were gearing up and getting ready to pull the Profiler back into human possession. The winch operator was in his place, and Stolp signaled him to run out the steel A-frame structure mounted above the stern. I was feeling a bit confused from that hit of Dramamine and the raw unfamiliarity of it all, and maybe that was why I didn't understand how they were going to retrieve the thing. There was nothing on the surface. To keep it safe from passing ships the mooring ball is fixed some fifty meters beneath the surface. I didn't want to interrupt the flurry of activity with remedial questions, so I settled for unobtrusive eavesdropping. Spotting John Toole and Scott Worrilow, chief sci-tech, standing by a computer terminal at the after end of the lab, I staggered that way to peer over their shoulders.

"It's an acoustic release," Scott offered. "There are two releases for redundancy. They're mounted at the bottom of the cable near the anchor. We just pinged them, told them to wake up. Hear those pings? Every ten seconds. That's the signal from the releases saying, 'We're awake and ready for instructions.'" Scott keyed in their coded instructions, then he and John waited silently for confirmation. "Done. It's coming up. It'll be away on the starboard side." We went topside to look for it.

The big orange float popped to the surface away to starboard, just where it was supposed to be. Captain Bearse deftly laid *Oceanus* alongside and held her there bow-on to the stiff wind. Bosun Stolp ordered the boom arm on the crane run out, someone got a line through the lifting ring on the float, and Stolp signaled the winch driver to take up. He called for a halt when the ball had risen above the rail, and the deck crew hustled to get lines on it to arrest its swinging. No words were needed. Everyone working together in sync with the thirty-degree rolls, Jeff signaled the winch driver to bring it inboard and lower it onto its dedicated rack, like a giant golf-ball tee, and then everyone relaxed. I felt like applauding, but this was just business as usual for these guys. The sci-techs unshackled the float, then led the wire to another winch bolted on the fantail. Stolp snapped his fingers against his palm, the universal "take-it-up" signal, and the winch driver, standing behind a metal-mesh screen for protection should the cable snap, engaged the four-foot diameter drum, and the retrieval process began. It took more than two hours to complete, and this was the shallowest of five moorings. One would not expect lubberliness aboard *Oceanus*, but I was filled with admiration that day and every other for the impeccable seamanship on the bridge and on deck.

The sci-techs trooped to the galley for coffee, and returning to the transom, they chatted about budget cuts, then fishing. One of the techs, a serious angler, had his rod and reel ready, expecting productive fishing here on the fringes of the Gulf Stream. The guys up on the bridge would be looking for fish, and they'd give a shout if they spotted something. I wondered what sort of fish he was hoping for.

"Blue fin," he said. "Big ones."

Jeff Stolp, a bosun with eighteen years' experience aboard *Oceanus*, lit a black cigar about the size of a pool-cue butt, and we chatted about Hunter Thompson, who had shot himself the week before, and about the Bush administration's anti-intellectualism and hostility toward science. At a sign I didn't see, everyone put down their coffee, replaced their hard hats, and assumed their posts. "It's coming up," said Jeff.

When the Profiler popped to the surface, Jeff closed his fist, the signal to stop hoisting. Worrilow and his crew went to the stern and detached the device from the wire, again without a word spoken, placed it on a little wooden wagon, and wheeled it into the hanger. I glanced at John, who seemed quietly confident as he waited to receive his device and extract its data. I hung around to examine the acoustic releases, twin cylinders about a foot long with heavy steel jaws at the bottom that latch onto the anchors, and then, upon receipt of electronic instructions, open to release the string of gear for its trip to the surface. Though I'd never heard of it, the acoustic release is common on research ships, another of the ingenious, specialized technical adaptations required to perform ocean science.

Not normally an effusive fellow, Toole positively beamed as he told me several hours later that the data was intact and that the Profiler had functioned flawlessly. He said that it had made 251 one-way trips up and down the line, a total of 748 kilometers. On this trip they would pull four more Profilers from the deep ocean, extract their data, and put them back down, the deepest in about 18,000 feet of water. All performed perfectly, and none was lost. The trip was a smashing success for John. But I found myself wanting answers of a childish immediate gratification sort. I wanted to know results, findings, declarative statements about the Deep Western Boundary Current, thermohaline circulation, hell, about the state of climate change. "So whattaya think, John?" That was the question I wanted to ask, even as I recognized that physical oceanography doesn't work that way. It would take months for John and his colleagues to parse the raw data, and even after they'd done so, they would not have definitive answers to the quality of questions I wanted to ask.

Physical oceanographers don't pull their instruments from the ocean, and exclaim, "Eureka, I've found it!" At least not these days. It would make a great story if they did, but that only happens in climate-disaster movies. Oceanography proceeds in small, patient steps, an expedition out by the bulge of Africa measuring sea surface temperatures, Line W scientists trying to grasp the variations in the DWBC, British and American collaborations to measure the North Atlantic basin-wide transport of heat energy. Little by little they compile information, and none of the oceanographers I speak with believes that all pertinent questions about the relationship between ocean circulation and climate stability will be answered in their lifetimes. The ocean is far too complex and variable to submit to quick answers, no matter how much we want and need them.

Chapter 12

THE SWITCH

"If you don't like the weather, wait fifteen minutes." One hears that said, often smugly, by people from all over the country, as if rapid changes in the weather were unique to their locales and they uniquely equipped to handle instability. Air is unstable stuff everywhere, and weather systems move quickly. Change is intrinsic to the very notion of weather, so let's define it as the behavior of the atmosphere in a particular region during a short time period, several days, a week at the most. Climate is different. Climate is the sum of the weather over a long period of time, decades, centuries, and millennia. The anomalous bits, that wet, chilly summer a couple of years ago and this year's unseasonably warm winter, are smoothed out over time; climate is the long-term mean of the weather. Weather is dynamic, which is one reason why we talk about it so often. But no one talked about climate, until recently.

We always knew that climate changed. Everyone has heard of that incident scientists call the Late Pleistocene Glaciation, the Ice Age. But climate, it was assumed, went about its business of change on a timescale that from the perspective of human history constituted stability. Climate was seen rather like a theater set, a backdrop before which the action—weather—unfolded, but the set didn't change from act to act, or even from play to play. Past tense is appropriate here because that view of a dependably stable climate is antique. It was an understandable error. Climate over the last ten thousand years, the Holocene period, during which agriculture was invented and civilizations arose and developed to the Atomic Age, has been consistently conducive, even beneficent to human expansion. But the Holocene, it turns out, is an anomaly, last year's unusually mild winter writ large.

It's a startling discovery, now seeping into the public consciousness, that what we call climate is an essentially unstable set of interdependent systems and feedback mechanisms. And when a certain combination of conditions collaborates, climate can change abruptly in a matter of years and remain changed for a long time. As Spencer Weart wrote in his fine book *The Discovery of Global Warming*, "Swings of temperature that were believed in the 1960s to take tens of thousands of years, in the 1970s to take thousands, and the 1980s to take hundreds of years, now [the 1990s] were discovered to take only decades."

One of the earliest glimmers of this possibility appeared in the 1930s, when Danish paleobotanists found grains of pollen from *Dryas octopetala*, a tough little flower native to permafrost tundra, in lake-bottom sediments laid down between twelve and thirteen thousand years ago at the end of the last ice age. At their maximum extent some 18,000 years ago ice sheets three kilometers deep covered most of North America south to the Great Lakes and most of Northern Europe south to the British Isles and the Ural Mountains. In the Southern Hemisphere, Argentina, Chile, New Zealand, along with parts of Australia and South Africa were subsumed by ice. Experts estimate that the total volume of ice ranged between eighty-four and ninety-eight million cubic kilometers during the crescendo of the Ice Age, this compared to some thirty million cubic kilometers remaining today. In the Northern Hemisphere, the ice retreat began about 16,000 years ago. By 12,000 years ago, more than half of the ice sheet had already melted, and hardwood forests had reappeared across Scandinavia. If the post–Ice Age warming was so well under way 12,000 years ago, why did contemporary lake-bottom core samples contain cold-adapted plant pollen typical to sub-Arctic tundra? Was it possible that the climate had abruptly shifted *back* to Ice Age conditions in such a short time?

That explanation fit the data, but it flew straight in the face of conventional thinking. If the *Dryas* evidence indicated that something had happened 12,000 years ago to cause a sudden flip-flop from one climatic state to the opposite state, then conventional thinking about climate change, about climate itself, would need to be revised completely. Like others, scientists grow testy in the face of evidence that their bedrock assumptions are wrong.

But it's too pat to say that scientists, taking collective note of the *Dryas* evidence and recognizing its implications, launched concerted research to find further evidence of rapid climate shifts in the past. (*Paleo* as a prefix to any branch of science refers to those who seek to understand conditions in the deep past, either for their own sake or for implications about the present.) Paleobotanists were digging for datable seeds and pollen; glaciologists were extracting ice cores; oceanographers were hauling up bottom cores from the abyss; astrophysicists were tracing changes in Earth's orbital relation to the Sun; geologists were chipping at the stratigraphy—all searching from diverse and ostensibly unrelated perspectives for clues to the question one historian called the "Holy Grail of climatology": What causes the ultimate climate change, an ice age? Since ice ages leave heavy footprints in ice, oceans, and rocks, *when* ice ages had occurred was reasonably well known— roughly every 100,000 years over the last 700,000 years, with dozens coming and going over the last five million years. But no one had isolated the specific mechanism or combination of mechanisms that triggered the rise of ice or its subsequent retreat. *Dryas* evidence said nothing about that, but, startlingly it seemed to indicate large and abrupt fluctuations of temperature *within* the glacial and inter-glacial periods.

Everyone knows that tree rings offer a handy means of back-tracking annual climatic conditions by measuring the relative size of the growth rings, but the view into the past is short, because trees don't live very long. Core samples of sediment accumulated on ocean floors offer far longer views of paleo-conditions. Since ocean-bottom sediment accumulates at a rate of about one inch every one thousand years, a core sample only twelve inches long reaches back to the close of the last Ice Age. But sediment isn't deposited evenly over ocean bottoms. In some places, for example, deep currents prevent any sedimentation at all; in others, worms and borers in the bottom disturb the pages of sedimentation. Paleo-records contained in ice-sheet glaciers in Greenland and Antarctica, however, suffer from no such disadvantages.

As annual snowfalls are compacted into ice under the weight of ensuing snowfalls, they leave behind layered signals of the past as distinct as tree rings, but far older. The Greenland Ice Sheet, two miles high, stores some 200,000 years of climate data. And since no life of any kind ever called an ice sheet home, annual sedimentation remains undisturbed by worms and things that burrow. Best of all, there is this fact of ice: Each season, as snowflakes fall through the atmosphere, they collect chemicals and minute particles, literal samples of ancient air, that are deposited and then preserved in minute bubbles beneath next season's snowfall, and the next, and so on. "Popping" and analyzing those bubbles, scientists can calculate to a high degree of precision the actual air temperature during a single winter 100,000 winters ago.

The Danish glaciologist Willi Dansgaard, who pioneered ice-core sampling in the 1950s, determined ancient temperatures by comparing the ratio of one type of oxygen isotope contained in the bubbles to another. When the ancient air was cold, the "heavy" isotope was present in greater quantity than when it was warmer. Dansgaard, in search of the grail, found in his ice cores supporting evidence for an earlier theory of the ice. In the late 1920s, the Serbian scientist Milutin Milankovitch, after calculating the distances and angles by which the Sun's radiation had reached Earth's surface, concluded that cyclical variations in Earth's orbit caused changes in the distribution of sunlight worldwide. If during those periods when Earth's spatial relationship to the Sun changed such that solar radiation decreased, then ice would tend to accumulate in the high latitudes. Being white, ice reflects sunlight ("albedo" is the scientific measurement of reflectivity; ice has a high albedo), and so the accumulation of ice would cause more ice, and this "positive feedback" process would continue year by year until the ice spread over the continents—an ice age. At the other end of the "Milankovitch cycle," when more solar radiation reached Earth, the ice would begin to melt, exposing more dark places with low albedo, such as ocean and land, and this would kick in the same sort of feedbacks going in the opposite direction. The waxing and waning of the ice ages more or less coincided in time with the respective swings in the Milankovitch cycle.

But Dansgaard found other more surprising evidence in his ice-core layers that recalled the *Dryas* findings. There had been large fluctuations in temperature, 10 degrees F. and higher, in the layers deposited *after* the Ice Age. And the sharpest variation took place twelve thousand years ago right at the end of the Ice Age—exactly consistent with the *Dryas* pollen evidence. Something had happened at that time, something serious, flipping the climate in Northern Europe from one state to a near opposite state in the course of a single decade. Some scientists, protecting the traditional notion of climate, cleaved to the view that this had to be some local Scandinavian anomaly—until other scientists, extracting ice cores from Southern Hemisphere glaciers found evidence of the same radical climate shifts at nearly the same time. This was a global event, and it quite clearly contradicted the traditional view of climate stability within the alternating glacial and interglacial periods. This would spell upheaval in the communities of climate science, but it took about three decades to settle in because there were so many different kinds of scientists sifting through such diverse paleo-evidence, and they weren't talking to each other in the natural course of their careers. Meanwhile, the evidence continued to accumulate like sediment on isolated glaciers.

Swiss physicist Hans Oeschger extracted an ice core he called Dye 2 over one mile long from the Greenland Ice Sheet, and in 1984, he presented his findings at the University of Bern. Dye 2 seemed to verify Dansgaard's findings as to the Milankovitch cycle, but Oeschger, using more advanced means of measuring that ratio of oxygen isotopes, also found abrupt, spiking changes in temperature on short timescales that could not be explained in astronomical or any other known terms. Oeschger's ice core, reaching back some forty thousand years during the peak of the last glaciation, showed swings of temperature of ten, twelve, even thirteen degrees occurring within a decade and lasting for one thousand years. And sure enough, the steepest, most pronounced and vivid shift in temperature took place as the ice was in full retreat during that time twelve thousand years ago, which by then had gained a proper name. It was called the Younger *Dryas*.

At about this point, one of the seminal figures in the climate revolution, Wallace Broecker, entered the story. Broecker had attended Oeschger's lecture at the University of Bern, and, struck by the Dye 2 implications, focused his expansive attention on the question *why*. What caused those jinks in temperature, which Broecker named "Dansgaard–Oeschger events"? To specify the question, Broecker asked what caused the most prominent Dansgaard–Oeschger event, the Younger *Dryas*? He had the idea that it was the ocean. His boss, chairman of the Lamont–Doherty Earth Observatory, Maurice Ewing, had been encouraging Broecker in that direction. Not everyone liked

Ewing's domineering personal style, but everyone respected his mind. Among a long list of accomplishments, he collected and badgered others to collect for him the largest array of ocean-bottom core samples in the world. In them Ewing had discerned the Younger *Dryas* transition along with other, briefer climate fluctuations, and he, too, believed that ocean circulation had to be reckoned in the causal question. Also, back in 1965—at a conference succinctly titled "Causes of Climate Change" held in Boulder, Colorado, to gather in one room the diverse field of climate scientists—Peter Weyl from Oregon State University had proposed that if the transport of saline water into Nordic seas somehow ceased, then, deprived of the necessary density, the water would not sink. That, in turn, would sever southward transport of cold bottom water, and the whole system would grind to a halt. The term and the very concept of thermohaline circulation were too new in 1965 for Weyl's idea to gain wide currency. But Wallace Broecker was listening.

Broecker, now in his seventies, had been thinking about thermohaline circulation since grad school days in the 1950s. After a string of technical papers, he presented his ideas to the public in a 1987 *Natural History* magazine article. In it, he coined the term "ocean conveyor belt" to refer to the worldwide ocean circulation driven by wind on the surface and density differences at depth, when the existence of global circulation was largely unknown outside the professional community. The article included the famous illustration that still troubles some physical oceanographers due to its extreme simplicity, though I think they've gotten used to it. It pictured a wide ribbon of warm surface water flowing north, sinking in the Arctic, and proceeding back southward as a cold, deep ribbon of water flowing down the middle of the North Atlantic toward Antarctica. It looped into the Pacific, where it upwelled to the surface, thence into the Indian Ocean, curling eastward around the bottom of Africa, and returning in the same sort of ribbon-like flow

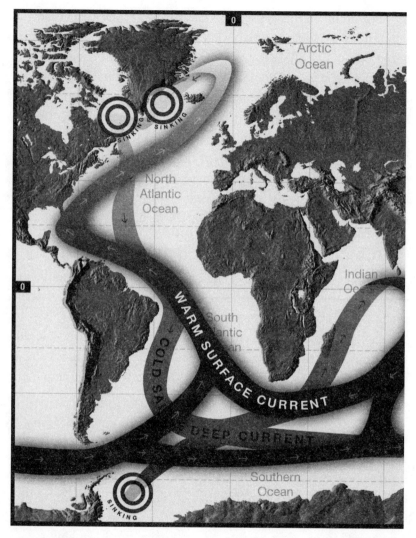

Great Ocean Converyor Belt

of water back into the Atlantic. One round-trip for a parcel of water would take about one thousand years.

Of all people, Broecker recognized that the illustration was only a caricature of the real thing, which is dizzyingly complex and as yet incompletely understood. But Broecker was addressing the public, not fellow scientists, and he had specific points to make in straight-forward, nontechnical language. First, he meant to introduce the existence of that conveyor-like process of world ocean circulation demonstrating the interconnectedness of all oceans. Second, this ocean conveyor was not solely an oceanographic function, but a fundamental climatological agent. By moving ocean water about the globe, the system also conveyed and redistributed heat, and by doing so it stabilized world climate. Third, he stressed that an appreciable change in either the *thermo* or the *haline* parts of the circulation could alter the balance enough to prevent sinking in the North Atlantic. That would deflect the North Atlantic Current, with its freight of highly saline water and warmed air, from reaching Northern Europe. We've been talking about the North Atlantic Current as the agent that initiates the sinking by delivering saline water to northern seas. The other way to see it is that the North Atlantic Current flows north *because* of the sinking—to replace the sinking water with surface water, thus conserving mass. If the sinking didn't happen, then the North Atlantic Current would remain in the mid-latitudes, perhaps bending southward with the rest of the gyre flow. In that case, Europe would be left out in the cold—just as it apparently had been during the Younger *Dryas*.

Maybe, Broecker and the others went so far as to suggest, there were only two climatic states: one with little ice and moderate conditions when the THC functioned "normally" and the other with a lot of ice and extreme conditions when the circulation shut down. Furthermore, maybe there was no gradual shift from one state to the other. Instead, the oceanic climate mechanism was rather like a light switch. You could apply gradual pressure to the switch without effect, but if you continue to press, at some sudden point the light will go out.

During that same year, 1987, an intriguing piece of collaborative evidence entered the mix when Lloyd Kiegwin (WHOI) and Ed Boyle (MIT) found clean footprints of Younger *Dryas* in ocean-bottom sediments they'd extracted from a mid-Atlantic plateau called the Bermuda Rise. Using the same dating technique Dansgaard and Oeschger had applied to the ice, Boyle and Kiegwin measured the ratio of oxygen isotopes contained in a certain variety of plankton. Among the myriad species of single-cell zooplankton, one, foraminifera, grows a hard limestone shell to protect its minute body. Like everything else that lives in the ocean, when "forams" die they sink to the bottom and accumulate in layers, oldest at the bottom of the sediment, youngest near the top. Unlike deceased soft-bodied animals that decay into ooze, foram shells are preserved intact essentially forever. Boyle and Kiegwin "took the temperature" of the ancient ocean by comparing the quantity of cold-adapted forams to their warm-adapted relatives containing the other "lighter" oxygen isotope. But the two scientists carried things a bit further. They discerned chemically the particular water mass absorbed by the shells when they were alive. There on the Bermuda Rise, in the mid-latitudes of the Northern Hemisphere, Boyle and Kiegwin found traces of Antarctic Bottom Water in the forams that died during the Younger *Dryas*. Under typical conditions, Antarctic Bottom Water remains in its own hemisphere, kept at bay so to say by North Atlantic Deep Water sinking in the Nordic seas and flowing south toward the equator as the DWBC. That Antarctic Bottom Water, the coldest and densest in the world, had seeped northward as far as Bermuda could only mean that, during the Younger *Dryas*, production of North Atlantic Deep Water had diminished if not entirely ceased.

Ten years later, in November 1997, Wallace Broecker published another article aimed at the public in *Science* magazine titled "Thermohaline Circulation, the Achilles Heel of Our Climate System: Will Man-made Carbon-dioxide Upset the Current Balance?" In it he posits that the integrity of the conveyor is most vulnerable right there in the Nordic seas where the sinking occurs, where we might say THC begins: "Variations in the conditions governing the density of high-latitude surface waters can lead to abrupt reorganizations of the ocean's circulation." Jochem Marotzke, ocean theorist and modeler at the Max Planck Institute for Meteorology, put it this way: "A wealth of model studies, ranging in complexity from the simplest imaginable to comprehensive climate models, have confirmed that such a THC collapse is in principle consistent with the physical laws governing the ocean."

Weyl, Ewing, and others, especially Wallace Broecker had been pointing to the melting ice sheets as the source of freshwater in quantities capable of decreasing the salinity, and therefore the density, of high-latitude water such that the sinking ceased. But the melting had been proceeding apace for some five thousand years before the Younger *Dryas*. Why after all that time did the THC suddenly shut down? Was it just a case of the freshwater reaching some critical mass? Or had something else happened? Solid-Earth geologists, working a half a continent away from the nearest tidewater, discovered the missing link, and it still sounds incredible.

In the rock strata and etched on the face of the modern landscape geologists found indications of an enormous ancient lake far larger than all the Great Lakes combined that had submerged some 180,000 square miles of present-day Saskatchewan, Manitoba, Ontario, the Dakotas and Minnesota—almost exactly twelve thousand years ago. So certain were geologists of its existence they gave it a proper name. They called it Lake Agassiz for Louis Agassiz, who essentially invented glaciology in the nineteenth century and who coined the term "ice age." There could, of course, be only one source for that much water: a melting ice sheet.

The appalling magnitude of the Ice Age glacier is hard to visualize, but fragmentary hints remain, most vividly as Antarctica, a continent of ice some ten thousand feet high subsuming an area the size of the United States and Mexico combined. Trying to picture Lake Agassiz and its source, we shouldn't confuse ice-sheet glaciers with mountain glaciers. Both are glaciers in that they move, they flow downhill; that's what distinguishes a glacier from a big chunk of ice. Flow is obvious in mountain glaciers that so clearly look like frozen cataracts. (Among the most powerful images of global warming are those photographs of today's vanishing mountain glaciers beside the same glacier thirty years ago.) Ice sheets cover entire mountains, entire continents under domes of ice that flow outward from the highest point, and transfigure the landscape with their passing. The Laurentide Ice Sheets ground all of Canada and half of the United States to a nub, peeling away everything above bedrock. Until the arrival of the ice, the Adirondacks and parts of the Alleghenies had been spired, alpine-style mountains. The rasping bottom of the advancing ice gouged out the Great Lakes basins, and at its maximum advance the ice dropped its rubble to form present-day Long Island and Cape Cod, to mention only a local fraction of its handiwork. And when the ice sheet melted, sea levels rose 120 meters worldwide, divorcing the British Isles from Europe and submerging the Grand Banks, where mastodons had lately foraged. So it strained no one's credulity that its meltwater could produce 180,000 square miles of lake. However, they were flabbergasted, upon further geologic inquiry, to discover evidence that the lake had emptied suddenly—in a matter of *weeks*, some experts contend. Where did all that water go?

Some of the lake water had drained down the Mississippi Valley, creating the riverbed as it went, but geologists, recognizing that no river on Earth could suddenly drain a lake the size of Agassiz, looked elsewhere. On the east side of the ancient lake near the present Great Lakes, they found remnants of what had been a gigantic dike of ice and rubble, which geologists dubbed the Superior Lobe. As the climate continued to warm, the Superior Lobe had suddenly collapsed. The resulting deluge may have been the most spectacular cataclysm involving water in all geologic time. Lake Agassiz cascaded through the Great Lakes and into the St. Lawrence Valley, widening it as it went—and then into the North Atlantic—in about two weeks. Here it was, the trigger, the light switch. The sudden mammoth inflow had stoppered the North Atlantic with freshwater and severed the thermohaline circulation. The wind-driven gyre currents didn't stop; they just realigned themselves farther southward. Starved of the North Atlantic Current's saline water, the Nordic Seas lost the density necessary to sink. The system lurched and sputtered for a time, then shut down. Within a decade, the feedback mechanisms tripped, and bad things began to happen, first in Northern Europe.

As noted earlier, that region's warm, moist maritime climate hinges on heat delivered northward by the Gulf Stream system, relinquished to the atmosphere, and then carried onto the grateful shores of Europe by the prevailing west winds. But the Younger *Dryas* deluge had shouldered the Gulf Stream southward. The westerlies still blew, but now, instead of warm and moist, they blew cold and dry. Temperatures plummeted. The fledgling forests in Scandinavia died off, replaced by tundra, *Dryas* habitat. Ice age conditions soon returned to Europe, which must have come hard to the modern human bands of hunter-gatherers who had huddled through the Ice Age and thought that gentler times had come. But these were only the local upshots of Younger *Dryas*.

Absent thermohaline circulation, no Deep Western Boundary Current survived to transport the cold water southward, and so it remained in the north, exacerbating the freezing. Dr. Broecker's ocean conveyor, "designed" to moderate extremes by distributing heat, backed up all around the world. Extremes predominated. As the ice locked up more and more of the world's fresh water, drought spread through the normally drier mid-latitudes. Scientists working as far afield of the Nordic Seas as the Chilean coast and Monterey Bay, California, have pulled up bottom cores deposited during the Younger *Dryas* containing elevated quantities of desert sand and dust. Some archeologists believe that the Younger *Dryas* prompted the development of agriculture thousands of years before its conventional birth date. The Akkadians, a shadowy culture hunting and gathering in the region now called the Fertile Crescent, were forced to experiment with hybrid grains when the wild strains they had subsisted on died of thirst, this based on fossilized traces of a hitherto unknown drought-resistant hybrid grain that scientists radiocarbon dated to the Younger *Dryas*. If it's real, this may be the first recorded instance of human response to climate change, and even if it's not, the story illustrates broadly the downstream result of climate change. Some organisms naturally flourish, some die out, and those that are able adapt.

A complete shutdown in the deep-ocean circulation plunging Europe into a renewed ice age, Younger *Dryas* is dramatic as well as illustrative. Yet I noticed that my oceanographer friends evinced a certain impatience when I brought up the subject. Was that due, I asked, to the doubt among some scientists about the direct correlation in time between the younger *Dryas* event and Lake Agassiz discharge? Or were they just sick of hearing about thermohaline shutdown? The *Dryas* shutdown comes up these days on quickie Science Channel documentaries. That's what Jack, the paleoclimatologist in *Day After Tomorrow*, was shouting about. Journalists tasked with explaining ocean dynamics and their influence on climate in too-short spaces gravitate to the shutdown for the sake of narrative obligations. Yes, my friends said, they were a bit weary of the subject, a worst-case scenario caused by an ice-related feature, Lake Agassiz, that no longer exists. But what irks them is that focus on the shutdown is reductive.

Look, they said, it's like focusing on the scary talk about rising sea levels. We hear from all manner of media, including scientific media, that if the Greenland Ice Sheet, which covers an area twice the size of California with enough frozen water to fill the Gulf of Mexico, were to collapse and melt, sea levels worldwide would rise twenty feet. (Antarctic Ice Sheet meltdown would add at least an additional twenty feet to world sea levels.) The ensuing catastrophe is scarcely imaginable. Millions drown; disease, dislocation, tens of millions of wandering refugees, social order collapsing worldwide—there's no reason to doubt the apocalyptic result of an ice sheet meltdown. However, it depicts the ocean as a crude, monosyllabic system—or entirely lacking a system, a dumb receptacle, like a pasta pot, that overflows its rim when the Greenland Ice Cap melts. In fact the ocean system is far more complex, delicate, sensitive, and dynamic. Many other changes, some only guessed at today, would reverberate through the links in the system as a result of the influx of fresh water long before the oceans overflowed their shores.

That said, having led us back from the precipice of catastrophe, scientists are worried about the potential of freshwater pouring into the North Atlantic from the Greenland Ice Cap to alter thermohaline circulation. Seemingly every month new reports by real scientists from universities, reputable scientific organizations such as NASA, NOAA, and their counterparts abroad, appear in the media to the effect that Arctic Sea ice and the Greenland Ice Sheet are melting at a rate far greater than the models had predicted. Then the next report appears saying, nope, it's happening even faster than that. Typical is this from a September 2006 report by scientists from NASA's Jet Propulsion Lab and the University of Kansas, who after studying satellite measurements from 1996 to 2005, con-

cluded that the amount of ice dropping into the sea from numerous
Greenland glaciers has almost doubled during that period. Eric
Rignot, the study's author, was quoted: "When you have this
widespread behavior of the glaciers, where they all speed up, it's
clearly a climate signal. The fact that this has been going on now
over 10 years in southern Greenland suggests this is not a short-
lived phenomenon."

We should distinguish between the melting Rignot is talking
about and the equally widely reported melting of Arctic Sea ice. Sea
ice is already afloat, like ice cubes in a glass, so its melting does not
increase sea levels. Melting sea ice, however, obliterates habitats
and ecosystems. Polar regions have been hardest hit thus far by
global warming, because the ice that defines those places is highly
vulnerable to rising temperatures for obvious reasons. A report issued in May 2007 by glaciologists at the National Snow and Ice
Center, in Colorado, predicted nearly ice-free Arctic summers by
2020, three decades earlier than previous models predicted. Though
we can only surmise the specific impacts, it's not hard to see that
the disappearance of a unique environment to which everything has
adapted will be dire. If polar bears can't hunt seals on the near-
shore ice, because there is none, then there will be no more bears.
The Environmental Protection Agency has officially recognized the
"endangered" status of that Arctic icon due to habitat destruction
(without actually addressing global warming), but that will not avail
the bear if the ice retreats beyond its reach. Common sense says the
same fate, with different depressing details, will fall on every crea-
ture in the ecosystems, just as it would in the forests of Amazonia if
annual rainfall were halved. On the other hand, human enterprise
might benefit from ice-free Arctic summers. If the old Northwest
Passage finally opens as a viable shipping route, Canadians,
Russians, and Americans will begin to eye the wealth of previously
unapproachable natural resources crying out for exploitation to

liberate us from the grip of foreign oil. And though all vestiges of their traditional lifestyle will have been obliterated, the Inuit might benefit from casino operations serving tourists and oil-field workers. But the real threat to the formation of water dense enough to sink looms in the form of ice-sheet glacier meltdown, the sort Rignot and colleagues referred to.

Greenland's vast ice sheet and the far larger Antarctic Ice Sheet are composed entirely of freshwater. Their melting would significantly raise sea level, and it would alter that delicately balanced combination of temperature and salinity on which the THC depends. In 2006, scientists were astonished by aerial photographs of a slab of ice the size of a small nation that had suddenly snapped off the Weddell Sea Ice Shelf, and they flocked to Antarctica to find out how that could have happened—everything like this comes as a surprise because nothing like it has ever happened before. Scientists learned that innocuous-looking puddles of meltwater forming on the top of the ice shelf during a warm spell had percolated down to the very base of the ice, thus weakening the structure and finally causing its collapse. Scientists then found the same pools forming on the Greenland Ice Sheet. Further, the scientists who conducted the NASA study quoted above suspect that meltwater forming at the bottom of the Greenland Ice Sheet has lubricated the intersection between ice and bedrock, causing the flow to speed up. Glacial ice doesn't need to melt to discharge freshwater into the ocean. When glaciers "speed up," their leading edges calve more and larger icebergs into the ocean. They might wander for a time around the Labrador Sea at the behest of winds and currents, but eventually the Labrador, Irminger, and other currents will carry them south into warmer climes where they all come to the same inevitable end—they turn to liquid freshwater. How much freshening does it take to interrupt the thermohaline circulation? The physics are unknown.

But no serious scientist is claiming that the freshening is about to sever thermohaline circulation in some *Day After Tomorrow* scenario. On the other hand, no serious scientist claims to know exactly what will happen as the melting continues. Ruth Curry, who was co-chief scientist on *Oceanus* during the Line W cruise, and Cecile Mauritzen of the Norwegian Meteorological Institute compiled oceanographic records to quantify the freshening of the northern North Atlantic between 1965 and 1995. Their study, published in 2005 in *Science*, concluded that "an extra 19,000 cubic kilometers of freshwater" entered the Nordic and subpolar seas during those thirty years. "The observed freshening does not appear to have yet significantly altered the MOC and its northward heat transport." (MOC stands for the Meridional Overturning Circulation, which we'll get to shortly, but for now, they're talking about the northward flow of warm surface water in the Gulf Stream system and the return flow southward of cold dense water in the Deep Western Boundary Current.) Curry and Mauritzen estimated that the rate of freshening they calculated would take a century to interrupt the MOC. But as they point out, this assumes that the rate of melting does not increase.

> Pooling and sudden release of glacial meltwater, disintegration of shelf ice followed by surge in glacier movement, or lubrication of the glacier base by increased melting are all possible mechanisms that could inject large amounts of freshwater from Greenland's ice sheet into the upper layers of the Nordic Seas. The possibility of such events precludes ruling out a significant slowing or shutdown of the overflows as a result of greenhouse warming.

Among the other worrisome factors, particularly in the Arctic, is the effect on the climate system of increased water vapor, a greenhouse gas far more potent than carbon dioxide. Increased warming causes increased evaporation, turning seawater into its gaseous state, which when it ascends into the atmosphere melds with tiny dust and other airborne particles, turns back into liquid, and falls as increased precipitation in those zones of already high precipitation, the tropics and the high latitudes. Then there is the question of clouds. Increased water vapor will increase cloud cover; everyone knows that, but the result is less certain. Low cloud cover will produce net cooling by blocking incoming solar radiation, while high cloud cover will exacerbate the greenhouse effect by trapping outgoing heat. No one knows, but we'll probably soon find out.

Although it seems embarrassingly obvious to say so, farsightful societies would rouse themselves to concerted, serious efforts to diminish the greenhouse effluvia they pump into the atmosphere. In a more farsighted society, money would pour into the hands of scientists, modelers, and geoscience institutions just as it did during the Cold War when ocean research was deemed essential to national security. On the plus side, it seems clear that distractions introduced into the fake debate over the anthropogenic causes of the warming, destitute of credibility, to put it more politely than the Inhofes and Dingells in congress, than Michael Crichton and the Al Gore haters deserve, is about to cease. If they had ever had a leg to stand on, the February 2007 report by the Intergovernmental Panel on Climate Change (IPCC) has knocked it out from under them.

The IPCC and its reports are a joint venture between the United Nations Environment Programme and the World Meteorological Organization. Their role is not to do science, but to collect and digest worldwide sources of scientific data produced by real scientists in peer-reviewed papers and to issue to the public an assessment of climate-change research. This was the IPCC's fourth voluminous report. In its 1995 report, the IPCC concluded: "The balance of evidence suggests a discernable human influence on global climate." In 2001: "There is new and stronger evidence that most of the warming observed over the last 50 years is attributable to human activities."

And in this the 2007 report, they wrote: "Most of the observed increase in globally averaged temperatures since the mid–20th century is very likely due to the observed increase in anthropogenic greenhouse gas concentrations." The likelihood of that, they concluded, is ninety percent.

Also the report made clear a fact of the ocean sometimes left out in the global warming discourse. There is a "time-delay" inherent in the oceanic system, which means that the climate is warming in response to carbon dioxide we spewed into the air and thence onto the ocean three or four decades ago; the carbon dioxide we're releasing today (twenty-five billion tons per year) will exert its effects about thirty years hence. And since the oceans have absorbed the vast majority of the carbon dioxide we've produced since the outbreak of the Industrial Revolution, we cannot assume that they will continue to save us from ourselves. Recent depressing studies have found that the carbon dioxide already absorbed by the oceans has altered their chemical makeup. It's being called ocean acidification, and no doubt we'll be hearing more about it in the near future.

Not a scientist in the world was surprised by the IPCC findings, nor were very many members of the public who have been paying attention. Scientists have been making these points for the last quarter century, and more recently the same points have been made by more accessible media, notably Gore's *An Inconvenient Truth*. The reason this report can't be easily shrugged off lies in the structure of the IPCC. Data are scrutinized by thousands of scientists and almost two hundred governments. Every verb and predicate in every sentence in the multi-volume report have been vetted and agreed upon by every participant. You can't get any more mainstream than the IPCC. In the face of this irrefutable evidence, certain prominent editorialists for the center-right establishment grudgingly admitted in print that, okay, global warming is real and due in great part to anthropogenic contributions, but there is nothing to be done about it except duck. Soon, one hopes, these retrograde responses and the administration they represent will be left behind by public concern and by corporations finally recognizing that bundles of money can be made by doing the obvious sensible thing.

For now the question hangs, how much freshening, how much carbon dioxide can the ocean handle before the feedbacks kick in? The term "tipping point," borrowed from epidemiology and recently popularized by Malcolm Gladwell's book by that title, has entered the vocabulary of global warming, referring to the threshold at which a series of relatively small feedbacks produce a sudden and disproportional impact. Another way to say it is that beyond the tipping point, past responses in the climate systems no longer predict future responses. Then, as scientists put it, things go all "nonlinear." The editors of *Nature* wrote in the June 15, 2006, issue: "Anyone claiming to know for sure when a particular tipping point will be reached should be treated with suspicion—and so must anyone who suggests that no tipping point will ever be reached."

I like the way Wallace Broecker famously put it: "The climate is an angry beast, and we're poking it with sticks."

Chapter 13

HURRICANES AND CTDs

Hoping to talk myself aboard, I phoned Chris Meinen, who was to be chief scientist on the NOAA ship *Ronald H. Brown*, at his Key Biscayne office in the Atlantic Oceanographic and Meteorological Laboratory (AOML), an arm of the National Oceanic and Atmospheric Administration (NOAA), which in turn is a branch of the Federal Department of Commerce, for some reason. The ship is named after Bill Clinton's commerce secretary, who was killed in a plane crash in Bosnia in 1996. I had a spiel all set about how I'd already been out on *Oceanus* with John Toole, and I'd been to sea a fair bit on sailboats, I'm not a danger to myself or others, and I'm trying to learn their science from the deck of—

"Will you work?"

"Work? Uh, sure. I don't know how to do anything." It would have come out.

"That's all right, we'll train you. We work twelve-hour shifts. Will you work, or do you need the time to . . . write?"

"Oh, no, I'll work."

"Did you do any CTDs on *Oceanus*?"

"No." In this acronym-peppered science, CTD stands for conductivity-temperature-depth, which is what the device measures, and CTD has become the name of the device itself. I had watched CTD operations aboard *Oceanus*, but amid all that was new to me on the trip, I had gleaned little about its true function and importance to ocean science beyond the rudimentary fact that it collected water samples.

"Fine. We leave from Charleston on September 9th and return to Miami on September 23rd."

That was a lot easier than I'd reckoned. But September? This was 2005, that bad hurricane year. Here in June, we'd already had two.

"I know," said Chris, "I know. I'll pick you up at the airport."

⌁

I met the ship at the sprawling, nearly defunct Charleston Navy Yard, where kudzu vines climbed the sides of naked cinder-block buildings with black holes for windows, rain-rotted roofs falling in, a dreary place to call homeport. With a pilot boat, Coast Guard cutter, and a navy troop ship, the *Ronald H. Brown* was tied to a hardcore concrete wharf known as Pier Papa. Unofficial flagship of the NOAA fleet, the *Brown* is 275 feet from the stem of her pleasing upswung bow to her low, flat transom, and she carries her 52.5-foot beam all the way to the square stern. Like her sisters *Atlantis* and *Revelle*, built in the 1990s by Halter Marine of Moss Port, Mississippi, the *Brown* can crank out fifteen knots if she must, but at that speed, she inhales 350 gallons of diesel fuel per hour. Typically, she cruises at a more economical eleven knots, about thirteen miles an hour. At that stately pace she has crossed and recrossed every ocean and nearly every marginal sea on Earth from the High Arctic to the fringes of the Antarctic Ice Sheet. Greater speed would always be desirable, decreasing steaming time to the work site, but hardly possible for a vessel displacing 2,250 tons, riding 26.5 feet deep in the water, while toting a staggering tonnage of winches, cranes, and other heavy-duty machinery on deck. Also, the quality of data gathered by the array of hull-mounted ocean sensors to measure temperature, salinity, and current velocity while the ship is under way would be degraded by higher speed. Her long-legged range of 11,300 miles and sixty-day endurance (limited only by the quantity of food she can store) are more important than speed for her work.

Excited to be going to sea again on a research vessel, while feigning old-hand nonchalance, I paused at the foot of the gangway to take her in and savor the beginning. Though her working life was evident in dents and scratches near the transom where the heavy lifting is done, she's scrupulously maintained, and to my eye a handsome ship with a well-turned sheer, pleasing proportions, and bright white topsides. There was a problem, however, with the beginning. Hurricane Ophelia, a category-three that had been tearing up the Gulf Stream on its way north, had paused overnight as if to marshal its forces and make up its mind. NOAA weather was predicting that it would jink west for a direct hit on Charleston. We might be delayed a day. Or two. The captain, Chris said as he led me down the main deck corridor toward my cabin, was waiting until mid-afternoon to decide whether to hunker at Pier Papa or run for sea room. I followed Chris past laboratories port and starboard, and by the time we went around a couple of corners and down a stairway to the science berthing area somewhere beneath the waterline, I was totally disoriented.

"Since we're only doing CTDs on this trip, no mooring operations, there aren't many of us. So you get a cabin to yourself," Chris said, opening a door with my name on it.

There are fifty-nine berths aboard the *Brown* in nine single and twenty-five double cabins to accommodate her twenty-one-member operating crew, six officers, and up to thirty-one scientists. Mine was typical of the science berthing area, with a double bunk, two institutional metal chests of drawers and a hanging locker, frilless but comfortable, and best of all, I had my own en suite head with shower. However, Chris warned, "These forward cabins can be really noisy." He nodded toward my bed. "The bow thrusters are right over there on the other side of the bulkhead." I had already noticed industrial ear protectors stowed in the rack with the life jackets and survival suits.

Among other specializations, ocean-research vessels do most of their work when stopped, "holding station," while technicians and scientists probe the depths. Measuring the characteristics of a column of water, you need to remain over that column of water. The *Brown*, like *Oceanus*, has no rudder, no propellers in the usual configuration, and no steering wheel. Instead, she has thrusters and video-game joysticks. There are two thrusters in the stern mounted in dogleg nozzles that can be rotated 360 degrees in unison or independently. Two more thrusters are mounted in recesses on either side of the bow. A good ship driver can spin her in her own length, walk her sideways, and perform other moves normal ships need not, the most important of which is to remain in one place when and wherever necessary. The new Dynamic Positioning System, a sort of autopilot, helps in this by automatically firing the thrusters when necessary to keep her on station; all the bridge officer needs to do is inform the machine of the coordinates of his desired position.

"Come on, I'll show you around," said Chris. "Then I'd better go talk with the captain."

He led me down corridors, up companionways from deck to deck, around corners, into and out of the main lab, the wet lab, the hydro and biochemical labs, and finally the computer lab. "This is our home," he said about the latter. "This is where we run the CTDs . . . It's freezing in here. Why's it so cold?" We went up to the 02 deck to see the galley and mess room, or maybe it was the 03 deck, thence down below the waterline to the laundry room next door to the little gym. He showed me the ship's store, closed now, that sold snacks, sundries, *Ron Brown* shirts and other regalia. By the time we finished the tour, I couldn't tell the pointy end from the square end. Excusing himself to go see the captain about a hurricane, Chris recognized my disorientation. "We're back on the main deck. Outside is through that door right there."

I seemed to be in the way of the hustling deck crew, lifting aboard pallets of gear and provisions with a crane, while others bolted down the deck gear already aboard with practiced competence. Just another trip for them, while I was feeling that old rush of romance I've known since dock-rat childhood in the presence of seagoing ships and boats, but of course it's easier for us amateur, dilettante seamen to retain our nautical romanticism. For me, this trip was different from my first aboard *Oceanus* peering over people's shoulders, separate. Now, a worker, I was part of the team, even if I had no idea how to do the work. Still, I was in the way of the real workers out here. I watched for a time, wedged in the corner of the hanger, a covered area opening at the aft end onto the transom, until the bosun came along to fetch some heavy-duty lifting strops from a rack behind me.

"You want a hard hat if you're out on deck," he said, pointing to a row of them on pegs.

Pleased with the unique combination of hard-assed industrial seamanship and pure science that goes on aboard these vessels, I hung around for a while watching departure preparations. I introduced myself to a couple of the deck hands who had just returned from a survey of the Southern Ocean in the vicinity of Cape Horn, and I was pleased to learn that Mary O'Connell, a retired teacher who'd signed on to see the world, and Phil Pokorski, a former dive operator and lifetime boat pro, had read my book about Cape Horn in preparation for the trip. They thought I was a celebrity. When they returned to work, I remained in the way, my potent celebrity notwithstanding, so I re-racked my hard hat and went below.

Wandering back into the freezing computer lab, I met Carlos Fonseca, an affable technician/consultant on whose experience and intelligence, it would soon become clear, everyone in the science staff depended. Carlos is responsible for CTD operations from initial setup to final data processing and quality control, but his heart remains in São Paolo, where he raises canaries with his father. Introducing me to the CTD console, a computer and VHF radio in a carrel near the door, Carlos explained that my job would be to direct the winch operator by radio to lower the instrument to within twenty meters of the bottom—try not to *hit* the bottom, he stressed—and then bring it up, stopping at predetermined depths to fire sampling bottles and to record temperature, salinity, and depth.

Brad Parks and Guilherme Castelão, doctoral candidates at the University of Miami's Rosenstiel School of Marine and Atmospheric Science (RSMAS, pronounced "Rasmas") and engineer Ben Kates straggled into the lab talking about surfing. Old hands at this "CTD console watch," they commenced telling horror stories about screw-ups on previous cruises who had crashed the heavy, delicate instrument into the bottom. I pictured the explosion of silt and mud in the deep darkness.

I went out to have a look at this CTD I'd be endangering, strapped for now to a wooden pallet on the starboard side. They call it the "package" aboard this ship, since it contains a multitude of instruments to measure *C*onductivity, *T*emperature, and *D*epth. The package is huge. You have to stand on a stool or something to reach the top, and it weighs about a ton. Standing off, I could see only the gray plastic water sampling bottles like skinny scuba tanks, twenty-three of them on this unit, mounted upright around the heavy circular frame. Kneeling, looking under the circle of bottles, I saw the array of instruments, the heart of the device, not a one of which I could identify. But I knew that their collective purpose was to determine the density of the water column from the bottom to the surface by measuring the components that determine density: salinity, temperature, and pressure. To learn the density—more precisely, the *differences* in density—along a particular strip of ocean reveals so much about the nature and extent of ocean motion that CTD operations are included in every cruise no matter its overall purpose.

Temperature is by far the most potent participant in the density mix. Cold water is denser (heavier) than warm water, just as cold air is heavier than warm. And since water and air are both fluids, they behave according to the same broad physical laws, the most broad of which states that warm fluid rises while cold sinks. Somewhere inside the circle of "Niskin" bottles, among the cables and connectors and instruments, there were two temperature sensors capable of measuring heat to a high degree of accuracy and reporting their readings in real time to our computer in the lab.

Salinity is the total quantity of dissolved solids contained in the water, including sodium, chlorine, calcium, magnesium, sulfur, about eighty in all, some in minute quantities. Rivers and rainwater runoff from land constantly pour more sodium and chlorine and other "salts" into the oceans, but this doesn't alter the total salt content because input is balanced by the tendency of heavier materials to sink to the bottom without dissolving. Salinity, therefore, has reached a "steady state." However, like temperature, it needs to be measured within fine tolerances. The total range from highest salinity to lowest is the difference between 33 and 38 parts per thousand. However, in more than seventy-five percent of the ocean, the salinity ranges between only 34.5 and 35 parts per thousand. In the old days, you had to boil off all the liquid in the water sample, then chemically analyze the solids left behind, a tedious and imprecise process. Late in the nineteenth century, the German chemist William Dittmar discovered that, while the quantity of salt constituents vary from place to place in the ocean, their ratio one to the other remains constant. This meant that you could measure only one constituent of salinity, usually chlorine, and extrapolate for the rest, an improved technique at the time, but an antique today.

In 1948, Henry Stommel wrote, "Due to the fact that water in the ocean is a conductor, and that it is everywhere under the influence of the earth's magnetic field, we should expect . . . that wherever the water is in motion electric potentials and currents will be established." To put it simply, when ocean water moves, it produces a slight electric charge. Since the electrical charge could be easily and accurately measured by adapting a common conductivity meter to survive a deep swim, oceanographers searched for a stable relationship between conductivity and the chemical constituents of salinity. When they were finished, they found that they didn't need to bother with chemical analysis at all. By applying an algorithm, they could accurately calculate salinity based on conductivity alone. And now conductivity readings, like temperature, are transmitted via the conductor cable directly to our computers.

Pressure, the other important element in the density mix, is a function of depth, a measure of the weight of water above a certain depth. This matters because seawater is slightly compressible, and when anything is compressed, a certain quantity of heat is generated. (That's the basic principle behind the Diesel engine.) The amount of pressure-generated heat needs to be learned so that it can be subtracted from the actual temperature.

As to this business of density, the normally recalcitrant ocean is remarkably cooperative. A water mass acquires its temperature and salinity signature at the surface, and when it sinks, as in thermohaline circulation, it maintains that characteristic combination of temperature and salinity as it moves about the ocean at depth. This, of course, allows scientists to follow its travels by identifying its "T-S profile."

⌒

"We're going," said Chris entering the lab. He looked at his watch. "At 1500. That's two hours."

What about Ophelia?

"It's veered a bit north, now predicted to hit Cape Hatteras tonight." The original plan had been to steam southeast from

Charleston directly toward the offshore end of the study line about three hundred miles east of Abaco Island and then work back westward along that same line of latitude (26.5 degrees North), CTD-ing all the way. Now, however, a southeast heading would present the ship's beam to Ophelia's hurricane swells. The motion would be untenable, gear and people careening from side to side in the deep rolls, a truly ugly and dangerous prospect. "The captain wants to run south, keeping the seas on her stern until we can turn safely east. It'll be plenty rough for a couple of days. So what we need to do is lash everything down in here and in the main lab. Okay?"

"Why's it so cold in here?" Brad wanted to know, pointing to a digital thermometer that read 55 degrees.

"Yeah, I'll ask somebody to look into it."

Chris assigned the lashing job to me, figuring that as a sailor, I probably knew a thing or two about lashing. He pointed me to a spool containing a couple of miles of cord and said I should use it all if necessary, just so nothing moves. Boy, did I lash. Feeling the engines rev, I took a break and went topside to watch us get under way. Everything that happens on deck, as separate from the engine room and the bridge, is the bosun's province, a capable man in this case clearly respected by the crew, with a Stetson-shaped hard hat and Maori tattoos ringing both legs. Line handling and the rest all deftly done, we steamed away from the pier out into the brown water of the Cooper River, heading toward the Route 17 Bridge. The captain had waited for low tide in order that the towering masthead array of atmospheric sensors, Doplar radar pods, navigation receivers, and long-range communication antenna cleared the bottom of the bridge span. Little harbor porpoise played in the bow wake as the *Brown* accelerated into the main channel. We passed the battleship *Yorktown* and a World War II submarine docked at the island museum on our port side. Fort Sumter came into sight, a vague lump in the muggy haze, away to starboard. The confluence of two rivers,

Charleston Harbor is broad but shallow, and the channel is still carefully marked with red and green buoys over a mile offshore. A long swell from the northeast finally signaled deep water.

Co-chief scientist Lisa Beal came on deck from the computer room, judging by her unseasonable wool sweater and hat. "We're going to have to live with it, I hear. Something's broken, and they can't fix it. We'll all get ice-cream headaches." Chris was trying out a new watch schedule, from 2 p.m. (1400) to 2 a.m. (0200), and Lisa was in charge of the second watch, 0200 to 1400. (Thankfully, I had drawn the first watch.) But, she explained, her main responsibility was the so-called ADCP, the Acoustic Doppler Current Profiler, and apparently it wasn't working up to snuff, if at all. I couldn't make out which because I wasn't too sure just what this ADCP was all about.

"It's another means of measuring deep current. You've probably heard the way the pitch of an ambulance siren changes as it speeds past. That's the Doppler shift. The ADCP senses ocean currents by bouncing acoustic waves off particles such as sediment or plankton drifting with the current. The wave arrives back at the instrument with a slightly different frequency than it went out with, and the difference tells us how fast the particles are moving. Oh, look, dolphins . . . Have you seen the ADCP?"

She led the way down the stairs from the elevated bow to the low main deck on the starboard side. Lisa knelt beside the CTD package and pointed to a three-foot-long yellow cylinder with four ceramic heads protected behind an epoxy lens aimed downward mounted among the rest of the stuff under the ring of Niskin bottles. This, she explained, was a "lowered ADCP." Like all the larger research vessels, the *Brown* carries another, a "shipboard ADCP," mounted in the hull peering downward. "This is useful because it can do its work while the ship is under way steaming between CTD stations. The drawback is the shipboard ADCP can only profile the ocean to a depth of 750 meters, while the average depth is around four kilometers, and that's where the lowered ADCP comes in."

Lisa didn't seem so fond of her lowered ADCP.

"It's great when it works."

There was a wooden picnic table aft on the starboard side in the shadow of the big main winch and its operator's house. Ben and Brad were sitting on the table talking longingly about the gnarly storm waves they were going to miss back in Miami. Brad was carrying, as he would through most of the trip, his copy of Joseph Pedlosky's famously difficult *Geophysical Fluid Dynamics*. "Have you read it?" he asked.

Afraid of the math, I had avoided the esteemed edition. The laws of physics determine the ocean's motion; the language of physics is math. I don't do math.

Guilherme Castelão, a bright, intense Brazilian who was dealing with these thorny concepts and their equations in a second language, would tell me later that "without math, I can't prove you anything." Luckily, I had nothing to prove.

Carlos and Chris came on deck followed shortly by Jon Molina, a RSMAS tech on the second watch who was to help Lisa collect and compile the ADCP data. Now the entire science staff had gathered around the picnic table. This cruise was part of an ongoing project called the Western Boundary Time Series (WBTS). Once or twice a year since 1984, scientists from AOML and RSMAS have been measuring the ocean dynamics along the same line of latitude, 26.5 degrees North. That study line—which cuts the Florida coast near Fort Lauderdale and extends eastward through Abaco Island several hundred miles out into the Sargasso Sea—was chosen by the AOML/RSMAS oceanographers partly because of a happy coincidence. Nearby, the telephone company had strung a cable along the bottom to connect Florida to the Bahamas, which, while performing its intended purpose, incidentally measures the voltage induced by the passing water. Applying some math to the voltage numbers, the scientists can calculate the water transport in the Florida Current, and so the cable happens to afford the Miami oceanographers a cheap but useful "time series" profile. However, the choice of 26.5 North as the focus of the Western Boundary Time Series was based on broader oceanographic considerations. The western side of the Atlantic at that latitude is richly dynamic. First, the warm Florida Current portion of the Gulf Stream crosses it from south to north. Also, along the seaward side of the Bahamas another piece of the Gulf Stream gyre, the relatively weak Antilles Current, flows northward until it merges with the Gulf Stream north of the Bahamas. And then, of course, there is the cold Deep Western Boundary Current flowing in the opposite direction beneath the Antilles Current. That profusion of flow, shallow and deep, warm and cold, makes this strip of ocean as relevant to the transport of heat, and therefore to climate, as any in the hemisphere.

At some point, we were going to retrieve a malfunctioning, inverted echo sounder, an acoustic device designed to rest on the bottom and measure the temperature and salinity of the water passing overhead. We would also deploy some drifters, Chris said, simple surface floats equipped with a temperature sensor and GPS receiver. Since CTD work was the main point of the cruise, we didn't need anymore people than could comfortably occupy a picnic table. We watched the low-lying Carolina coast fade to a wavering smudge on the western horizon, and the *Brown* powered through a long, ominous swell rolling in from the northeast out Ophelia's way. It might be worse tomorrow.

"Well, it's that time," someone said. "Dinner." It was 4:30. One gets used to it.

Throughout much of the cruise, Chris and Lisa generously held fizzo lessons for me. At my request, the first night's lesson was "Geostrophy 101." Geostrophy was another of those fundamental principles of ocean behavior I'd never heard of before I began trying to see the ocean through oceanographer's eyes. And at that time, September 2005, vision was still blurry.

"Remember, Ekman transport piles up water near the center of the gyre, and gravity takes it away," said Chris. "So geostrophy is a steady state in which the pressure gradient and the Coriolis force fall into balance." He wrote it as an equation: (1 / rho) dp / dx = fv. "Oh, that's right, no math."

"Sorry."

"'Geostrophy' is borrowed from meteorology. The hill in the ocean is basically the same as a region of high pressure in the atmosphere. Air wants to flow away from the center of high pressure outward toward regions of low pressure, but Coriolis bends the flow to the right in the Northern Hemisphere, and the winds then spin in a clockwise direction along lines of equal pressure. Same thing happens in the ocean. Look at it this way: I'm standing in a boat at one point in the ocean, and you're standing in another, say, sixty miles away. Suppose the sea surface is one meter higher under your boat than it is under my boat. That means there is more water under you than me, and so there will be a pressure gradient between us. Water will want to flow from beneath your boat towards mine. Now because of Coriolis, the flow will be turned to the right, so in effect the current will flow perpendicular to the line of sight between our boats. Our purpose is to measure the slope of the pressure gradient in order to learn the velocity of the current. That's where the CTD comes into it. The CTD measures salinity, temperature, and pressure. If we know those things, by applying a couple of equations, which I won't mention, we can calculate density. By comparing the density between this CTD station and the next one and the next, we're able to measure the slope—the horizontal pressure gradient—between them. If we know that, we can calculate the flow between stations, arriving at the so-called thermal wind equation. If we run about fifty stations, like we're doing on this trip, across a specific strip of ocean, we get a broad picture of the current. But then we have to do it again six months later and six months after that to make sure we're not mistaking temporal variations for the mean flow. That's what this Western Boundary Time Series Project is all about. We've been measuring this strip of ocean since the early eighties."

That was clear enough. From the CTD data, you can learn the differences in density between stations, and from that information you can calculate the current's velocity without having to measure it directly. Right?

"Well, yes," said Lisa. "But it's not quite that simple."

I was afraid of that.

"After we do the math, we still don't know the absolute velocity of the current. We only know the relative flow between the measured stations."

Yes, I'd read about that. "Is this the reference-level problem?"

"Exactly," said Chris.

Lisa said, "The density gradients in the ocean can tell us how geostrophic velocity varies with depth, but it can't tell us the absolute velocity—because we can't measure the actual sea surface slope. What would we measure it against?"

As Chris put it, "If the material that makes up the Earth were perfectly uniform and Earth were perfectly spherical, then in order to talk about sea-level differences we would need to measure sea-height relative to a circle that is everywhere equal distance from the center of Earth." The problem for oceanographers is that Earth isn't entirely spherical, and the material comprising Earth's surface is not uniform. There are mountains in some places, valleys in others, and a lot of ocean everywhere. Scientists have long struggled to find a level surface or something to represent it—the so-called geoid—that could perhaps be measured from space by satellites, but at this writing, everyone agrees, the range of error is too great to be completely reliable. The geoid is sort of an idealization, and reckoning a level surface remains tricky.

Over the years, Lisa pointed out, oceanographers have tried myriad ways to "reference" geostrophic velocities: various kinds of neutrally buoyant floats, moored current meters, shipboard and lowered ADCPs, bottom-mounted pressure sensors, and so on. But all these methods have a similar problem, the same one we've "referenced" earlier, that is, the constant variability of the ocean's circulation. The geostrophic currents, those calculated from CTD measurements, are being constantly confused by small-scale perturbations from, for instance, tides and other waves bouncing around through the interior of the real ocean, what scientists call "noise."

So what's the poor oceanographer to do?

He or she tries to determine a "level of no motion" or "reference level." Chris explained that early oceanographers just assumed that the current velocity at the bottom of the ocean was zero. But as time passed and technology advanced, they learned that the deep ocean was indeed moving, so they had to look elsewhere for their level of no motion. Once scientists learned to identify individual water masses by their temperature-salinity signature, they found points where one water mass was flowing north, for instance, while another, deeper mass was flowing south. It stood to reason, then, that there should be a point of zero velocity between the two masses, and that point could be found by detecting changes in temperature and salinity. That determination works in places where adjacent water masses move in distinguishably different directions, but that's not the case everywhere in the ocean. In some places, as we've said, the so-called surface current carries all the way to the bottom. And in other places, the water masses move with uncooperative variability in relation to each other. For instance, time-series measurements along 70 degrees West, the longitude of Cape Cod, show that while most of the time the Deep Western Boundary Current flows in the opposite direction from the Gulf Stream, it doesn't always. Occasionally it changes direction as well as depth. There may still be a level of no motion somewhere in the mix, but it's hard to find because it moves around and up and down.

"So how do you solve the reference-level problem?"

"You can't entirely," said Lisa. "There will always be a degree of uncertainty in the geostrophic velocities, but our objective is to reduce them as much as possible. That's one of the reasons why we measure this 26.5 North line twice a year. Where we have moored current meters in place over the long term and, say, repeated ADCP measurements, we gain a pretty accurate idea of the actual current. We can use those places where we know the current as benchmarks to figure out a level of no motion with simple arithmetic. It's not one hundred percent accurate, but we can get close. Occasionally we just have to take an educated guess and say, okay, three thousand meters is our level of no motion. Over time," Lisa said, "we can refine our assumption or find a better one."

"So theoretically, if you put current meters on moorings all over the ocean, you wouldn't need the CTDs?" I asked.

"Theoretically, yes. But there aren't enough ships and oceanographers in the world to tend all those moorings even if somebody agreed to pay for them," said Chris.

"And still," said Lisa, "you'd have to come out here, say, once a year, to replace the batteries. Besides, current meters need to be pulled out of the water and taken ashore for servicing and recalibration from time to time. The conductivity sensors, for instance, which measure salinity, lose accuracy over time. So we have to take water samples with the CTD bottles and analyze the salts in order to know how to recalibrate the current meters."

"Where do you analyze the salts? Back ashore in the lab?"

"No, we'll do it right here aboard. Have you seen the salinity lab?"

I hadn't.

"It's this little closet just across the corridor. No place for those prone to seasickness. In fact, when you get up to speed on the CTD console, I'll have Guilherme run salts, and you can do the CTD alone."

Oh. I didn't really want that responsibility, but then that's why I was aboard.

"Don't worry, you'll be an expert in no time."

"All you need to remember is—"

"Don't hit the bottom. I know, I know."

Oceanographers like it when outsiders seek to understand their work. Since much of this country's oceanographic research is paid for by the National Science Foundation and NOAA, supported in turn by taxpayer dollars, scientists are, to some extent, obliged to speak to the rest of us. They call it "outreach," and everyone I met approves of the concept, but in practice outreach is problematical on a couple levels. To translate esoteric principles into popularly understood language without draining the integrity from the principles requires pedagogical technique, not part of the research scientist's job description. Then there's the "forum" question. Where would this pedagogy take place? I can't picture my fizzo friends calling a news conference to report their research findings, to keep us posted as it were, short of something really dramatic. That they don't keep us posted and that we don't ask that they do so have provoked a level of confusion as to what, actually, is going on in ocean and climate science. For instance, these same scientists from RS-MAS and NOAA who are working jointly on another ocean/climate project have had to draft a press release to clear up the murk generated by a string of erroneous press reports. They had to say in effect, no, we're not talking about the Gulf Stream shutting down. But oceanographers aren't yet used to their new relevance and its attendant relationship to publicity. Lisa, Chris, and other young oceanographers said that ten years ago they would never have imagined that the press, let alone the public, would want or need to hear from them.

Also militating against organized outreach, the culture of science doesn't reward those who try to address the public. I suppose things have lightened up in this respect since fellow physicists excoriated Carl Sagan for his television series *Cosmos*—particle and theoretical types going around saying mockingly, "*billions* of stars"—but such efforts are still faintly disrespectable. Maybe this exclusive spirit will evaporate as oceanographers absorb their new role—or as we absorb the relevance of their research. But scientists will still need to maintain their professional skepticism, and it's not exactly fair to ask them to become advocates for, say, emission caps on greenhouse gasses. Advocacy and intellectual objectivity are hard to reconcile. Also, political advocacy, at least for now, is professionally injudicious for a scientist whose funding proposal might be judged yea or nay by someone who disagrees with the position advocated or disapproves of advocacy, period. This, I'm told, is less a factor in climate science, since there are no climate-change dissenters among real scientists, only those who dislike the language and syntax of the present climate-change "debate."

Be that as it may, Lisa and Chris were reaching out to me beyond the call of duty. This level of time and concentration would be available only here aboard ship. I hoped to be a quick study, but I felt like going outside to make sure the ocean was still there. We could feel its actuality in the windowless lab, the *Brown*'s stern rhythmically rising to the following seas and sagging back. (There are several large portholes in the lab's outboard wall, but these are routinely covered at night with blackout plates to prevent light spill that might interfere with visibility from the bridge.) And occasionally we could hear the ocean wash along the starboard side, but I still wanted to go outside and look just to be sure. Fading, we concluded the lesson about midnight. I walked out on the transom, stepping gingerly around various objects and shin-cracking protuberances barely visible in the shadowy light spilling from the hanger, until I remembered I had a flashlight in my pocket. Alone out there—everyone else who wasn't on watch was asleep or watching *Meet the Fockers* in the crew lounge—I stopped six feet from the lifelines strung across the stern for safety's sake.

Marble-sized globules of green phosphorescence churned in the white wake. The moonlight, bright and shimmering two hours ago, was diminished now to a dull loom near the top of a towering black cloudbank. I panned my light across the wake searching for a sense of the sea state that I could correlate to the wind, but the puny beam illuminated nothing. I longed for something from the ocean. I distracted myself for a while concentrating on the seeming dissonance between the scientific explanation of the ocean and the other more personal, evocative view unexpressible in the language of physics. I knew this same vague longing as a kid scuba diving in the Gulf Stream and earlier, a child standing on a Florida beach in late-afternoon shadow, and it has been aboard with me on every ocean trip since, particularly at night when the ocean reveals almost nothing of itself. As a child, I dreamed of living in the ocean, drifting through the mid-water where sunlight barely penetrates in a sort of particulate suspension to watch ocean creatures materialize from the gloom, pass, and disappear again. Clouds pinched off the loom of the moon.

"Do you need some light?"

I jumped.

"I saw you out here on the screens from the bridge." It was Lieutenant Elizabeth Jones. "I came down to see if you needed light."

Since there were no unobstructed sightlines from the bridge to the transom or the side decks, the ship was being scanned constantly by video cameras. I knew that, but it hadn't occurred to me that my presence on the transom would excite concern on the bridge. Just being here, I had made Liz trek down numerous flights of rolling stairs to see if I needed light. I apologized for the inconvenience and said that I was just looking.

"Well, if you need anything, you can call the bridge from one of the telephones. Just dial 125."

"Thank you."

"No problem."

Next morning, we were in the Gulf Stream. It wasn't necessary to see the water to know that. Humidity signaled its presence. Several engineers standing around in the hanger having coffee and a smoke ignored me as I passed through their conversation onto the open transom. The Gulf Stream is blue, as everyone knows, but there is no other blue like it in nature. It's not a light-hearted hue like the blue of a cloudless sky on a June morning, but dark and dense, more sensation than color, as if consciously, artistically designed to evoke extravagant response. *Gulf Stream* blue.

Removing myself to the starboard quarter (the right rear corner of a ship), beneath the boom arm of the big black crane I watched those straight shafts of sunlight shimmering down into the depths. Actually, the water isn't blue at all, but gin-clear, transparent, due to near absence of organic material in suspension. Blue is the collaborative trick of water and light. When sunlight penetrates the surface, the water strips the spectrum of reds and greens and yellows, leaving behind only the blue. But the trick doesn't diminish the evocative power of this Gulf Stream blue, and the feel of the heat engine running full blast affirms its power. A deckhand climbed into the driver's compartment and fired up the crane engine. He leaned out the window to ask me to move before he swung the boom arm inboard, but I was already on my way.

Chris Churylo, taking the air on the transom before his shift began, introduced himself, and when asked about his role aboard, said, "If it has electronics, it's mine to repair and maintain—radars, computer networks, communication, entertainment, and science equipment." That seemed a lot for one man to know. He didn't actually *know*, he said, but he could read a manual.

The hurricane avoidance plan had been to carry on south to about 28 degrees North, the latitude of Cape Canaveral, Florida, before turning east toward the survey line. But Chris had just heard that, since the seas weren't as bad as suspected, we might make the eastward turn seventy miles or so north of that latitude at around 1500 today. He had heard, also, that a tropical storm named Rita was expected to turn into a hurricane by midnight and head west, passing between our survey line and Cuba in the next several days. Had he heard anything else?

"There's going to be a surprise abandon-ship drill before lunch."

I went below to my cabin to check my assigned muster station posted on the door for abandon-ship and fire drills just as the claxon went off and an intercom-voice said, "Abandon ship, abandon ship. All hands report to your abandon-ship stations. This is only a drill. Repeat: this is only a drill." Yes, but it's taken very seriously indeed aboard these vessels. I put on a long-sleeved shirt and hat, as required, collected my immersion suit and life jacket and made my way back up the stairs to our assigned place at the after end of the main lab on the starboard side.

James Brinkley, a tall young ensign uniformed in crisp khaki, was in charge of the science abandonees. He asked Meinen to count heads, and when that was complete, Brinkley informed the bridge that we were present and accounted for. James told us to don life jackets, make sure that there was a whistle and strobe light attached and that the strobe worked. Then, with apologies, he told us all to climb into our Gumby suits, and we waddled around for a while sweating profusely as James checked us out. "Any questions?"

"Secure from abandon-ship drill," said the voice from on high. "Prepare for man-overboard drill."

Uninvolved in that, Chris, Lisa, Brad, Ben, Carlos, Guilherme, and I sat around on the picnic table to watch. A crewman carried a life-size dummy named Oscar in a Gumby suit and red helmet onto the transom and waited for radio instructions from an officer. When they came, he heaved Oscar over the side.

"Man overboard!" said the intercom voice. "Away on the starboard side."

As she slowed to a stop, four crewmen rushed up the stairs to the O2 deck and clambered into the boat, descriptively called a rigid-hull inflatable, or RHIB, slung outboard from the O2 deck on an ingenious hoist. The winch driver lowered the RHIB into the water, and it sped away toward the MOB, a speck in the distance, appearing and disappearing with each wave. The sobering lesson—*stay on the ship*—was not lost on the picnic-table audience. Everyone involved in the recovery knew the drill was coming; the boat crew was geared up and ready; the ship had stopped immediately, but the MOB dummy was already so far astern we had to stand on the table to see it in fleeting glimpses. Without a life jacket, a real man overboard would be in serious trouble, even in these warm waters; a man or woman who went over the side at night would likely become part of the deep-ocean circulation we were out here to study. Later, I asked around to learn whether anyone had ever been lost off the *Brown*. Apparently not, but the question brought up the "swim-call story."

"Swim call?"

At the captain's discretion, research-ship personnel were allowed to take a swim while the ship was stopped, "vastly agreeable in these torrid zones," as Captain Ellis put it a couple of centuries ago. That policy was terminated not long ago when during a swim call somewhere in the equatorial Pacific, a tiger shark removed a scientist's leg in a single pass. "She survived, but swim call didn't," as someone put it.

The captain made his left turn toward the east before dinner, and the seas, seemingly negligible when they were on the stern, set her rolling as they passed under her port beam. Shortly after dark on the second night out, still short of the study line, the *Brown* came to a stop. We were going to make a practice CTD cast. The main purpose was to test the salinity and temperature sensors and the ADCP return, secondarily to teach the volunteer to make himself useful. When Carlos and Chief Survey Tech Jonathan Shannahoff donned life jackets and hard hats and headed out to launch the CTD, I followed them onto the open starboard-side deck.

Carlos double-checked the connections and the arming mechanisms on the bottle caps, and when he signaled all was in order, Jonathan radioed the winch driver, out of sight one deck above, to take it up. Carlos and Jonathan steadied it by hand against the building roll until the winch operator swung it outboard, and Jonathan ordered the winch to dunk the package. I returned to the computer lab to learn my new job. While I had expected to watch over someone's shoulder, Carlos asked me to take a seat at the controls, which consisted of a computer screen and radio mic to talk to the winch driver.

With the package awash just below the surface, it would be up to me to make sure all the sensors were working. "Okay," said Carlos, peering at the screen "everything is fine," though I couldn't tell how he knew that. "Now tell the winch driver to take it down to ten meters. Just say, 'Winch, down to ten.'" I did so, authoritatively. "We wait at ten meters for two minutes to let the instruments adjust, then tell the winch to take it down at thirty meters per minute."

"Down at thirty, please."

Mary, the winch driver, clicked the mic button twice as acknowledgment. (We're instructed by Jonathan not to converse with the winch person even if we're buddies, stick to business.) We watched the depth increase. At one hundred meters, we increased the speed to sixty meters per minute. The CTD measures pressure instead of depth in a unit called decibars, but "d-bars" coincide closely with meters. Carlos switched to another computer screen that registered in the form of a line graph changes in temperature, salinity, and pressure with a different color for each. This visually revealed the broad stratification of the ocean.

As Ellis and others noticed centuries ago, the Sun warms directly only the uppermost sliver of seawater. Solar heat is churned deeper beneath the surface by wind-driven waves, resulting in a well-mixed layer with constant temperature and salinity, but seldom below three hundred meters and often no more than seventy-five meters. This is called straightforwardly the "mixed layer." Below the mixed layer lies the "main thermocline," ranging in depth from two hundred meters to as much as one thousand meters, depending on local conditions. Temperature decreases rapidly in the main thermocline. Beneath the thermocline, in the deep layer, temperature remains nearly constant (cold) all the way to the bottom. The visual representation of the ocean layers appears on the monitor in the shape of a champagne glass—straight down from the lip, bending inward, then straight down the stem—as the package passes down through the mixed layer, thermocline, and into the deep layer, respectively. "That's what you look for on the downcast," said Carlos, "that champagne shape." He pointed to another instrument in a bulkhead lined with instruments and black boxes called the "bathy" that acoustically measures the bottom depth. We were in 4,450 meters of water, according to the bathy on the bulkhead. "You want to stop the package twenty meters above the bottom, but don't use the bathy for that. I show you when we get there."

Brad and Guilherme wandered off as the package proceeded through the lightless depths. I stayed and watched the layers resolve, pressure increasing as temperature decreased. Jonathan bustled nervously around the bank of instruments. Lisa joined him and they watched skeptically as the ADCP data came in. Something was amiss, but I never learned just what. As the bottom approached, Carlos told me that there was a down-looking altimeter mounted on the package, and it would kick in at 250 meters above the bottom. If it doesn't, he said, I should stop everything and call him or Chris. An hour or so later, the altimeter had dutifully joined in, and the CTD, it said, was one hundred meters above the potential crash site.

"At forty meters, tell Mary to stand by, and she'll slow to thirty meters a minute."

"Winch, stand by."

"Standing by," she replied.

Chris joined us and sat down behind me. "Don't think I'm paranoid or anything," he said.

"Make sure that she actually does slow down," said Carlos pointing to the decreasing altimeter numbers. "Then at twenty meters, say, 'aaaaand stop.'"

I said so, and it stopped after bouncing for a bit on the long cable.

On a standardized form, the "CTD Log sheet," Chris had listed about a dozen bottle-stop depths. The water is sampled on the way up, of course, because if you closed a bottle on the way down, the pressure would crush it flat. (Among the amusements apparently universal on research cruises is to write greetings to friends ashore on Styrofoam cups and send the cups down with the CTD; they come back up squeezed to thimble size.) Adhering to radio protocol, I was to stop the package at each depth, record temperature, pressure, salinity, and then "fire" the bottle with a mouse click to close the bottle stoppers trapping in situ water.

"And that's pretty much it," said Carlos. "Make sure you fill out all the information on the sheet for each bottle stop. Let's see, I'll show you how to log off the computer and shut down the package when it comes up. What else?"

"Don't hit the bottom."

"Yes. Don't."

A few minutes before our watch ended at 0200, Chris asked me to help him deploy the first of a series of "drifters," and I followed him out to the hanger where they were stored in stacked cardboard boxes. Simple inner-tube size floats, Chris explained, drifters are an inexpensive means of measuring sea surface temperatures (SSTs). Satellites do this most efficiently from space, but direct measurements by drifters and things are used to validate (or invalidate) satellite readings. Scientists are keeping a sharp eye on SSTs, because rising surface temperatures mean increased evaporation that pours more moisture into the atmosphere and, in turn, leads to more severe storms among other feedbacks. And then there's the matter of sea-level rise: Heat causes water to expand—"thermal expansion" is the straightforward technical term—so if SSTs rise, sea levels will rise as well.

Drifters also measure surface current velocity, Chris was explaining. "Well, not literally the surface, but fifteen meters down. It carries a sea anchor—we call it the holy-sock—to keep the drifter from riding with the wind rather than current." Above water, it carries a GPS-style receiver that updates its position several times a day, and from the changes in position between fixes, current velocity can be easily reckoned. Chris phoned the bridge, where every activity is logged, to inform them that we were about to deploy the drifter. We carried it, about the size of a coffee tabletop, out to the stern, where I began opening the box.

"That won't be necessary," he said. "We just toss the whole thing over the side. The cardboard disintegrates, leaving the drifter to do its work. Ready? On three?" The box disappeared into the darkness.

I humbly agree with John Swallow that the purposeful structure and repetition of shipboard life clears the mind, affording new perspectives on shoreside life. I, for one, love shipboard routine, its orderliness and efficiency, watch-on–watch-off, no matter what, twenty-four hours a day. Others would rather not go to sea for that same reason. Mealtimes are fixed. The evening meal is over at 5:30. I never eat three meals a day at home; out here I wouldn't miss one, in addition to our ritualized post-watch snack. The galley itself is off limits, but the mess-room pantries are always open. We eat, sleep, and run CTDs for twelve hours and repeat the process. I was tense the first time running the console by myself, but I didn't bury the package in the bottom, and by my third cast—the deep casts took three hours to complete—I had the hang of it. At the completion of each cast, with the package lashed aboard, Guilherme, Carlos, and I go out to extract water samples, one round for oxygen, one for salts, and the deeper into our watch, the funnier our own patter seems to us. I've noticed on sailboats as well as these research vessels that a "trip joke" inevitably evolves, and we find it endlessly hilarious even as we run it into the ground (deck). But it's impossible to retell to those ashore. I used to try, but no longer. Trip jokes make no sense except to those who were sampling salts and oxygen at 0100 in 25 knots of wind, their ankles awash on a rolling deck. I miss the jokes and the shipmates and the ocean when the trip is over.

At sea, weather, which is to say wind, determines the sea state (waves) and thereby the quality of life, and so a flutter of excitement ran through the science staff when Chris Churylo passed around the latest NOAA Tropical Weather report. Rita had indeed matured into a category-three hurricane, and was heading west northwest at

20 mph. I plotted the coordinates of its reported position on my chart and compared that to our present position. It was heading right for us. Hurricanes focus people's minds when floating in their paths. I measured the distance between it and us. If Rita maintained that course and speed, she'd be on us the day after tomorrow. We went back to work dipping and retrieving the package. I admit to a certain curiosity about how the *Brown* would behave in really heavy seas, but that's not something someone in the moment says out loud. Swells from Rita's direction were already changing *Brown*'s motion. (The lab never warmed up; we wore four layers and foul-weather jackets at the console, then took it all off to go outside to sample salts and things in the path of a hulking subtropical disturbance.)

By the afternoon, September 19, NOAA's weather update reported that Rita had turned due west, now predicted to pass through the Old Bahama Passage between the lower arm of Great Bahamas Bank and the north coast of Cuba. Only its fringes, tropical-storm conditions, would brush our position out on the 26.5 North line. By dark, we were experiencing 30-knot winds with higher gusts and spectacularly beautiful seas, though I would not have used that word had we been aboard a 40-foot sailboat. The *Brown*'s decks were constantly awash, and the package was swinging wildly, threatening its own well-being and ours, when we hoisted it off the deck. By 2100 (9 p.m.), Chief Survey Tech Jonathan Shannahoff had seen enough and called a halt to operations. Heartbroken, our watch played poker until 0200, for funzies, no gambling allowed on NOAA ships. Routine resumed the next day in sparkling sunshine, no wind, but a residual southerly swell kept us moving from handhold to handhold.

CTD ops were suspended for several hours on the 20th in order to retrieve one of Chris's Inverted Echo Sounders (IES). "Observational" oceanographers like Meinen are in the business of figuring out how to measure the ocean, what combination of instruments might best gather the desired data, and then going to sea to gather it. Think of the IES, he said, like a stereo speaker keyed to a stopwatch. The IES sits on the bottom on an expendable metal rack and shoots sound pulses up at the surface that then bounce back to the instrument. When it emits a pulse, it starts the stopwatch; the return pulse stops the watch. These many thousands of "travel-time" measurements provide information about the total heat content of the water because the speed of sound in seawater is a direct function of water temperature. Chris conveyed instructions via computer to the acoustic releases telling them to let go of the rack, and they obeyed. About an hour and a half later, Mary spotted the strobe light pulsing on the black surface, and an hour after that, we had hooked it back into human hands.

Starting at the farthest seaward point on the 26.5 North line 274 nautical miles east of the Bahamas, we did some forty CTD casts, working westward watch-on-watch-off. Ten days later, by the watch change at 0200, we could see intermittently between passing squalls the dull loom from two lighthouses on Great Abaco Island. The plan was to run CTD casts on through the Northwest Providence Channel and then across the Florida Straits right up to the continental shelf off Ft. Lauderdale. I was surprised to learn, however, that before we could work in Bahamian waters, we would be required to clear customs. This would take at least half a day. *Brown* stopped tantalizingly close to the seaward edge of the coral reef off Abaco Island where the salmon-colored water turned abruptly deep blue. The executive officer, with our passports in a waterproof packet under her arm, joined the boat crew already aboard, and they lowered away. A hot southwest breeze was kicking up little steep waves too tightly packed to fit the boat between the crests; its crew would have a molar-jarring ride to the customs office. Meanwhile, members of the science staff peered down into the gorgeous azure water.

"Swim call!" someone shouted wishfully.

"Perhaps we could sign a shark waver."

"Sure, you write it up and take it to the captain."

Five hours later they retrieved the RHIB with its wobbly complement, and we got under way into the Northwest Providence Channel, the deep trench through the middle of the Bahama Islands. After dinner, we had the CTD back in the water.

The stations came fast and furiously in the shallow continental slope water, none deeper than eight hundred meters. The ship headed for the next stop the moment we had the CTD back on deck. By the time we'd extracted our oxygen and salt samples, emptied the bottles, and rearmed their triggers, she was maneuvering into position for the next cast. We'd been hoping that the shallow-cast rush would fall to the other watch. By midnight, we could see headlights turning onto A–1A in Ft. Lauderdale. By 0200, the last cast—the fifty-fourth—was complete. Our work was finished. The *Brown* turned south and we headed for Government Cut, Miami, and the Coast Guard dock near South Beach. I don't like the endings. I'd grown weary with CTD routine, like everyone else, but I wouldn't have minded a few more days at sea.

I walked forward to the point of the bow and stood for a time watching Broward County slide by and growing nostalgic. I grew up on that coast and fell under the ocean's spell; my mother had died there several months earlier. But I decided not to dwell on nostalgia, turned aft, and joined the science staff telling stories in our arctic lab while wearing coats and woolen caps. A couple of hours later, after waiting her turn out by the sea buoy, *Brown* steamed into Government Cut. Gathered along the starboard rail, we watched the pastel neon on the deco hotels behind Lummus Park and the hot discos at the foot of Ocean Drive. Lisa, who lives there, named them for us. Nikki Beach Club, with the South Sea motif, that was *the* place for Sunday-night partying on the beach beneath the firmament or in teepees, cabanas, beds.

Coast Guard Station Miami occupies multibillion-dollar real estate across the channel from South Beach, but the atmosphere is different, destitute of cabanas and teepees. Coasties on the wharf awaited our lines. As the captain edged her sideways, harbor mud billowing outboard in the thruster wash, a salsa party aboard an awninged pontoon craft passed astern. Laughter, music, bottles clinking, dancing revelers in white suits and dresses, someone singing about his broken *corazon*—we were far from the ocean now.

"So are you willing to go out again?" Chris wondered, salsa fading.

"Sure."

"The next trip is in March. Same ship, only more crowded, and same study line, but this will be a different project. It's a collaboration between us and British oceanographers called RAPID/MOCHA to measure the MOC all the way across the North Atlantic."

"MOC?"

"The Meridional Overturning Circulation."

I had never heard of the Meridional Overturning Circulation at the time.

"Molly Baringer will be chief scientist. She'll be here tomorrow to help us pack up. I'll introduce you. She'll sign you on."

"Well, okay."

Chapter 14

"GRAVEYARDS OF THE ATLANTIC"

Amid the science of ocean currents, it might be illustrative to glance at the mariner's relationship to currents. It's not been congenial. Currents have caused much maritime grief over the centuries, and still do. I'll bet if we remove intoxication and headlong idiocy from the statistics of inshore boating accidents, look only at those with inherently nautical roots, we'll find "groundings in current" at the head of the list. The captain, crossing the current, thinks he's going in the same direction as his bow, but he's not. He's crabbing sideways. If he's not paying attention, telling hairy sea stories to his guests from Tulsa, then: the vicious sudden stop, the sickening hollow thunk of fiberglass meeting rock. It happens all the time. But if he strikes bottom, that means he has screwed up in a tidal current. They're easier to judge than ocean currents because fixed visual reference points are usually available. You can eyeball an inshore current by lining up, say, that nun buoy with the church steeple at the head of the harbor, a "range" in nautical parlance. If they fall out of line, then a current must be setting you sideways. (To get back on range you steer toward the nearest mark.) At sea, however, without any reference points fixed to the bottom or mounted on land, not even the most talented and experienced old salt can judge the set of an ocean current. Absent some visual clue such as a change in water color, he can't even tell that a current is present.

Then there is the blunt trauma of wind-against-current conditions. Inshore or off, when the wind blows against a current, two things happen, both unpleasant and, in the extreme, unhealthy. First, the wind peels up steep, flat-faced waves. Second, but simultaneously and building with time, the wind retards the flow of the current, waves stack up, and the distance between their crests decreases. These are said to be "short seas." The boat has no time "to find her head" before she's slammed by the next wave. Short seas can be nasty in bays and sounds, like running into rock walls on a Vermont dairy farm. Wind blowing against an ocean current does essentially the same thing but everything turns out much bigger. Like many green kids, I received my first real pummeling in a little boat when a stiff northerly blew up in the Gulf Stream. I couldn't believe the way my beloved Gulf Stream was treating me. When really heavy wind blows against an ocean current for a prolonged period of time, waves turn monstrous, *averaging* fifty feet in extreme conditions with "rogues" twice that height scattered through the wave train. At least in most instances of ocean-current violence, with plenty of sea room and with nothing hard to hit, one usually emerges unscathed and a little wiser. But in certain places, when ocean currents approach shallow water, they conspire with geography to lay exquisite traps for mariners. Cape Hatteras, among the most exquisite, has therefore earned the title "Graveyard of the Atlantic."

This is an unlikely graveyard. It lies not in the angry, icy high latitudes isolated from the boon of civilization and any hope of rescue, as one might suppose, but in the moderate mid-latitudes. While the appellation evokes a vision of doom and gloom in shades of gray, wet swirling fog, black basalt lurking to leeward, ghosts of dead mariners flitting in the spindrift, Cape Hatteras is a bulge near the bottom of the Outer Banks of North Carolina, a picturesque arc of white-sand barrier beach fronting soft, marsh-fringed lagoons and sounds with pretty names, Albemarle and Pamlico. Dense with holiday homes and motels and marked by that lovable barber-pole lighthouse, the Outer Banks evokes images of toddlers and sand castles, cookouts and beach volleyball of a Saturday afternoon, not broken-backed ships and corpses rolling in the surf zone.

On the other hand, if the sheer number of wrecks in its waters is a measure, Cape Hatteras has earned the appellation. The *Tiger* was the first, part of Richard Grenville's 1585 expedition delivering colonists to Roanoke Island. The damage repaired, she managed to sail back to England, taking a rich Spanish prize on the way—in Elizabethan times there was negligible difference between explo-ration, colonial settlement, and piracy. But when she ran up on the shoals and the seas holed her, *Tiger* had lost most of the food and supplies that were to see the Roanoke colonists through the first winter. That loss was one of the central reasons why the colony foundered. Francis Drake rescued the famished survivors in the spring and returned them to England. One published report holds, hyperbolically, I suspect, that during the ensuing centuries 2,200 ships followed the *Tiger* onto the graveyard sandbanks now called Diamond Shoal and Frying Pan Shoal. A more credible record counts 230 ships of more than fifty tons dying on the banks between 1866 and 1945, but that's still a lot of nautical grief. Why? What makes this place so mean to mariners? Why not just sail out around the damn thing? It's not like Cape Horn; you don't need to round it to reach your destination.

Consider the problem from the deck of a wind-driven vessel, a schooner, say, from Maine carrying lumber to Miami during the building boom of the 1920s. Upon approaching Cape Hatteras from the north, her captain was confronted with three navigation alterna-tives, all rotten. He could stand far enough offshore to avoid the shoals, but that would put his bow dead into the foul northerly set of the Gulf Stream. A coastal trader under sail might average six knots in a fair wind, but if she tried to stem the Gulf Stream current of three knots and more, she would be stripped of half of her "velocity made good" over the bottom. Using those figures, her day's run would be reduced from 144 nautical miles to seventy-two. To sail knowingly against a heavy current was a stupid alternative. Instead, the captain could decide to sail seaward away from the danger, cross the Gulf Stream, and then head south out in the Sargasso. This was the safe alternative, at once avoiding bad ground and foul current. However, it added more than two hundred miles to the trip, perhaps a full week depending on the wind. His profit margin sliced paper thin even in good times, the otherwise prudent captain would be tempted, therefore, to take the third alternative—to sail the course that earned Hatteras its nickname.

That is, he might opt to duck inshore and sail south between the north-setting Gulf Stream and the deadly clutch of Diamond and Frying Pan. Because the inside edge of the Gulf Stream wavers and the shoals relocate with each autumn gale, we can't say precisely what his margin of error might be, but ten to twenty miles is a good guess. That was quite enough for safe passage in clear visibility and fair wind. However, to a sailing vessel in unfavorable conditions— fog, rain, snow, a dying breeze or strong onshore winds—twenty miles is nothing. If his navigation proved faulty or the weather took a turn for the worse, he might easily fetch up on the shoals. Once hard aground, beaten by incessant waves, his ship was a goner. In fair weather, the crew might manage to launch the lifeboats; in heavy weather, they wouldn't stand a chance. A century on, a November blow might disinter her ribs.

Some people, Canadians mostly, might say, wait just a moment, there is another place called the Graveyard of the Atlantic, and it's been so called longer than Cape Hatteras. They would be referring to their own Sable Island, and they have a point, though their claim is hopeless. Sable Island will continue to lose the battle for the brand because it's an uninhabited little sandbar, a beach without a shore, a speck in the ocean right on the edge of the continental shelf

180 miles east of Halifax, Nova Scotia. Wild horses live on Sable, and the Canadian government maintains a tiny research station, but without tourist emporiums or gift shops to dispense coffee mugs and T-shirts that say "Sable Island: Graveyard of the Atlantic," it will remain obscure. Most Canadians west of Toronto have never heard of it, I suspect. But as a nautical deathtrap, Sable Island, in recognition of its extreme insidiousness, takes the Graveyard Prize hands down.

Just look at the thing—you need a big-scale map of the Canadian Maritimes to find it at all—alone out in open ocean south of Newfoundland and east of Nova Scotia. About thirty miles long, no more than two wide, the island resembles a well-trimmed upside down eyebrow. There is no other land anywhere nearby, deep water everywhere around. This wouldn't matter to mariners if Sable Island were situated in some remote untraveled piece of the North Atlantic. Instead, it's poised like a pirate fleet athwart the most practical, busiest sea-lane between Northern Europe and the Northeast Coast of the Untied States. One moment you're sailing fast in bottomless water, "off soundings," and suddenly, implausibly, land appears dead ahead. And it appeared only to the lucky sailors; the others, at night or in fog, never laid eyes on the low-lying beach until they crashed on it.

As a rule, the weather is not ferocious compared to other places of legendary lethality like the Bering Sea and the high Southern latitudes. But the potential for extreme violence in these waters, made famous for a time by *The Perfect Storm*, is built right into the normal atmospheric conditions. Warm, moist air riding southwest winds up from the Gulf of Mexico encounters cold and dry continental air from Quebec as if they were roving street gangs itching for a fight. Cold and dry, warm and moist wherever they meet abrade each other belligerently, due to their gaping differences in pressure. The encounter turns particularly volatile in autumn and winter, when the lows are lower and highs higher, and soon it's blowing forty-five knots from the northeast in a tightly wound gale, visibility zero. No one is surprised when an October nor'easter exceeds hurricane velocity. But in such weather as that, you don't need to hit an island to go down. Records are sketchy because the little island is so far from everywhere, but of the three hundred to five hundred ships said to have been lost on Sable Island, most probably ran up on it in the fog. This whole region from southernmost Nova Scotia to L'Anse aux Meadows (where the Vikings settled) in northernmost Newfoundland is the birthplace of fog. This is so simply because the water is frigid while those southwest breezes are warm and moist. Cold water plus warm air equals fog all over the globe, but here both sides of the formula are extreme. In summer, entire months pass thick o' fog. In those conditions, hard places in the open ocean loom murderously.

Currents, however, may be the most insidious of the collaborators lurking at the graveyard gates. In this case, a duet of surface currents conspires against mariners. The Gulf Stream brushes the sourth shore of Sable Island as the current sweeps east toward the Grand Banks. Meanwhile, the frigid Labrador Current from out of the High Arctic brushes Sable Island as it slides along the north side of the Gulf Stream. But these two currents do not glide past each other like two impermeable panes of glass. The boundary wavers, meanders, and wanders. Therefore, whether inbound from Europe on the great circle route or outbound from U.S. ports, the ship's course over the bottom, the one that counts, will be skewed by one current or the other as she approaches Sable Island. The captain knows its position (44 degrees North by 59.5 degrees West), but he may not know his own. In fair weather, daylight, watches posted, the island sighted, he can relax. But if he's been sailing for days in fog or foul weather, or even overcast skies that have prevented him from obtaining a celestial fix, then he can only guess at his position. He can have no idea what one current or the other has done to his desired course. And up ahead somewhere, he knows, lurks dry land. It's only a spot of land, but it must have seemed like a jagged continent if measured by the scale of threat to life and limb.

We can argue academically, American and Canadians, which is the more dastardly trap, which claimed more wrecks, but from a maritime perspective the concept of the graveyard of the Atlantic is antique. No ship has been lost on Diamond or Frying Pan shoals off Hatteras or on the sands of Sable Island since the late 1940s. Nothing has changed geographically, meteorologically, or oceanographically in either place; the elements of menace remain in force and exquisite in their confirmations. We have changed. Except for those few who still go to sea in sailboats for kicks, today's ocean traffic consists of big steel ships with plenty of reliable power to overcome tides and currents. Most important, today's mariner, including those in small sailboats, need never want for a spot-on accurate position fix, thanks to GPS and affordable radar. The mariner who knows his position from moment to moment (and keeps track of it) will not run aground on little islands or shallow shoals, no matter the configuration of the currents. Still, even with the threat deboned by technology, only a damp-souled literalist devoid of romance and a sense of history can approach these places from the sea without a shiver running up his spine.

In certain respects, it's the same with the science. There at Hatteras, the Gulf Stream, bringing around sixty million cubic meters of water every passing second, heads seaward for Europe. Thousands of meters down and transporting about sixteen million cubic meters a second, the Deep Western Boundary Current crosses under the Gulf Stream heading for the equator with a different kind of water. Several hundred miles downstream, the Gulf Stream passes Sable Island and, further down, the Grand Banks, while rubbing against the cold flank of the Labrador Current, their waters swirling, mixing, squabbling, exchanging fluids and thereby nurturing one of the richest marine habitats on Earth, before we fished it out. Imagining all this activity going on out there, one can't help thinking of the ocean as a living, breathing organism, to express unscientifically sentiments evoked by the science. Either Cape Hatteras or Sable Island might be more appropriately called "The Place Where Currents Collide," as WHOI scientist Bob Pickart titled a popular article about Hatteras, but that just doesn't have the same ring on T-shirts and coffee mugs as "The Graveyard of the Atlantic."

Chapter 15

CHOICE

B y around 600 A.D., Europe's climate began to change for the better. By 700, the so-called Medieval Warm Period was in full swing, and the quality of life on the continent improved significantly. Swamps dried up, alleviating the scourge of malaria. Pitiless a century earlier, the land gradually grew generous, nurturing reliable harvests and enough fodder to feed farm animals through the winters. Infant mortality decreased, lifespan increased, and European population ballooned by forty to sixty percent as average annual temperatures climbed four degrees Fahrenheit. Changes came more slowly to the higher latitudes of Scandinavia, but come they did, and its population also surged. However, while the land grew more fruitful, there was still not enough of it for everyone, particularly in present Norway, where only the terraces on the fringes of the fjords could reliably produce enough food crops and hay to support the bucolic lifestyle. Norway's mostly vertical geography and its social structure of isolated villages in remote fjords had always induced farmers to look seaward for supplemental protein and a means of communication. Around the year 600, sail technology, originating with the Arabs, had filtered from the Indian Ocean to the Mediterranean, thence northward to Europe, and the sea-adapted Scandinavians took to sailing in a big way.

Their cultural need for boats, more pressing than in the flatlands to the south, the availability of building materials in vast stands of forest, and the presence of skilled carpenters combined to produce a nautical masterpiece. By the early decades of the eighth century,

Scandinavians had fashioned the knorr and its faster, lighter cousin the longship, the finest specimens of sea-boats ever seen to date in Europe, perhaps the world. Strong and flexible in the open ocean, shallow drafted for inshore work, exceedingly fast under sail and oars, these vessels altered the course of Western history.

Probing the coastlines of the British Isles and North Sea shores of Europe during early trading and reconnaissance forays, Norse sailors couldn't help but notice that, first, these places were far wealthier than their homeland and, second, that the wealth was owned either by the nobility or the Church. The nobility usually pro-tected their riches with men at arms, but the Church did not. Monasteries were sitting ducks, unarmed and isolated without hope of help along the remote coasts of England, Scotland, and Ireland, only a couple of days' sail from the Hardanger Fjord. Feeling no compunction about hacking up defenseless monks for their silver chalices, golden crosiers, and bejeweled reliquaries, the Norse be-came Vikings ("raiders") on June 8, 793, when suddenly they stormed ashore to sack and pillage the monastery on Lindisfarne Island in northeast England.

Monastic records for the next century and a half are filled with gory descriptions of bellowing barbarians—Berserkers—materializing from the mist aboard incredibly fast boats to slaughter every Christian in sight. "From the fury of the Northmen, good Lord, de-liver us." Europe far and near quaked in fear of longships in the off-ing. In 793, the English scholar Alcuin wrote, "It is nearly 350 years that we and our fathers have inhabited this most lovely land, and never before has such a terror appeared in Britain as we have now suffered from a pagan race, nor was it thought that such an inroad from the sea could be made." (There's the story for instance about the Viking called by his fellows "the children's man," referencing his reluctance to toss captive children into the air and catch them on the point of a sword.) But not all Norse were Vikings, and few were full-timers. Most were practical traders, and they saw themselves as farmers who sailed, not vice versa. Nonetheless, Norse influence spread by force and by trade to all parts of Europe accessible by navigable water. Their culture, language, and bloodlines enriched the Western world, since the Norse, faced with overpopulation at home, tended to settle and meld with the local populations. Swedish Vikings headed east across the Baltic, via rivers, deep into Russia, founding trading centers as far away as Kiev. The Danes sailed south down the North Sea coasts of England and France, settling at the mouths of the Loire and Rhine rivers and in Normandy, from which one of their direct descendants, William the Conqueror, would invade England in 1066—the final Viking raid, according to some historians. Meanwhile, Norse from modern Norway settled in Scotland, western England, and Ireland, and, uniquely, sailed westward into the open Atlantic in search of living space.

Evidence suggests that westward expansion happened by accident. A ship bound, say, for the trading post at Dublin was blown off course and then, in clearing weather, sighted the Faeroe Islands. Once the Faeroe's were colonized, the same mishap resulted in the discovery of Iceland. But one wonders if there was more intentionality to their ocean exploration. Irish monks in skin boats had most likely discovered the Faeroes during a string of evangelical voyages in the seventh century sometimes lumped together under Saint Brendan's name, and quite possibly they had reached Iceland. The North Atlantic was spattered with islands on contemporary maps, which at that time were more acts of imagination and religious fealty than practical documents. Word had been around since Greek times of an obscure land to the north called Thule and later about islands, some imaginary, some real, lying off in the west, and there is no reason to discount purposeful voyages of exploration by the Norse. Though we'll never settle the true chronology of medieval discovery in the North Atlantic, we know that the Norse had settled in the

Faeroes about A.D 800, and by 870, they had colonized Iceland, both previously uninhabited.

Among the Icelandic settlers was Eric the Red, who had emigrated in 982 after being banished from Norway for killing a man with influential friends. This, it turned out, was no aberration. He was soon banished from the original Icelandic settlement after another fatal quarrel, and he moved to the other side of the island, to a place called Breida Fjord. But when he killed still again, the pattern was clear: This Eric the Red was a sociopath who had to go. But where? The authorities didn't care as long as it was elsewhere.

Eric had heard rumors of another large island out in the west, and, lacking alternatives, decided to give it a try. Five hundred miles later, he sighted an enormous ice-choked coast and followed it southward until it came to an end. He liked what he saw down there: game aplenty, foxes, bears, caribou, fish, and birds, and at the foot of the inland mountains, there were grassy slopes where animals could graze and crops grow. The place probably reminded him of his native Norway, but most appealingly this new land was bereft of people. It was Eric's land; he wouldn't have to fit in. Leniently, it would seem, Eric had been sentenced to a three-year banishment, during which he and his followers surveyed and planned the new settlement. Then, having paid his debt to society, Eric sailed back to Iceland to promote the new fruitful land and enlist settlers. He called it Greenland.

That was beautiful, those of us interested in exploration once thought. Here's this habitual criminal who returns to the scene of the crime, and, like some Florida real estate huckster, hawks a new development in an ice-clogged wilderness by marketing it as *Greenland*. But that was kind of dumb of us. Norse settlements in Greenland lasted for 450 years, impossible if it had been nothing but a frozen boondoggle. On the other hand, reckoning climate into the strains of human history is relatively new. In fact, Greenland *was* green, its climate only slightly cooler than today's. In 986, Eric returned to Greenland leading a twenty-five-ship fleet of immigrant families and their animals. Eleven ships were lost en route, but about 450 people arrived safely and set to work on the business of survival.

They had not come to Greenland to start something new. They meant to replicate the hierarchical social structure (chiefs-commoners-slaves), the bucolic lifestyle, values, customs, indeed all aspects of Norwegian culture they had left behind. For instance, when they had attacked Lindisfarne, the Norse were pagans. Eric and his Greenlanders were pagans. When in 995, Norway officially converted to Christianity, so did the Greenlanders; they were, after all, Norwegians. And periodically some church official would visit the Bishopric of Greenland to look things over and tote up the tithes, paid in walrus tusks and polar bear furs. As time passed, Eric's successors, including his son Leif, who sailed to North America, founded two Greenland colonies called the Eastern Settlement, sited on the southern point of the big island near Cape Farewell, and the Western Settlement, in a fjord about three hundred miles up the west coast. At its peak, population in both settlements totaled about four thousand, most in the Eastern Settlement where the living was easier.

When the Norse arrived, southern Greenland was uninhabited. A shadowy culture called the Dorset People lived in the north, but they died out or were displaced by modern Inuit. In the course of normal life, Norse and Inuit did not interact. Each autumn, however, male members of the European colonies piled into (wooden) boats and rowed up the west coast to the "Nordrseta," or northern hunting grounds. There began the long, sad history of encounter between European voyagers and far-flung Arctic cultures. Not surprisingly, the Norse did not evince empathy or attempt diplomacy during that first meeting on the hunting ground. Several Inuit wound up dead.

From the Norse perspective, they were there first, and the Inuit were the interlopers. And of course, the Norse viewed the Inuit as smelly primitives, as *skraelings* (roughly, "wretches"), and as pagans, just as Christian monks had viewed the Vikings.

Unlike the Inuit, the Norse weren't food hunting at the Nordrseta. They were gathering trade goods—live gyrfalcons, polar bear skins, and occasionally a live cub—for export to Norway. Their other export commodity, walrus-tusk ivory, had soared in value since the Moslems, controlling the Mediterranean, had severed the supply of elephant tusk ivory to Europe. Focused on trade and continued communication with the homeland, the Norse habitually bypassed potential food sources during the Nordrseta. In the good years, they could afford it. The same thinking shaped the content of their imports. They wanted European stuff, luxury items by which the chiefs signaled their status, and they wanted religious implements, jeweled reliquaries and silver scepters, the same items their ancestors had looted from the monks. During the Medieval Warm Period, before the stress of survival clamped down on the colonies, the Norse could retain the ways and means of European Christians without great cost.

The homes, churches, and boats of Western European civilization were made of wood, and Greenland, nearly destitute of trees to begin with, was soon deforested. When farming families moved to fresh pastures, they removed from their abandoned earthen dwellings irreplaceable lintel beams, frames, and other large pieces of wood and took them along. That they owned iron tools, while the dumb *skraelings* had only bone, was another indication to the Greenlanders of their own cultural superiority. But medieval toolmakers used low-grade bog iron, the smelting of which required a lot of charcoal, leading to further deforestation. The Greenlanders might have imported iron tools from home or from Iceland, but they chose instead to import religious trappings and status symbols. The colonists had made sporadic voyages west to Labrador for timber, but the voyage was too long and their ships too small to import sufficient quantities. Time passing, their elaborately constructed boats inevitably deteriorated for want of wood, and for that reason they had to discontinue their voyages to acquire it. Environmental feedbacks were beginning to engage even before the cold bit down.

The change began around 1300. By 1400 the Medieval Warm Period had given way to the Little Ice Age. Though not all are convinced, some scientists contend that the change in climate was caused by diminished sun spot activity, which decreased the amount of solar radiation reaching Earth's surface during the Little Ice Age, about 1350 to at least 1800; it's called the Maunder Minimum. Oceanographers have found evidence to suggest a concomitant slowdown in the thermohaline circulation, but it remains uncertain whether that was cause or effect. In any case, Earth grew colder, not suddenly and not without variation, but decidedly colder. The stresses mounted against the bucolic lifestyle. Winters growing colder and longer, the animals had to be brought inside earlier and put out later. But as a succession of wet, cold summers ruined hay harvests, more animals had to be slaughtered before spring, and as average annual temperatures continued to fall, as the circle of want tightened, the Norse began to kill their breeding stock. That was the beginning of the end. There was no hope of rescue from abroad, since the Icelanders were also starving, and annual visits by ships from the mainland had essentially ceased as ice clogged the seaway. Then a round of the plague wiped out half of the Norwegian population. Archeological evidence—farm buildings abandoned with the precious wooden lintel beams still standing, the skeleton of a man left unburied on a farmhouse floor—suggests that in Greenland the end came quickly.

Jared Diamond in his book *Collapse* points out that, while it's easy for us to see how the Norse refusal to digress from the terms of European religious and farming culture caused their demise, we should also recgnize that the cohesive strategy and shared values contained in their transplanted culture enabled them to survive four and a half centuries in marginal conditions. Life in Greenland was never easy. The Dorset people had apparently responded to a far colder climate in northern Greenland by developing survival strategies similar to the Inuit, but the Dorsets vanished, perhaps when some local, temporal jink in climatic conditions altered their prey animals' migration patterns. The Inuit were also stressed to the brink, starving to death in large numbers during the hard times. But the cold fact remains that the Inuit survived, while the Greenlanders died out.

Diamond cautions against imagining that the Norse could simply have become Inuit and lived happily ever after. That the Norse would choose to do so was no more likely than the Massachusetts Bay Colonists deciding to relinquish their culture, religion, status, material goods, and basic self-assumptions to become Wampanoags after recognizing that their way of life was better suited to the environment. Yet even if they had wanted to, Greenlanders could not have become Inuit. Inuit technology and methods of survival had evolved over millennia, and young Inuit had to be assiduously taught where, what, and how to hunt, how to build shelters and boats, and how to process furs for clothing. Only by becoming something akin to wards of the Inuit could the Greenlanders have learned their modes of survival, and that, of course, was out of the question. Further, the Greenlanders lacked the knowledge that the Medieval Warm Period had, in fact, given way to the Little Ice Age. (Just look at the problem we're having with the whole idea of climate change, even with the benefit of science and historical hindsight.) Greenlanders had reason to hope that next year would be better;

after all, there had been poor years in the past, but conditions had always improved eventually. No need to do anything radical.

On the other hand, at some point during the late 1300s, the Greenlanders must have noticed that the growing cold was no aberration and that their bucolic lifestyle was faltering. At that point, they were presented with a choice. They had observed the Inuit in their marvelous kayaks darting around the ice floes like sea-adapted animals; they had watched the Inuit hunt walrus and ringed seal with their toggle-tipped harpoons, seen their successful fishing methods, and their mode of dress. It wasn't that the Greenlanders were too dim to notice the efficacy of Inuit technology or dietary strategies, but that they decided not to adopt any of them. Greenlanders starved to death in the presence of available food sources. That was a choice.

To compare then and now, as if one directly reflects the other, is usually a misuse of history, and admittedly, there are more differences than similarities between medieval farmers in Greenland and contemporary industrialized societies in the temperate zones. But there are similarities between them and us around this matter of choice. Greenlanders were resolutely, unbendingly farmers. Farming was a matter of identity; farming made them what they were. (*Skraelings* were subsistence hunters.) Similarly, fossil fuels made and make us what we are today. Almost everything we own is rooted directly or indirectly in burning fossil fuels. Yet, now, scientists are bringing us the unwelcome news that continuing to burn those fuels will, at best, alter our environment and, at worst, cause widespread dislocation and destruction. In a sense, it's no wonder that some among us recoil in disbelief, like Columbus insisting, to the moment of his death, that he had reached Asia despite the evidence of his own eyes. Metaphorically, at least, the terms of our choice are similar to the Greenlanders': We can adapt to a changing world by relinquishing, for the greater good, for what used to be called the "commons," some of the things that make us who we are, or we can cling to our engines and our devices and rationalize our intransigence on political, economic, or ideological grounds.

In our own recent history there are encouraging precedents of adaptability. Despite the usual hue and cry from vested interests that it would destroy our economy, we passed the Clean Air Act in 1990, when we recognized that we were poisoning ourselves. Ice core samples from Greenland and from Antarctica show a sharp black line with white ice above it marking the very year that the Clean Air Act took hold. It mattered; it worked. And then there was the ozone hole. When scientists revealed the degradation of the ozone hole and its relevance to our eyesight, we listened. And when they proved that the ozone hole was caused by PCBs, we banned them, despite warnings that doing so would raise prices, cost jobs, and sap our precious bodily fluids. Now, nature has all but repaired the rent in the ozone layer, and our economy survived. It mattered. Remember catalytic converters? They, too, were supposed to destroy the American auto industry.

Also, we've grown used to the concept of ourselves as custodians of nature. Not so long ago, we commonly held the assumption that God had created the world to serve the needs of man, His favorite piece of creation, and so we had no compunction about "improving" nature. Indeed, it was almost an obligation. If we could drain and reclaim "useless" swamps such as the Everglades to make new land for farmers and developers, then that's what we should do. If we needed coal to improve our lives, and if that Kentucky mountain contained coal, then there was every reason to tear down the mountain to get at it. By the late 1960s, almost no one was viewing nature as the servant of man, a resource to be done with as he wishes. When we recognized that it was within our power to eliminate any ecosystem that stood in the way of "progress," we altered our old definition of progress. When we recognized our capacity to exterminate the large predators our ancestors once feared, we decided to protect, by force of law, at least a few of the animals and their habitats.

Now we're called upon again to shift our concept of nature and our relationship to it. However, the necessity of our transition from the pioneer ethic to the conservation ethic, to custodianship, was relatively easier to grasp and to install, since the deleterious aspects of progress appeared on a local, visible level. I'm not suggesting that the battles to protect nature from short-term profiteers have been won, and now we can rest on our laurels, only that the battles are usually focused pointedly on this span of wetlands, that wild river, the old-growth forest, or the coral reef. We know what to do individually and politically. Climate is far harder to see and to understand, the fields of engagement harder to isolate.

At this writing, the IPCC has just issued its promised addendum to the 2007 report, *Summary for Policymakers* (SPM). Its title notwithstanding, the SPM makes no policy recommendations, but states explicitly at the top: This is what we all agree on; of this we are certain to a "ninety-nine percent degree of probability." And what all those governments, all those scientists agree on is this: The warming is real; it is not part of any natural oscillation; and it is caused by us. To deny that in the face of the IPCC report, the consensus of two hundred governments and many hundreds of scientific advisors, not to mention the voluminous evidence on which it was based, is an act of stubborn faith, not rationality. And before any sensible, meaningful shift in our relationship to nature can proceed, we'll need to recognize, admit that the evidence is conclusive, that there is no doubt about global warming.

One salient feature of the document is a number we're going to be hearing more about in the near future: the measure of "climate sensitivity." This is the extent to which climate will grow warmer if the amount of carbon dioxide emitted since the beginning of the Industrial Revolution doubles to something around 580 parts per million, while presently our atmosphere contains 380 ppm of carbon dioxide, and rising steadily. The IPCC is "virtually certain" that the climate-sensitivity turning point lies between 2 and 4.5 degrees C., with a three-degree hike being the most likely number. But, the report adds, "Values substantially higher than 4.5 degrees centigrade cannot be excluded." At that point, we will experience increased precipitation in the form of downpours, more heatwaves and droughts to disrupt agricultural patterns; there will be more tropical storms and floods; sea levels will rise between eighteen and fifty-nine centimeters due to thermal expansion alone. (Sea-level rise due to potential melting in Greenland and Antarctica was not included in the report for lack of consensus in the models, but the last time carbon dioxide levels reached their present extent, during the inter-glacial period about 125,000 years ago, sea levels were some fifteen feet higher.) On all of this the IPCC is sixty-six to ninety percent certain. That should end the debate. We can't hide behind the incomplete-science dodge, at least not rationally, and we need to dismiss as cranks those who continue to do so.

Perhaps even after we quit debating, we will still need to take the intellectual, if not spiritual step, to recognize that we, *Homo sapiens*, have so successfully expanded our capabilities since, say, the Little Ice Age that we have become a genuine geophysical force. There isn't a forest in the world we can't cut down, no river we can't dam, no wetlands we can't replace with real estate, but these are mere ecosystems and geographical features. Now we hold the capacity to change the entire world. The difference between us and other geophysical forces such as volcanoes is sentience. We have a choice. We'll have to give up things we like right now and pay real money to find alternatives to our present mode of life to forestall a dark future. But that's been said hundreds of times, almost as often as it's been said that if we do nothing our grandchildren will revile us for our blindness and selfish intransigence.

Then to hell with our grandchildren. That can be our choice. All we have to do is nothing, cling resolutely to our present technologies and our gas-guzzlers, because how else will we get around? Besides, the economy's been good to us, and now we're supposed to shake it up with newfangled notions, spend a lot of money on stuff that might not work based on the predictions of scientists we can't even understand. Only fools kill the golden goose. And even if we decide to do with less, while spending more on research, those Chinese are still pumping out greenhouse gases like crazy, so why should we sacrifice? Our grandchildren will surely understand that. Also, climate change will land hardest on the uninsulated poor countries first—Bangladesh, hapless places like that—before it clamps down on us, and in the meantime someone may come up with a technological fix, a vaccine. It's our choice. Metaphorically, we can be Greenlanders clutching a mode of life that no longer suits reality, or we can decide to imitate the Inuit. But we can't say that we don't know.

Chapter 16

OVERTURNING

The project is called RAPID/MOCHA, and in many ways it represents the future of ocean research. RAPID/MOCHA aims to apply the methods of oceanography not exclusively to understand
ocean behavior per se, but to find in it signals of climate change.
The objective of the project is to measure from one side of the
ocean to the other the velocity and the temperature of all the permanent currents in the North Atlantic flowing on the surface and in
the abyss. Together those currents—from west to east: the Gulf
Stream, Antilles Current, Deep Western Boundary Current, and the
Canary Current—comprise the so-called Meridional Overturning
Circulation, or MOC. Because all the currents in the MOC vary in
temperature and velocity (particularly velocity), RAPID/MOCHA
scientists will need to maintain near-constant vigilance over them
for years to come. But if their techniques work, if they can measure
a line across the entire ocean, scientists will gain a picture of the
"normal" basin-wide circulation. This in hand, they'll then be able to
recognize pertinent changes in the circulation. So important is this
particular circulation in this particular ocean that any sustained
change will signal (or cause) climate change. To say it differently,
oceanographers will be positioned to *predict* climate. Hanging
around oceanographers, one grows skeptical of the categorical and
prone to employ qualifiers. The project participants might fidget in
the face of bald statements about their future, but I think we can
venture to say that this represents an historic shift in the practice
and objective of oceanography from an observational science to a

predictive one. And as a veteran of CTD ops, I had been invited to ply my trade on the thirty-day RAPID/MOCHA cruise departing Bridgetown, Barbados, on March 8, 2006.

The *Ronald H. Brown* had been measuring sea surface temperatures off the coast of Chile, and since we were bound back out on the 26.5 degrees North line, she had availed herself of the deep-water harbor and big-ship facilities in Barbados instead of returning to Charleston only to backtrack. She reflects in that sense the heritage of the old tramp steamers Conrad and London wrote about that follow the work from ocean to ocean wherever it leads, only occasionally touching home. But quite unlike the tramps, she has no trouble finding employment. It takes $35,000 per day (not counting science costs) to keep the *Brown* at sea, and she's out there more than two hundred days a year every year.

I had met co-chief scientist Lisa Beal and her father, Mick, for a tour of the island, and now it was time to report aboard for tomorrow morning's departure, but the treacherous midday heat had turned the air viscous, and the *Brown* was tied way at the far end of the long wharf. After trudging the lengths of two cruise-ship behemoths tied nose to tail and a tough seagoing tug, we seemed no closer to our ship, receding in the haze. Living in Miami for these last several years, Lisa, acclimatized, strode purposefully, while, Mick and I, from colder climes, fell behind. Mick Beal had traveled from his home in England to volunteer aboard the *Brown* in order, he said, "to understand what my daughter does for a living." A delightfully open-minded guy, Mick was to be my cabinmate.

I was pleased to board the ship again, when finally we arrived at the gangplank. I greeted Phil and Mary, deckhands on the September trip, who told me that my buddies Chris Churylo, technician in charge of shipboard electronics, and Chief Survey Tech Jonathan Shannahoff were still aboard, and most of the same NOAA Corps officers—new captain, though.

The back deck was bustling with people and crowded with new machinery. *Brown* crew were going about their departure preparations, bolting heavy objects to the deck, winching aboard pallets full of boxed provisions, including sweating cartons marked Häagan-Daz. (Everyone hated the generic ice cream on the September cruise.) Bruce the bosun, under his Stetson-shaped hard hat, was directing traffic and signaling instructions to two separate winch drivers. And then there was the dozen-member British mooring team stepping lively about the transom, sweating profusely as they squared away their mounds of gear, which had only just arrived in the orange shipping container mounted on the port side.

RAPID/MOCHA is a collaborative venture between British scientists from the National Oceanography Centre, Southampton (NOCS) and Americans from NOAA working jointly with their friends on the other side of Biscayne Boulevard at the University of Miami. The Americans and the Brits have essentially divided the Atlantic in half, the former measuring activity on the western boundary (Gulf Stream, Antilles Current, and Deep Western Boundary Current), while the latter measure the interior middle of the ocean and the Canary Current on the eastern boundary of the gyre. So there would be two separate science staffs. NOAA's Molly Baringer would head the American team, Stuart Cunningham the British, while Molly would serve as onboard Chief Scientist. University of Miami oceanographer Bill Johns is overall head of the MOCHA program, while Harry Bryden runs RAPID; neither of them was to be aboard for this trip.

Lisa had explained this multilayered system as we trudged down the wharf.

"Complicated," said Mick.

"What about the mooring team?" I'd asked. "What are they going to do?"

"The RAPID people have set several moorings arrayed with current meters and miniature CTDs and things on the west side of the line. NOAA's basically contributing ship time so they can pull the moorings for servicing."

Due to some misunderstanding or late change in plans, the Brits had received word only a few days ago that they were to be aboard in Barbados with all their equipment ready to go. Loads of arcane gear, instruments, tools, hardware, spools of rope and oceanographic wire, and things I couldn't identify poured from their walk-in container as the team tried to figure out what they had and what they'd left behind. We dodged two guys dragging a chain of "hard-hat floats" to the other side of the transom. These are glass spheres about twice the size of bowling balls protected in heavy plastic casings, bolted in pairs to steel frames, and then chained together in a string of about ten. Several strings are typically toggled to the mooring cable providing extra flotation to keep the cable vertical. The chief mooring tech, Ian Waddington, a man respected for his skill and long experience—this was his last rip before retirement—checked things off on his clipboard as he directed the placement of gear. Two other guys dragged the hard-hat string back across the transom to its original location.

Lisa, who had worked for a time at NOCS, knew most of the mooring guys from other cruises in other oceans, but this clearly was no time to renew acquaintances. Some rolled their eyes and shook their heads when she greeted them in passing. Among all the smaller stuff in the container, the mooring team had brought two huge winches already bolted to the deck, along with a complex, inscrutable system of blocks and fairleads to spool and unspool several miles of oceanographic wire. That made five heavy-duty winches aboard this vessel. All that sophisticated solid-state, acoustic, Doppler-radar, hypersensitive, gee-whiz technology on which ocean science is founded would be useless without the brute lifting power of winches and cranes. When Lisa stopped briefly to greet Colin Hutton, a burly shirtless fellow (the Brits were very concerned with their tans) who was nursing a mending broken ankle, the result of overzealous dockside jumping, Mick and I dodged below to stow our gear.

The submarine-style door leading from the hanger into the main deck corridor is to remain closed and dogged (nautical for "latched") at all times to preserve the air-conditioning without which below-deck survival in these latitudes would be unlikely. We slipped into the line of busy crewmen in the crowded corridor, keeping right as we made our way forward, then through the door marked "Science Berthing," down a flight of stairs, and after a couple more turns, Mick was as confused as I'd been on my first trip. Relishing my pretense as an "old hand," I assured him the layout would soon reveal itself and she'd feel like home. I love going to sea.

Lisa came down from her lofty co-chief scientist single cabin three decks above as Mick and I finished stowing our stuff. Departure was set for 1000 tomorrow, and there was to be a science staff dinner somewhere in the hopping clubby section of Bridgetown, but right now, since we were generally in the way, why don't we go for a swim? She had a nearby public beach all picked out on the map. We stepped lively over the transom and down the gangplank trying not to look to the sweating workers like science staffers going to the beach.

Next morning, Mick and I and a few others made a quick foray to the duty-free pavilion of potential bargains at the head of the dock. Some among *Brown*'s complement availed themselves of reduced cigarette and rum prices, but there is no drinking allowed on American research ships. You can bring alcohol aboard, but it is to be relinquished to an officer who will seal it for the duration in a dedicated "spirits locker." No doubt everyone complied. And now at 1000, right on the dot, the crew began readying the deck for departure. Captain Gary Petrae appeared on the portside bridge wing three decks above and spoke by radio to the bosun, who gave quiet orders to his crew. I introduced Mick to my friend, shipmate, and our CTD captain, Carlos Fonseca. (We hereafter were known proudly as "Carlos's Boys.") Then we leaned on our elbows on the second-deck railing, the traditional posture of departure on a sea cruise, watching the crew winch the big metal gangway aboard and lash it against the portside bulwark. In practiced order they took in the dock lines, thick as rolling pins, and coiled them in figure eights around heavy cleats on the fantail. The three of us weren't alone up there, idly watching the work, since all noncrew had been invited by the bosun to get the hell off the way. Even the mooring team had stopped work, sunning themselves in beach chairs at the aft end of the hanger, as the *Brown* steamed out between the breakwaters and headed north up the west side of the island.

Sited smack in the easterly Trade Wind belt, Barbados has a windward side and a leeward side, and the difference is absolute. Over here on the leeward side where the tourists go, the ocean is lagoon flat, but the east side, in the teeth of the Trade Winds, is too rough to swim. This wind is an impressive phenomenon, so different from a temperate-zone wind of equal velocity. Up there the prevailing westerly feels separate from the body of water it blows over, two different mediums, but not here in the tropics. The incessant Northeast Trades carry enough water vapor drawn from the whitecaps they generate to feel like part of the sea, a layer of water in the process of turning into actual air but quite there yet. Experiencing the magnitude of the Trade Winds from the deck of a vessel at sea, particularly a small sailboat, you begin to understand how these winds can power that great circulatory machine the North Atlantic Subtropical Gyre. Here in the tropics, you can feel the volatility in the air-sea interface, and you can see the immediate result in the often intense, isolated rainsqualls that pop up so suddenly. When one parks over the ship, the noonday sky turns to twilight, and rain sweeps the decks, runs out in rivulets through the scuppers. Then it's gone, and thirty minutes later the sun has steamed the decks bone dry. (Some climatologists think of the ocean as "wet air.")

Clearing the northern point of Barbados, we left our sheltered lee behind. The wind blew people's hats off, and endless trains of six-foot waves surged under *Brown*'s starboard beam. She commenced to roll. Conversations faltered. There were several students aboard from Southampton and Miami as well as two "Teachers at Sea," part of a NOAA outreach program, and two ocean chemists from Texas A&M, not all of whom had their sea legs, and one by one they went down to seasickness. Several of them would not be glimpsed again for days. Mick, on the other hand, who'd never been to sea, was unfazed. When the rolling increased by ten degrees as the higher ridges on Barbados dropped beneath the horizon, we staggered like drunks on the open deck.

A chain of volcanic mountaintops known appropriately as the Windward Islands (Barbuda, Antigua, Guadeloupe, Dominica, Martinique, St. Lucia, St. Vincent, and the Grenadines) arcs southward 650 miles between Puerto Rico and the coast of Venezuela. Though part of the chain, Barbados lies off by itself nearly one hundred miles east of the arc. The Windward Islands, most discovered and named by Columbus, form the eastern boundary of the Caribbean, separating it as if with a picket fence from the open Atlantic. In the wind-exposed channels between the islands, open-ocean conditions exist. Likewise, the current activity is intense. The North Equatorial Current, "forced" across the ocean by the Northeast Trades, plows between the islands and into the Caribbean. In the 1970s, WHOI oceanographer William Schmitz proved that almost one-third of the water flowing between the islands comes from the Southern Hemisphere, from the South Equatorial Current. Like their mirror-image twin in the Northern Hemisphere, the Southeast Trades push a current toward the west. But things are different down there. The Bulge of Brazil protrudes far out into the Atlantic toward its kin on the other side, the Bulge of Africa, forming the narrowest stretch across the Atlantic. Schmitz and colleagues showed that, when encountering this pointed shoulder of South America, the South Equatorial Current splits, and some of its transport circulates southward along the coasts of Brazil and Argentina as the Brazil Current. The rest of the South Equatorial Current, however, slides northward up the Brazilian coast in the form of the North Brazil Current—which then bends eastward. The sharp turn, or retroflection, casts off those ring formations akin to Gulf Stream and Agulhas rings, and these deliver Southern Hemisphere water into the Caribbean, thence the Gulf of Mexico, and by that route into the Gulf Stream system. Here's another way that rings and eddies enable currents to make "difficult turns," though in this case, rings enable water to make the move across the equator, not commonly accomplished in any ocean due to the required change in vorticity from one hemisphere to the other.

The captain intended to run up the east side of the Windward Islands and on north to the study line at 26.5 North latitude. Barbados lies at 13 degrees North. Since there are sixty nautical miles in each degree of latitude, we had an eight-hundred-mile steam before the work would begin, at least three days of leisure, plenty of time to pick scientific minds. Not only were they plentiful, they were conveniently arrayed, MOCHA in the computer lab, RAPID with all their instruments laid out on tables in the main lab. They had no means of escape.

Molly Baringer pointed out that the ultimate objective of the project was to measure the total *heat transport* northward across 26.5 North. That's the "function" of the Meridional Overturning

Circulation, to move heat around the North Atlantic. That, broadly, is how oceans influence climate, but in this the MOC is special because it encompasses thermohaline circulation, the sinking. The Gulf Stream system transports warm water northward along the western boundary into cold Nordic seas. There, in winter, the saline water grows dense enough to sink—that's the *overturning*—and then flows back southward across the equator. A quantity of the southward transport also occurs on the surface in the Canary Current, the eastern boundary of the gyre. So if you pick a (west-east) line of latitude, 26.5 North, for instance, then you have a platform across which all those currents will pass, a sort of cross section of the entire ocean basin. Since all that transport runs either north to south or south to north, it's said to flow *meridionally*, that is, along meridians, another word for (north-south) lines of longitude.

RAPID/MOCHA will succeed in understanding the heat transport if its members can manage to measure entirely all the currents in the MOC. That assumption is based on a fundamental principle of ocean physics: Water temperature multiplied by the velocity of the flow equals the total heat transport. Look at it this way, Molly suggested. Normally, there is a heat gain to the ocean in the tropics and a net heat loss in the high latitudes—but together the gain and loss on a basin-wide scale cancel each other out, and the net change is zero. If, say, the poleward heat transport across our latitude increases, then one of two things will happen to the north of our latitude: Either the ocean must transfer the excess heat to the atmosphere, or sea level temperatures must rise. We're talking here about significant changes, not natural variations or oscillations that balance out in the long term, but if the change is large enough and lasts long enough, then it will register in the climate; we'll feel it in various forms on the surface of Earth. That's what we're looking out for, said Molly, and that's what we don't want to see.

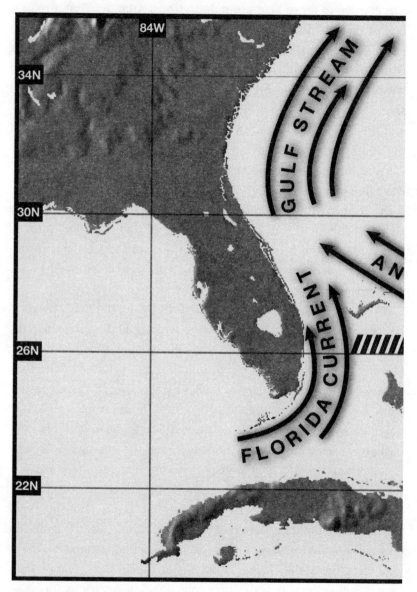

RAPID/MOCHA Study Line

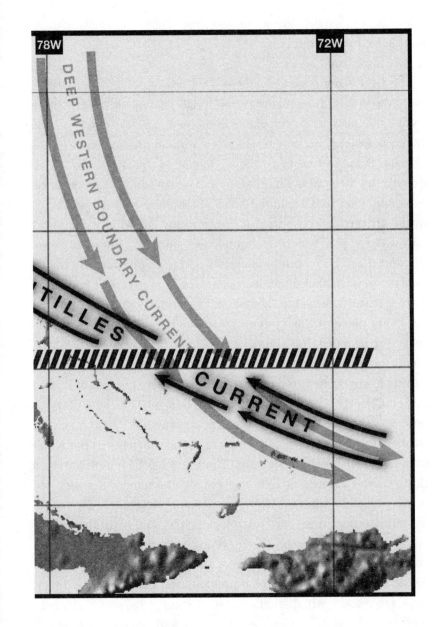

Just how much heat are we talking about being moved along those meridians, I wondered.

"Oh, huge," said Molly.

The Gulf Stream system moves a bit over one petawatt—that's one followed by fifteen zeros—the rough equivalent of the output from 1,000 nuclear power plants combined, a hell of a lot of heat, which helps explain how ocean circulation impresses itself on the climate. Some of that heat, she explained, is transferred to the air directly, by the simple fact that air and ocean touch at the surface, "sensible" heat transfer in the lingo. Much more heat is transferred to the air through evaporation. Evaporating, seawater transforms into water vapor, which then condenses into droplets of freshwater, and these go to produce clouds and precipitation and sometimes storms. At that point, the ocean's heat, stored thus far as if in a great battery, turns into actual energy; at that point it warms the air. Every piece of this system is huge, hard to grasp in its magnitude. For instance, the annual transfer of ocean water to freshwater in the atmosphere would be great enough to lower sea level worldwide by some three feet, except that ninety percent of it is returned directly to the oceans as precipitation. The remaining ten percent falls on the land and makes its way back to the sea via rivers carrying a load of salts, minerals, and nutrients in the water to enrich near-shore ecosystems. There has been no new water on Earth for the last several billion years; it is the same water recycled time and again endlessly. We've heard something of this process in the climate literature—the hydrologic cycle. The hydrologic cycle per se will never change; the recycling will never stop. However, continued warming will likely alter the global distribution of that water, specifically by changing precipitation patterns, and this, it stands to reason, will disrupt or destroy some ecosystems. Broadly, increased moisture in the atmosphere will aggravate extreme weather conditions, but the models show differing results depending on how the patterns of precipitation change. The point, for our purposes, is that a change in the oceanic heat transport will result in an altered hydrologic cycle that will inevitably manifest itself in the climate humans and animals actually feel. Those in some locales will benefit; others will die.

Myriad ocean and atmospheric mechanisms are all interlocked; everything is connected to everything else, yet the exact *how* of the connections remains obscured by layers of complexity that blur the distinctions between cause and effect. Someone likened the intimacy of the relationship between air and ocean to two coats of paint on the same croquet ball. Further, every piece of activity in both "coats" is an arc of a larger circle without a beginning or an end. Is the ocean in control, or is the atmosphere driving the ship? And then there is the problem of scale. This intricate exchange of heat and moisture goes on simultaneously all over the globe. The Sun's uneven heating of Earth's surface sets up pressure gradients, and wind results as air flows from high pressure to low. Strong, steady winds, like these Trades, engage currents that carry heat from the low latitudes to high latitudes. On the way northward, the ocean relinquishes heat and moisture to the atmosphere, and then the prevailing westerlies carry it away to bless Western Europe with a mild, wet climate when by dint of latitude it should be frozen solid in winter. This theme occurs in general all over the world, but its variations are infinite.

Sometimes the variations are short and, for now, inexplicable. For instance, at a 2006 climate change conference in England, Harry Bryden, RAPID's leader, reported that the Deep Western Boundary Current had shut down for ten days—just quit, stopped. The English press misunderstood what he was getting at and waxed hysterical. The *Guardian*, for instance, wrote that the Gulf

Stream had shut down for ten days. (The British are understand-
ably concerned about the continued health of their warmth-
delivery system, and the issue is more immediately pressing than
on the west side of the Atlantic.) But then ten days later the DWBC
was chugging along at twice its "normal" velocity. Nothing in the
system changes without cause, even if the cause is inscrutable, but
not all changes have climatic effect; some merely confuse and
complicate humans' attempts to measure the meaningful changes.
"Noise," as scientists say.

On the other hand, some seemingly small, temporal variations ric-
ochet through the atmosphere/ocean system to enormous effect. El
Niño is the classic example of that. Under normal circumstances,
the Trade Winds systems literally push the surface of the warm
Pacific Ocean water over to the west side of the Pacific basin such
that sea level near the equator is literally higher on the east coast of
Australia than on the west coast of South America around Peru and
Ecuador. By shifting the warm surface water away from the South
American coast, the winds expose the colder thermocline layer, so
we have warm water piled up on the west side of the ocean, cold water exposed to the atmosphere on the east side—when the system is
governed by normal atmospheric conditions. But look what happens
when, periodically, the Trade Winds relax due to changes in atmospheric conditions. Then, no longer pressed westward, the warm
surface water "sloshes" back to the east. This is El Niño. The visita-
tion of this huge mass of warm water changes the whole thermal
structure of the eastern Pacific. The ocean transfers this heat to the
atmosphere through evaporation, and that in turn significantly
changes atmospheric pressure conditions—what had been cool and
dry suddenly becomes warm and moist—and the change alters
weather patterns on a hemispheric scale, at least. Lately, the results
have been disastrous.

The 1982 El Niño event brought prolonged drought and near-famine conditions to the Philippines and the Asian subcontinent, while floods raged in Southern California. The Peruvian anchoveta fishery, once the largest by volume of catch in the world, totally collapsed when the fish, a cold-adapted species, fled the suddenly warm water. The economic impacts reverberated throughout the region, plunging people into poverty. It happened again in 1998. El Niño inflicted droughts on Russia, China, and other parts of Central Asia. Drought in the American Midwest had never been so severe since the Dust Bowl days of the Depression, and the mighty Mississippi was reduced in its upper reaches to an unnavigable stream. Meanwhile, torrential rains flooded India and Bangladesh and vast tracts of central Africa. In his book *Our Affair with El Niño*, the Princeton climatologist and oceanographer George Philander puts the death toll from extreme weather conditions directly attributable to the 1998 El Niño at 21,706, the displaced and homeless at 117,863,114. Philander, who refers to El Niño in the third person, writes, "He teaches us that changes in weather and climate are not merely local phenomena that profoundly influence the traditions and culture of the people in a region; they are aspects of continually changing global patterns that connect us all." However, Philander also points out that the name "El Niño," originating in Peru and Ecuador, referred to the welcome warmth that usually arrived around Christmas time. "The transformation of a regional curiosity, which we used to welcome as a blessing, into a global climate hazard happened recently, during the second half of the twentieth century." Vicious El Niño events beginning in the early 1970s, as much as any other single influence, brought the fact of global warming into the public consciousness. Further, El Niño devastation in the 1980s prompted research (by Philander among others) that divulged the true identity of the phenomenon and the direct link between extreme El Niño events and global warming. Also, its associated death and devastation moved ocean and atmospheric scientists to explore means by which they could predict El Niño's arrival.

On the other hand, "he" can be generous. With all their reliable indicators stacking up in an alarming pattern, meteorologists predicted that 2006 would be a very bad hurricane year. Sea surface temperatures were higher than normal in the tropics near Africa, and atmospheric pressure was lower. Despite solid evidence to support it, the prediction was wrong. Far fewer named storms and hurricanes developed, and none struck the United States. Some scientists contend that El Niño helped us out by creating upper-atmosphere conditions that essentially chopped the tops off potential hurricanes before they could mature. But the point is, changes in the atmosphere prompt big changes in the ocean's thermal structure, which cause still bigger changes in the atmosphere, both connected, two coats of paint on the same ball. El Niño is neither an ocean phenomenon nor an atmospheric one, but an inextricable ocean-atmosphere phenomenon.

Because oceans are so much denser than air, they are able to contain and store far more heat than the atmosphere. The atmosphere is nimble, heating or cooling on the spot, depending in part on ocean temperatures, and moving of course far faster than oceans. Yet it takes ages for the atmosphere to change the surface temperature of the ocean over any significant area. So the atmosphere is running the show in the short term. In the long term, the ocean rules. What ultimately determines climate as far as humans and the rest of life on the planet are concerned is the long-term temperature at the surface of Earth. Yet that temperature is related to the ocean and its transport of heat poleward from the equator. And around we go. That brings us back to RAPID/MOCHA, which seeks to understand variability in the heat transport by measuring the entire range of currents across the Atlantic from Ft. Lauderdale, Florida, to Agadir, Morocco. As Molly, Carlos, and Lisa explained the goals and scope of the project, I visualized hundreds of moorings festooned with current meters, Profilers, and miniature CTDs, thousands of instruments picketing the entire ocean basin plus repeated CTD and ADCP transits aboard ships. How else could it work? So I was surprised and a little confused to hear that the Brits had about ten moorings across the ocean, only three out in the vast middle.

Among the other ample brains I picked aboard the *Ron Brown*, one belonged to the German scientist Jochem Marotzke, professor at the Max Planck Institute for Meteorology, in Hamburg. Jochem is an ocean theorist. Though the boundaries are permeable, the theorist is different from the "observational" oceanographer, who does the actual measuring. The theoretician, whose primary tool is the numerical computer model, focuses on the mathematical equations that describe the physical processes in the ocean in order to determine how it works. Before moving to the Max Planck Institute in 2003, Jochem held a professorship at the National Oceanographic Centre, Southampton where, with Harry Bryden and Stuart Cunningham, he helped found the RAPID program. Jochem conceived the theoretical underpinnings of the project, the next best alternative, as it were, to measuring the entire basin directly.

He and I customarily met on the fantail after meals to talk about politics, baseball, and oceanography. (Throughout the cruise, Jochem wore a New York Yankees cap, the same one he wore while working with Carl Wunsch at MIT, until some gentle Red Sox fan explained the risk he was incurring.) Jochem explained that at a 1998 World Ocean Circulation Experiment conference in Halifax, he had proposed the possibility that the MOC could be monitored without stringing instruments all the way across the North Atlantic. His idea was that the temperature and velocity could be determined by measuring the currents in the western and eastern boundaries, where the action occurs, with only a few moorings in the vast middle of the ocean, and from those "endpoint" measurements the total transport could be inferred.

"How?" I asked.

"Are you familiar with geostrophy?"

"Yes."

"Well then, my point was that if our computer model could predict separately the eastern and western boundary layers, using CTD and any other data, then we could learn the density differences on the boundaries. From that, we can apply the old geostrophic equations to calculate the relative flow between the stations we measured. Remember," he added, "I was speaking in theoretical terms about a model. I never thought observationalists would take this seriously as a strategy." But enough did to encourage Jochem, then at MIT, and a colleague, Detlef Stammer, to draw up a proposal for just such a study and submit it to the National Science Foundation, which rejected the idea.

Oh, well. Jochem accepted the position at NOCS, and his co-applicants went their separate ways. Publicity plays a role in this story, and one suspects that the role will expand with time as our encounter with climate change, which really has only begun, develops. In 1999, a new chief executive, John Lawton, took over the Natural Environment Research Council (NERC), the British version of the NSF. I'm not suggesting specifically that Lawton was motivated by a bevy of "Oh, my God" press reports when he approached the Southampton oceanographers asking if anyone in the UK was working on MOC shutdown, but there was plenty of talk in the British press about collapsing ocean circulation and the imminent arrival of another ice age. In any case, the NOCS officials responded that, yes, they have this new hotshot German scientist, Professor Marotzke, who has been working on that very thing. This—the shutdown of the

MOC, or THC—was not the thrust of his work, but sometimes the uneasy relationship between the media and scientists serves science, particularly its funding; and Jochem was asked in late 1999 to prepare another proposal based on endpoint monitoring. He fully expected that observationalists would shoot it down on the grounds that the entire MOC could not be accurately measured by measuring the boundaries, geostrophy or no geostrophy. But Harry Bryden and Stuart Cunningham, among others, embraced the idea. In 2001, they submitted a proposal to NERC to monitor the entire basin along 30 degrees North.

Around the same time, on the west side of the Atlantic, Bill Johns (and later Lisa Beal) at Miami, with Molly Baringer at NOAA, were proposing to the National Science Foundation a project to monitor the MOC from the western boundary. It's not surprising that such a complex project requiring the collaboration of three proud, top-flight oceanographic institutions would engender a certain level of turf-centric politics. NOAA and University of Miami scientists have worked side by side for years, but this, an international project involving NOCS with its own funding source, required a new level of cooperation and flexibility from all involved. So it's to make a long story short to say that, as time passed, British and American scientists and their program directors from the two funding bodies recognized the efficacy of dividing the Atlantic between them. Naturally, they needed to choose a baseline latitude situated in the region of greatest heat transport, somewhere between 25 and 30 degrees North. They settled on the 26.5 North line specifically, because scientists from NOAA and RSMAS had been measuring the western boundary currents along that line since 1982. (That's what we were doing on the September Western Boundary Time Series cruise.) RAPID/MOCHA, one of the largest current experiments in the world, first went to sea, actually submerging instruments in the MOC, in March 2004.

There are, of course, other large ocean-monitoring projects presently in force. The Tropical Atmosphere Ocean (TAO) array uses seventy moorings with current meters and other instruments to span the entire Pacific astride the equator between 8 degrees North and 8 degrees South. But among its main objectives is to predict El Niño events, and for that TAO does not need to measure activity below about five hundred meters. And there is the ARGO project, which at this writing has deployed about 2,000 of an intended 3,000 neutrally buoyant, free-drifting, expendable floats—contemporary descendents of the Swallow float—to measure temperature and salinity profiles between the surface and 1,000 or 2,000 meters over the world ocean. If, however, comprehensiveness is the size criterion, then RAPID/MOCHA, not only covering an entire ocean basin, but also measuring it full-depth from the surface to the bottom, is the largest current study in the world.

"I think," said Jochem one evening as we watched an extravagant sunset of the sort only seen at sea, "that after we analyze the data from this cruise, we'll know whether we're successfully measuring the MOC."

"Really? How?"

"You're probably familiar with the conservation of mass?"

"Yes."

"How about the 'Sverdrup' as a unit of measurement?"

One Sverdrup (Sv.) equals one million cubic meters of flow per second. The Florida Current portion of the Gulf Stream system alone transports thirty-two Sverdrups within the Florida Straits. Then there's four to six Sv. going northward in the Antilles Current, which runs along the east side of the Bahamas Banks. That makes about thirty-six million cubic meters of ocean water a second crossing 26.5 North heading toward the Pole. Common sense tells that an equal quantity of water must return south. Otherwise northern Europe would flood, "and there's no evidence of that," said Jochem. A bit more water moves north in the ocean's interior due to Ekman transport and other technicalities, but let's ignore that to say if 36 Sv. go north, then we have to find 36 Sv. of southerly flow.

"The Deep Western Boundary Current and the Canary Current, on the eastern boundary of the gyre, each transports about sixteen Sverdrups back towards the equator. There's the balance, 36 Sv. We know that mass must be conserved. That becomes a kind of benchmark for us. If we measure the MOC for, say, two years and find 36 Sv. flowing north across the line, but only 31 Sv. coming back, then we know our measurements must be wrong—unless the Netherlands goes under. If, on the other hand, our transport measurements turn out within a Sverdrup or two of zero, then we can be fairly certain our measuring technique works, and the project will be successful."

By 0800 on the second day, we were abeam of Guadeloupe, and twelve hours later, we climbed abeam of the U.S. Virgin Islands, well out of sight to the west. We were growing used to our leisure. By breakfast time on the third day, the wind had relaxed after twenty-four hours at thirty knots. The fallen began to emerge from their darkened cabins sporting that ruddy glow particular to those who have recovered from a presumably fatal bout of seasickness with giddy delight at life itself, hungry. We congratulated them on resurrection.

At 275 feet overall, *Brown* is among the larger American research vessels, but she was feeling small. There aren't many places to *be* aboard these ships. There are the labs, the mess room, the lounge, or the transom; privacy is available only in one's cabin. Though this worked just fine for my interrogatory purposes, I couldn't help but notice that we had fallen into separate camps. No one was unfriendly or rude—these people are professionals who know how to behave at sea—but with so many different groups aboard, gravity pulled us to our own. I hadn't noticed cultural separation aboard *Oceanus*, perhaps because she's one hundred feet smaller, or aboard *Brown* last September, because she was so sparsely inhabited. The British mooring team sort of stuck to themselves in the main lab, and so did those of us in the computer lab. I noticed this as I willfully crossed the borders (they're separated only by a corridor) to corner sources. The crew, appreciably the same as on September's trip, also seemed less forthcoming. For them, again, this was no different from any other trip. Watch on, watch off, their job is to get the ship where the science requires with all her systems in order, and it matters not to them where she goes or why or for whom. Our watches had not yet begun; theirs never stop, not even in port where they maintain a skeleton watch. Further, in our leisure, we tended to loiter on the transom in fine weather, where we were often in the crew's way. As we steamed, the mooring team worked feverishly, assembling instruments and stringing miles of wire around this winch to multiple-part turning blocks, back to a different winch on to some other device, getting it ready to go over the side. (Their tans were well under way before we'd reached the first station.)

Word filtered around the ship that the original plans had changed, or they hadn't, it was not clear which. In any case, we were going to steam out to the end of the line at 69.5 degrees West longitude, 408 nautical miles east of Abaco Island, and work back west toward the Bahamas doing CTDs. Then we would reverse course, steam back along 26.5 North to do the mooring work. The two tasks can't be done simultaneously for various technical reasons. The mooring team, thinking they would go first, had been hurrying to get ready, and this resulted in some reserved murmers of dissatisfaction. I fully recognized on this trip the logistical complexity of the large oceanographic expedition, all the coordination, organization, and good luck required to get the data, as well as an insight into the allure of the old days when simpler ocean objectives were in force.

⌐◡⌐

There had been a quiet controversy spinning around certain oceanographic circles before the *Brown* sailed from Barbados and continuing after her return to Charleston. It's worth parsing not for controversy's sake itself, and certainly not to cast aspersions, but because it illustrates something about the present practice of big-science oceanography, the media, and our own understanding of our relationship to climate science. In 2005, the RAPID leader Harry Bryden published a paper in *Nature* contending that the Meridional Overturning Circulation had "slowed by about *30 percent* between 1957 and 2004" (Vol. 438, December 2005, with coauthors Hannah Longworth and Stuart Cunningham—italics mine). Bryden wrote, "Whereas the northward transport in the Gulf Stream across 25 degrees North has remained nearly constant, the slowing is evident both in a fifty percent larger southward-moving mid-ocean recirculation of the thermocline waters, and also a fifty percent decrease in the southward transport of lower North Atlantic Deep Water between 3,000 and 5,000 meters in depth." Let's take that statement apart; it's only our unfamiliarity with the language that complicates the principle.

Bryden is saying that the surface current flowing across 25 North, that is, the Gulf Stream, has not changed in velocity or volume. However, Bryden found a significant change in the surface circulation downstream of Cape Hatteras: "In 2004, more of the northward Gulf Stream flow was recirculating back southward in the thermocline within the subtropical gyre and less was returning southward at depth." This is to say that some significant portion of the North Atlantic Current was circulating southward over the top of the gyre, instead of proceeding northward into the Nordic Seas where the

sinking takes place. The result of this, Bryden contended, is a thirty
percent decrease in the cold water carried southward by the Deep
Western Boundary Current. This was startling, indeed. Changes of
that size in the mass transport of the Meridional Overturning
Circulation must have large effect on the heat transport and, therefore, on climate. Mustn't they?

Harry's paper produced two separate and very different responses
from the mainstream press and from his colleagues. First, the press:
The *Los Angeles Times* reported, "The ocean currents that transport
heat around the globe and keep northern Europe's climate relatively
mild appear to be weakening, according to a new scientific report"
(November 30, 2005). Said the *Times* of London on that same date,
"The Gulf Stream currents that give Britain its mild climate have
weakened dramatically, offering the first firm scientific evidence of a
slowdown that threatens the country with temperatures as cold as
Canada's. [An] even deeper freeze could follow if the Gulf Stream
system were to shut down entirely." CNN reported online, "If the
Atlantic conveyor belt were to break down, many scientists say it
could trigger an ice age in which Europe comes to resemble Siberia.
The data in this study suggest the conveyor is not breaking, but it is
slowing down." These are only three of about fifteen articles I saw in
various media within two days after *Nature* hit the newsstands, and
there must have been more. This was extraordinary. Oceanographic
research is not typically such hot stuff in the mainstream media, and
many people in the field were surprised by their sudden public
prominence. Harry told me that he had to excuse himself from this
RAPID/MOCHA cruise in order to stay on the beach and field calls
from reporters.

It's no fault of his that the press soared right over the top or that
some reporters misunderstood what he was actually saying. For instance, he never claimed that the Gulf Stream system was shutting
down; it will not. ("The only way to produce an ocean circulation

without a Gulf Stream is either to turn off the wind system, or to stop Earth's rotation, or both. . . . The occurrence of a climate state without the Gulf Stream any time soon—within tens of million years—has a probability of little more than zero," as Carl Wunsch put it in his inimical style in a letter to *Science*.) This initial flurry of alarming publicity prompted a second round of more measured essays cleaning up the science reporting, but these were read by far fewer members of the public. The problem for even the most intellectually rigorous journalists is that the ocean features and principles involved in the MOC do not fit conveniently in the typical newspaper-length article, as you may have noticed. However, though they skewed some of the facts, the reporters' sense of urgency was cued by Bryden's words, not by a false infusion of drama to make a good story. Reporters got his point that if the ocean's circulation patterns had, in fact, changed to that magnitude, climate would also change. In this light, it's notable that Bryden published his findings in *Nature*, readily available to the public, not in the *Journal of Physical Oceanography*, *Deep-Sea Research*, or one of the other technical journals read only by oceanographers. By publishing in *Nature*, it seems fair to say, Bryden meant for the public to notice.

Now as to his colleagues, who had a very different response to the "Slowing of the Atlantic meridional overturning circulation at 25 degrees North": Criticism from the dozen or so oceanographers I spoke with was universal. It wasn't necessarily Bryden's conclusion they quarreled with, but with the sparseness of his data, insufficient, they said, to support his alarming conclusion. These people speaking in private did not expect to be quoted, and so they will not be, but they all said the same thing, agreeing in principle with Wunsch, who put it more harshly in a letter to the editors of *Nature*: This, he wrote, was "a very extreme interpretation of the data . . . It's like measuring temperatures in Hamburg on five random days and then concluding that the temperature is getting warmer." Though Wunsch's skepticism about the threat of THC shutdown is well known, his problem, like others, was that Bryden's data were derived from five "snapshots" of the ocean over fifty years, not nearly enough to isolate a long-term trend in the MOC from natural variation. As we've stressed more than once, the ocean varies on all timescales. If it did not, if the ocean were cooperatively consistent, it would be far easier to follow the water. Obviously, Harry, a respected, experienced scientist with an impeccable reputation, was well aware of the ocean's variability. And so despite the sparseness of his sampling, Harry believed that he was seeing a broad trend, not merely a temporal variation here today and gone tomorrow (like that ten-day shutdown the Deep Western Boundary Current).

Harry's article made international news not because editors perceived that the public was clamoring for up-to-the-minute information about mass transport in the MOC. It was international news because he found signals of climate change in the mass transport. Harry has since backed away somewhat from the thirty percent decrease in the MOC claimed in the *Nature* article, agreeing that subsequent data have revealed that such heavy variation is built into the ocean system. That alone is an important result of RAPID/MOCHA research. And that's an example of how oceanography and other climate-related science work. Someone draws a hypothesis from available data and submits it to a peer-reviewed journal that vets the content, asks for changes, if any, based on the (anonymous) reviewers' comments and then publishes the paper, usually read only by other oceanographers. Research continues, and more data come in that corroborate, contradict, or develop the original hypothesis. As people, scientists are prone to the same foibles and distractions as the rest of us, but the process is inherently rational, and given time to unfold, it reaches a level of knowledge capable of supporting a theory—the highest level of scientific certainty—to explain nature's systems. The naysayers, ideologues, and apparatchiks have cleverly exploited the very process of science, the step-by-step unfolding of knowledge, to say, see, even the scientists disagree, implying that science is a matter of opinion.

There have been numerous excellent examples of climate-change journalism, and solid information is available across a wide range of media to members of the public who want to know what's really going on. That said, media and science don't operate on the same terms. In the case of the *Nature* article, the media more or less misunderstood what Bryden was saying, but it sounded like news, and indeed it would have been. However, when it became clear that such variations in the transport might just be an inherent part of the ocean system, the same press that reported the news did not follow up on the story. The extent of ocean variation is less newsworthy, but to ignore it is to sever the scientific process, and therefore to feed the mistaken idea that, well, we can't really rely on the experts, because they say one thing one day and something different the next.

Our relationship to our own climate lies stalled somewhere around the second-date level of intimacy, and there it will remain until somehow we learn to communicate with real scientists. We can expect nothing but continued foot-dragging and dim philistin-ism from the Bush administration, whose idea of a climate scientist is the fiction writer Michael Crichton, but that crowd will soon be gone. The resolute naysayers are still blathering, still scurrying to devise reactionary strategies to distract us, but there are hopeful signs that fewer normal people are listening. State governments, el-ements in Congress (the recently established House Committee on Energy Independence and Global Warming, for instance), major corporations such as Alcoa, BP America, Sun Microsystems, Merrill Lynch, and others, including segments of the evangelical Christian movement, have called loudly for alternative energy research and mandatory cuts in greenhouse gas emissions. These are all solid reasons for optimism that rationality will obtain, and in the development of clean energy sources, American industry might even revitalize itself. However, as all sorts of people have been exclaiming in all manner of media, that will not solve the problem.

Like it or not, we are married to our climate for life. "Mitigation," as it's coming to be called, in the form of solid, sensible legislation, alternative energy, conservation, and new ideas about "sequestering" carbon emissions underground, if put into practice, will signal a maturing relationship. However, if by some magic we could shut down today all present emissions, relegate to history the internal combustion engine and dirty power plants, the climate will continue to warm, triggering feedback mechanisms, some of which are predictable, and others not. As if looking out for our interests, the ocean, for instance, has been absorbing tons of our carbon dioxide since the dawn of the Industrial Revolution, and some scientists are predicting that, approaching its saturation point, ocean chemistry has shifted toward acidification, which is already wrecking ecosystems such as coral reefs. We'll be hearing more sad news about that as new data come in.

Involving so many interlocked systems and requiring such elaborate technology, climate research and particularly its ocean component is expensive. If we believe that research is valuable, then we'll have to pay more for it. The acceptance rate at the NSF for proposed projects in oceanography—those that actually get funded—runs about eight percent, and one hears talk about doubling the rate in 2008 to a whopping sixteen percent. That's not enough. Money matters. There is no technological reason, for instance, why today's ocean-sensing gear was not developed and in the water fifteen years ago, only want of funding. Across-the-board budget increases for good climate research will signal political will and public awareness. But there is more to this relationship than money.

If our climate relationship is to mature, then we need to insist on a more sensible, reality-based discourse, recognizing that we'll have to sustain it for the rest of our lives. If we appreciate that climate, generally, and climate change, specifically, have nothing at all to do with ideology and everything to do with science, then we'll find some mechanism by which to invite scientists back from their marginalized position on the fringes into mainstream culture. (It's darkly ironic that one of the few real scientists we've heard from in the recent round of congressional hearings in the wake of the IPCC report has been NASA's James Hansen. Here is a man who has been thinking about climate mechanisms for decades, who has much to tell us, but the only reason we know his name is because he complained publicly when he learned that some political hack was rewriting his science.) But if we decide we need to include scientists, then we will need to exert a certain intellectual effort to keep up with their evolving discoveries.

That said, let's look at this question of communication from the scientist's perspective. One complained that people sometimes talk about scientists as though they were members of some different subspecies with shared, classifiable traits; and as if science itself were monolithic. In Darwin's day, a determined student could learn by reading published material all that was known about, say, geology and, if he had some spare time, botany, too. That would be preposterous today. So much knowledge has been accumulated in all the separate genres of science that almost no one can cross the borders. But the segmentation of science runs deeper, as oceanography so thoroughly illustrates with its several arms—physical, chemical, geological, and biological. Physical oceanographers are concerned with the dynamics of the water, while geological oceanographers would like all that pesky water to part so they might observe their subject, the rock and sediment on the bottom, more conveniently.

Chemical oceanographers analyze the properties that comprise salt-water, while biologists study the organisms that live in it. I met a couple of interesting people working on genetic dispersal among reef fish at the Marine Biological Laboratory, one of the preeminent institutions in the field, which is situated on the WHOI campus. I was surprised at first to learn that they did not know the interesting people I'd met in the physical oceanography department, though they work every day in buildings about two hundred yards apart, fronting the same street in tiny Woods Hole. This is not a matter of tribalism, simply that in the normal course of their careers neither encounters the other any more routinely than, say, test pilots encounter airline pilots, though both fly airplanes. This, too, exacerbates the marginalization of science and scientists.

Another factor separating climate scientists from the rest of us is the very messy state of the climate debate, or to put it differently, the very fact that there is a debate at all. They don't want to participate in that, quite rightly beneath their dignity. And as a related factor, the oceanographers I've met are mildly mistrustful of the media; they shrug and assume they'll be misquoted, but they don't take it too seriously because all their colleagues have already been misquoted. Additionally, they know they will be asked, "So what's going to happen to us as a result of global warming?" The question makes most climate scientists edgy; they stiffen and tend to qualify carefully every noun and verb in their sentences. They know what the models show; they have their own ideas, but they aren't going to stick their necks out for attribution while the whole issue remains so politically fraught.

Aboard ship, where they were trapped, I pressed them about the general question of addressing the public. One said, "The only way I can learn anything new is to talk with my peers. Everything else is teaching." Teaching, all agree, is a good thing, but careers advance by performing research, composing technical papers, and writing successful grant proposals, and that keeps them busy enough. But one consensus among oceanographers I questioned was always the same: The public doesn't seem all that interested. Culturally, our scientific illiteracy is axiomatic, though perhaps not permanent or inevitable. If we decide to clean up the debate and learn something for ourselves about how science works, we have at least cleared the decks of impediments to sensible, measured dialogue. Scientists need us, and we need them, but the exchange is stalled at the moment, partly because neither has had much practice talking with the other. Perhaps when we look back at this fledgling point in our climate relationship from, say, fifteen years on, we'll see it as similar to the early years of the modern conservation movement when John Muir, Aldo Leopold, and others were introducing us to the concept and the word ecology while striving to convince government and the public that some things were more precious than profit and must be protected, preserved forever by law. Al Gore's *An Inconvenient Truth* will probably be viewed from a distance as a milestone in the "climate movement." It's still turning the Gore-haters and the ideologues apoplectic. But let's skip that boring chorus and glance at another reaction by honest scientists moved to point out that Gore brushed over the details of the science to reach an alarmist conclusion (particularly as to sea-level rise). Discussing this aboard the *Brown*, someone suggested that Gore felt a genuine moral obligation to convince the public that global warming is real and anthropogenically caused. What if we step beyond that point, remove the advocacy aspect, free Gore and others from the polemical need to convince? We're not there yet, but perhaps when we look back on these years, we'll see a distinct point beyond which we quit arguing and started learning.

One morning after a breakfast discussion about *An Inconvenient Truth*, publicity, and money, when scientists and volunteers straggled topside with coffee, we suddenly noticed that the ship was leaving an enormous wake, a veritable rooster tail. The deck vibrated as she powered along about five knots over the cruising speed we'd grown used to. And then we noticed that the sun was astern. We were heading *west*. Chris Churylo ("Sparks"), who, with a direct line to the bridge always knew what was happening or about to happen, explained our new course. A young engineer had just received word that her sister was seriously ill (*Brown* is set up to send and receive e-mail round the clock), and we were taking her back to Abaco at the western edge of the line to catch a plane for home. The sad young woman, whom we had not met, stood at port rail and stared seaward. Chris walked over to console her.

On the fourth day out, we reached the first CTD station at the east end of the line, and the pace of life for the volunteers changed abruptly. Time pressing, Molly considered dispensing with the practice cast and get right to the real thing, but since the console would be operated entirely by first-time volunteers (with the exception of me), a practice run, she decided, would be judicious. Then CTD ops began in earnest, twenty-four hours a day for the next week. The station stops at the east end of the 26.5 North line are spaced about fifty kilometers apart (I never got used to the scientists' use of kilometers instead of nautical miles to measure horizontal distance at sea). Out there in depths around 5,200 meters, each cast required three to four hours. Then with the CTD back on deck, the chemists and volunteers lined up in a prescribed order to extract a full range of water samples. First, we sampled oxygen, followed by two types of CFCs (CFC-11 and CFC-12), organic nutrients, freon, and finally salinity. "Milking the CTD," they call it, and in this case the process was complicated enough to require the oversight of a designated "sampling cop." Since each of the CTD bottles had been "fired" at different, known depths, the cop's job was to coordinate the bottle number (1–23) with numbered vials for each separate sample to prevent mix-up. That usually took another hour while the *Brown* steamed toward the next station. Cast by cast, twelve hours on watch, twelve off, the days bled together in that unique, pleasing (at least to me) rhythm of at-sea oceanography.

Leisure returned to the CTD crew when we dipped the package at the last stop within easy sight of Abaco Island. We still had the final string of stops in the Northwest Providence Channel and the Florida Straits, but we would pick those up after the mooring guys did their work. We waited almost a half a day while Molly and the executive officer sped ashore with the boat crew to clear Bahamian customs. After seeing so much deep-blue, open-ocean water, fascinated and frustrated, we lined the rail staring down into that wonderful turquoise of tropical shallows, longing for a swim or a dive, hang the sharks. As soon as they had the RHIB back aboard and secured, the *Brown* turned around and headed back toward the end of the line and the beginning of mooring operations.

The team had laid out all its instruments side by side on tables in the main lab. They had three different types of current meters, miniature CTDs about the size of rolling pins, and bottom-pressure sensors to help determine the reference level. I'd visit the lab to chat about oceanography with Jochem and Stuart Cunningham (Stuart, a big cricket fan, and I tried to engage in a comparison between cricket and baseball until we recognized that neither of us knew a thing about the other's game). Jochem gestured toward the display of fizzo instruments and said, "You know, this stuff in such quantity would knock the eyes out of most every oceanography institution in the world." Two days later, the mooring team swung into action.

Nothing was visible on the surface when *Brown* settled to a stop. Someone talked by computer to the submerged array requesting the acoustic releases to relinquish their grip on the anchor, which is abandoned on the bottom, more than four thousand meters below. Mick, the chemists, two women from Texas A&M, and a few of the other volunteers gathered on the 02 deck to watch the show. But it got off to a slow start. The audience waited nearly an hour for the great orange float at the top of the mooring to break the surface. The bridge maneuvered to put the float in reach of the stern winch, and working in practiced silence, the Brits captured the ball and hauled it aboard. Now the mooring and its array of instruments hung vertically several thousand meters beneath the ship, and after detaching and stowing the ball, the team ran the wire to another winch to begin the long retrieval process. The gallery retreated from the sun to await the next step.

The instruments are strung at intervals on the wire, and as each came aboard, Ian, the mooring chief, signaled the winch operator to stop while his guys removed the instruments one by one. Now the task was to reattach fresh instruments and sink the mooring back to the bottom, retrieval in reverse. They attached the topmost float and winched it over the stern. Stopping to connect and record each instrument and the strings of hard-hat floats, they paid out the mooring step by step until the ball was barely visible astern. And now, "seeing" the length of the mooring, rather than just hearing about its length in meters, we recognized anew that the ocean is very deep indeed. Reaching the bottom end of the mooring, Ian and his team shackled on a fresh pair of acoustic releases, then connected the wire to the anchor, a stack of locomotive wheels, and winched it outboard. Everybody ready? With a long pole, someone popped the shackle connecting the winch to the anchor, and it vanished with a great splash. We watched the ball off in the middle distance while the anchor dragged the bottom part of the mooring toward the bottom. After about a half an hour, the ball was yanked beneath the surface. And we steamed toward the next mooring.

We reveled in our leisure until it was announced that the Brits wanted to test their fresh instruments before they dunked them against the highly accurate temperature and salinity sensors on the CTD. Carlos removed about half the Niskin bottles to make room for the mooring team's instruments, which they lashed to the CTD frame. Then we heard that the Brits wanted us to leave the package at each depth for five minutes, instead of the usual thirty seconds. That was beyond the pale.

"This is an egregious case of CTD exploitation."

Mick agreed. "We need to stand up for the rights of CTD operators worldwide."

"Perhaps a work stoppage is in order."

"Our duty is clear."

A week later, the mooring ops were complete. A few instruments had been lost to the ocean, but not many, and everyone was happy with the work. "Carlos's Boys" wrapped up the final shallow CTD stations through Providence Channel and the Straits of Florida in one watch. With the package back on deck after the last cast, we hugged each other and went up to the mess for a last midnight snack. The *Brown* turned north in the Stream and steamed for Charleston.

Next evening Molly heard that the movie was to be *The Day After Tomorrow*. "Come on," she said. "It'll be fun."

⌒

Some months after the trip I phoned Bill Johns, the University of Miami oceanographer who heads MOCHA, to hear what the future might hold for the project. I wondered if their data indicated whether or not the endpoint-measurement technique was working.

"Yes," Bill said, "Our transport measurements are working out to near zero. We're all pleased about that. Actually, we're hoping we'll be able to remove a couple moorings." They would be particularly interested, he said, in removing those on either side of the Mid-Atlantic Ridge.

The Ridge, the largest single geographic feature on Earth, is a submerged mountain range that rises some six thousand feet above the seafloor and weaves its way sinuously from the High Arctic (Iceland is perched on the Ridge) to the doorstep of Antarctica. Geologically, the Ridge is a seam in Earth's crust where two great tectonic plates are pulling apart, thus releasing magma from the bowels of Earth to create new rock, a process called seafloor spreading. (The Atlantic is expanding ever so slightly, while the Pacific is contracting.) These two moorings are expensive to maintain, because the Mid-Atlantic Ridge is situated in the middle of the ocean on the way to nowhere, and to turn them around, a ship must make a special trip of about two weeks mostly spent steaming. However, the Ridge is so high the project had to assume that it exerted some influence on the deep circulation.

"Now we're waiting to hear whether the National Science Foundation will approve the next round of funding. If so, and if NERC [NSF's British counterpart] approves, then RAPID/MOCHA will be funded through 2014."

"How does it look?"

"It looks good, but we can't count on it until we hear for sure."

"When will that be?"

"Mid-May."

Since this book had to go to press before then, I called Miami again in late April, speaking with Molly Baringer, hoping, as a preeminent CTD jockey, I might be privy to some inside information.

"No," said Molly. "We haven't heard anything definite yet, but it looks very good. You've probably heard about the Ocean Research Priorities Plan?"

In 2000, Congress instructed the U.S. Commission on Ocean Policy (USCOP) to consult with a broad range of federal organizations including NASA, NSF, the Coast Guard, and NOAA and prepare recommendations for "a coordinated and comprehensive national ocean policy." The commission went to work and came back several years later with some two hundred regions and subjects that warranted study, and then they began the culling process. In early 2007, the Ocean Research Priorities team published a document listing and explaining their final priorities. There were four short-term priorities warranting concerted, immediate research: forecasting the response of coastal ecosystems to "persistent forcing" and extreme weather events; developing a comparative analysis of marine ecosystem organization; developing sensors to observe the content and condition of near-shore ecosystems; *and* "assessing the variation in the Meridional Overturning Circulation for implications about rapid climate change."

"That," said Molly, "leads us to believe we'll get the funding. But we won't know definitely for several weeks."

I had heard via the grapevine that optimism prevailed at RAPID as well. Harry Bryden and his colleagues in Southampton were confident enough about renewed funding that they were already requesting ship time.

"Oh, and speaking of variability," said Molly, "we've found a very interesting result from the data collected so far including the cruise you were on. We see in *one year* the same high range of variability that Harry found over the fifty-year period he wrote about in the *Nature* article."

"That alone is a significant discovery, right?"

"It sure is. Everyone is surprised."

Encouraged by the success thus far of the RAPID/MOCHA concept and techniques, the British and American team is discussing extending a similar project into the South Atlantic, using 30 degrees South latitude as the baseline. That latitude cuts through the border between Uruguay and Brazil on the west side of the basin and South Africa on the east side.

"The circulation is different down there than at 26.5 North, isn't it?"

"Quite different," said Molly. The deep circulation is somewhat different, but perhaps the most significant difference, she explained, is the absence of such a well-defined western boundary current. Also, people are talking about expanding and developing instruments to include chemical sensors on the moorings to afford long-term measurements of oxygen to understand the "age" of deep-water masses, nutrients, trace elements such as CFCs and tritium, and carbon dioxide sensors to study the growing problem of ocean acidification and other results of CO-2 uptake. Full-depth, basin-wide projects to study heat transport and the chemical composition of the ocean in various locations probably constitute the wave of the future for ocean research. That will require a new level of international cooperation involving South American scientists and governments, new and various instruments, scientific ingenuity of which there is no shortage, and money of which there is usually a shortage.

When I began this project, I was used to viewing currents and waves from a sailor's perspective, but I soon appreciated the extent to which sailors and oceanographers ask different questions about their shared medium. Sailors need to know the current's direction and velocity but they need not concern themselves with why the currents flow in the first place. Likewise, they need not accommodate in their navigation plans abyssal circulation; only dead sailors go that deep. I came away from the study of oceanography and my small participation in its practice with an enriched intellectual understanding of the ocean—inevitably, since I began with a high degree of ignorance. But I also came away with deepened love for the ocean, an unscientific sense of it as a living, breathing organism, along the lines of James Lovelock's Gaia principle, even as I know that it is not.

It's not hip in sailing circles to say you love the ocean. Those who watch the ocean from the beach, Melville's "water gazers," say things like that. The implication is that if you've been out there, incurred its pummeling, you may have a range of feelings about the damn thing, but love can't be among them. Maybe, but people who go out there time and again knowing they're likely to be bruised, bilious, and occasionally frightened don't do so because they're mildly interested in the ocean. There is a deeper attraction at work, even if the "code" requires it to remain unarticulated. Like mountains and deserts and other works of pure nature, the ocean can reach out and clutch a person at a very young age, and never relinquish its hold on mind and heart. And now we learn that the ocean, all this time, has been moderating, stabilizing climatic conditions as if somehow consciously to protect us from extremes of hot and cold, wet and dry. Even we romantics know that it does so without consciousness or intentionality but by lucky coincidence. Those who have been out there, particularly in small boats, recognize, on a very personal level, that the ocean doesn't care whether we live or die. On a scientific level, we know that the ocean will generally continue doing what it does as long as the Sun shines and Earth rotates. We're also beginning to recognize that if we continue doing what we do, the ocean may well change its ways long enough to produce conditions less generous to human habitation. But I'm a bit troubled by that as the sole reason why we ought to protect oceans and their ecosystems.

I recently watched a beautifully shot, well-meaning television documentary on the Amazonian rain forest that revealed the awesome diversity of its life forms and the web of life connecting one to the other and all to the trees. Concluding, the narration made a plea for the preservation of the jungle in part on the grounds that somewhere among its still unknown myriad of botanical species we might find a cure for cancer. That would be a fine thing, of course, but the implication was that we ought to refrain from cutting down all the trees because they might serve us at some point in the future. That same human-centric argument gets applied to the ocean. We should protect the ocean and its diversity of life from our effluviants, because if we don't, it may rise up, in the worst-case scenarios, flood our shores or plunge us into an ice age. This is of course is a compelling reason, yet it is also a reflection of the ethical perspective that brought us to this juncture in the first place: that nature is first and last about us.

Our brains and our hands have made us the first and only animals on Earth able to exist separately from any specific ecosystem, and certainly the only animal able to study other ecosystems. I hope one of things we learn—and articulate—is that the oceans (and the Amazon) have intrinsic value as magnificent works of nature in and of themselves unrelated to our own value. And we ought to protect them simply because we share the same Earth and because we can.

ACKNOWLEDGMENTS

I've never before done a piece of work that, for its very existence, depended on the assistance of so many people. For their patience, sustained generosity, and indeed their friendship, I am deeply indebted to a group of physical oceanographers who made this book possible: Molly Baringer and Chris Meinen at NOAA/AOML; Lisa Beal and William Johns at the University of Miami; John Toole at WHOI; Wilton "Tony" Sturges, Professor Emeritus at Florida State University; and Jochem Marotzke at the Max Planck Institute for Meteorology. However, any mistakes or infelicities in the text are my fault and none of theirs, nor that of any other oceanographer with whom I communicated, including Frank Bohlen, Stuart Cunningham, Robert Molinari, Phil Richardson, William Schmitz, and Peter Wiebe.

For reading the text at various stages of construction, my deep appreciation to Dick Drinkrow, Nick Lansing, Eugenia Leftwich, Robert Hogan, David Konigsberg, Jochem Marotzke, Carl Wunsch, and Chris Meinen for his unflagging willingness and generosity.

I wish to thank my science-staff shipmates aboard r/v *Ronald H. Brown*: Mick Beal, Tania Casal, Brad Parks, Ben Kates, Guilherme Castelão, and especially "Captain" Carlos Fonseca, who taught me everything I know about CTDing. I owe thanks also to the captain and crews aboard that vessel, shipmates Phil Pokorski, Mary O'Connell, Jonathan Shannahoff, especially Chris Churylo, and to NOAA for allowing me aboard. Likewise, my thanks to captain and crew of r/v *Oceanus*, to Jeff Stolp, and to the people at WHOI for allowing me aboard.

My thanks also to Nan North for the graphics.

A big thank you to Chris Greenberg and the good people at Perseus Books (I wish I could thank Elizabeth Maguire in person), and to Lori Hobkirk at The Book Factory.

Thanks, too, to my agent Lydia Wills.

For their various valuable contributions, I owe thanks to Jelle Atema, Warren Brown, Paul Bushman, Jenifer Clark, Steve Cohen, Philip Cronenwett,

Ruth Curry, William Curry, Shelly Dawicki, Kathy Donohue, John Farrington, Alan Friedman, Gabi Gerlach, Dan Goldner, Thomas Herrington, Nelson Hogg, Robin Hurst, James Kent, David Kriegel, David Langhorne, Bob Leban, Jim Ledwell, Harvey Leifert, Rick Lumpkin, Nick McKinney, Tim Millhiser, Tim O'Mera, Tracey Poirier, Darren Rayner, Jerry Roberts, Audrey Rogerson, John Rousmainiere, Jonathan Russo, Sarah Shankman, John Thackray, and Joanne Tromp.

BIBLIOGRAPHY

Books

Apel, J. R. *Principles of Ocean Physics*. New York: Academic Press, 1987.

Bombard, Alain. *The Bombard Story*. London: Grafton Books, 1990.

Boorstin, Daniel J. *The Discoverers*. New York: Random House, 1983.

Braudel, Fernand. *A History of Civilizations*. New York: Penguin Books, 1993.

Brown, Sanborn C. *Benjamin Thompson, Count Rumford*. Cambridge: MIT Press, 1979.

———. *The Collected Works of Count Rumford*. Cambridge: Belnap Press, Howard Press, 1968.

Burroughs, William James. *Climate Change: A Multidisciplinary Approach*. Cambridge: Cambridge University Press, 2001.

Calvin, William H. *A Brain for All Seasons: Human Evolution and Abrupt Climate Change*. Chicago: University of Chicago Press, 2002.

Carson, Rachel. *The Sea Around Us*. New York: Simon & Schuster, 1950.

Carter, Edward C. *Surveying the Record, North American Scientific Exploration to 1930*. Philadelphia: American Philosophical Society, 1999.

Chapin, Henry, and F. G. Walton. *The Ocean River*. New York: Charles Scribner's Sons, 1952.

Christiansen, Eric. *The Norsemen in the Viking Age*. Oxford: Blackwell, 2002.

Clark, Ronald W. *Benjamin Franklin*. London: Phoenix Press, 1983.

Cowen, Robert C. *Frontiers of the Sea*. Garden City: Doubleday & Co., 1960.

Deacon, Margaret B. *Oceanography: Concepts and History*. Stroudsburg, PA: Dowden, Hutchinson & Ross, 1978.

———. *Scientists and the Seas, 1650–1900: A Study of Marine Science*. New York: Academic Press, 1971.

Diamond, Jared. *Collapse*. New York: Penguin Group, 2005.

Douglas, Marjory Stoneman. *The Everglades, River of Grass*. Sarasota: Pineapple Press, 1997.

Drake, Frances. *Global Warming*. London: Arnold, 2000.

Durbury, A. C. *An Introduction to the World's Oceans*. Dubuque: William C. Crown, 1989.

Fagan, Brian. *The Long Summer*. New York: Basic Books, 2004.

———. *Floods, Famines, and Emperors*. New York: Basic Books, 1999.

Gelbspan, Ross. *Boiling Point*. New York: Basic Books, 2004.

Gore, Al. *An Inconvenient Truth*. New York: Rodale, 2006.

Gould, Stephen Jay. *Time's Arrow, Time's Cycle: Myth and Metaphor in the Discovery of Geological Time*. Cambridge: Harvard University Press, 1987.

Gurney, Alan. *Compass*. New York: W. W. Norton, 2004.

Heezen, Bruce C., and Charles D. Hollister. *The Face of the Deep*. London: Oxford University Press, 1971.

Helferich, Gerard. *Humboldt's Cosmos*. New York: Gotham Books, 2004.

Huntford, Roland. *Nansen: The Explorer as Hero*. London: Gerald Duckworth & Co. Ltd., 1997.

Jardine, Lisa. *Ingenious Pursuits*. New York: Random House, 1999.

Klein, Bernhard, and Gesa Mackenthum, eds. *Sea Changes: Historicizing the Ocean*. New York: Routledge, 2004.

Jones, Gwyn. *Vikings: The North Atlantic Saga*, second ed. Oxford: Oxford University Press.

Leip, Hans. *River in the Sea*. New York: G. P. Putnam's Sons, 1957.

Lewis, David. *We, the Navigators*. Honolulu: University of Hawaii Press, 1972.

Limburg, Peter R. *Oceanographic Institutions*. New York: Elsevier/Nelson Books, 1878.

Linklater, Eric. *The Voyage of the Challenger*. Garden City: Doubleday & Co., 1972.

Maury, M. F. *Physical Geography of the Sea*. New York: Dover Publishing, 2003.

McPhee, John. *Annals of the Former World*. New York: Farrar, Straus & Giroux, 1998.

Philander, George S. *Our Affair with El Niño*. Princeton: Princeton University Press, 2004.

Morison, Samuel Eliot. *The European Discovery of America*. New York: Oxford University Press, 1974.

Murphy, Dallas. *Rounding the Horn*. New York: Basic Books, 2004.

Nansen, Fridtjof. *Farthest North*. London: Gerald Duckworth, 2000.

Ocean Navigator Magazine, eds. *Navigator's Gulf Stream Companion*. Portland: Navigator Publishing, 1992.

Oceanography Course Team. *Ocean Circulation*. Walton Hall: The Open University, 1989.

Oelschlaeger, Max. *The Idea of Wilderness*. New Haven: Yale University Press, 1991.

Parry, J. H. *The Discovery of the Sea*. New York: The Dial Press, 1974.

Piccard, Jacques. *The Sun Beneath the Sea*. New York: Charles Scribner's Sons, 1971.

Pirie, Gordon R., ed. *Oceanography: Contemporary Readings in Ocean Sciences*. New York: Oxford University Press, 1977.

Pittock, Barrie. *Climate Change: Turning Up the Heat*. CSIRO Publishing, 2005.

Rousmaniere, John. *A Berth to Bermuda: One Hundred Years of the World's Classic Ocean Race*. Mystic: Mystic Seaport/Cruising Club of America, 2006.

———. *After the Storm: True Stories of Disaster and Recovery at Sea*. New York: McGraw-Hill/International Marine, 2002.

———. *The Annapolis Book of Seamanship*. New York: Simon & Schuster, 1989.

Rozwadowski, Helen M. *Fathoming the Ocean*. Cambridge: Harvard University Press, 2002.

Schlee, Susan. *On Almost Any Wind*. Ithaca: Cornell University Press, 1978.

———. *The Edge of an Unfamiliar World*. New York: E. P. Dutton & Co., 1973.

Schmitz, William, Jr. *On the World Ocean Circulation: Vol. I*. Woods Hole: Institution Technical Report, June 1996.

Shapin, Steven. *The Scientific Revolution*. Chicago: University of Chicago Press, 1996.

Springer, Haskell. *America and the Sea*. Athens: University of Georgia Press, 1996.

Stommel, Henry. *The Collected Works of Henry Stommel*, Volumes I, II, and III, Nelson G. Hogg & Rui Xin Huang, eds. Boston: American Meteorological Institution, 1995.

———. *A View of the Sea*. Princeton: Princeton University Press, 1987.

———. *The Gulf Steam*. Berkeley: University of California Press, 1966.

———. *The Starbuck Essays*. Woods Hole: Friends of Starbuck, 1992.

Sverdrup, Harald. *The Oceans, Their Physics, Chemistry, and General Biology*. New York: Prentice-Hall, 1942.

Teal, John, and Mildred Teal. *The Sargasso Sea*. Boston: Little, Brown & Co., 1975.

Thurman, H. V. *Essentials of Oceanography*, fourth ed. New York: Macmillan Press, 1993.

Trujillo, Alan P., and Harold V. Thurman. *Essentials of Oceanography*. Upper Saddle River: Pearson, Prentice Hall, 2005.

Van Dorn, William. *Oceanography and Seamanship*. New York: Dodd, Mead & Co., 1974.

Vetter, Richard C. *Oceanography, the Last Frontier*. New York: Basic Books, 1973.

De Villiers, Marq, and Sheila Hirtle. *Sable Island: The Strange Origins and Curious History of a Dune Adrift in the Atlantic*. New York: Walker, 2004.

Von Arx, William S. *An Introduction to Physical Oceanography*. Reading: Addison-Wesley Publishing Co., 1962.

Williams, Frances L. *Matthew Fontaine Maury, Scientist of the Sea*. New Brunswick: Rutgers University Press, 1963.

Withey, Lynn. *Voyages of Discovery*. Berkeley: University of California Ress, 1989.

Technical Periodicals

American Geophysical Union, NASA Jet Propulsion Laboratory. "Arctic Sea Ice Diminished in 2004 and 2005." September 13, 2006. Press release.

Broecker, W. S. "The biggest chill." *Natural History*, October 1987, 74–82.

Broecker, W. S., and G. H. Denton. "The role of ocean-atmosphere reorganizations in glacial cycles." *Quaternary Science Reviews*, Vol. 9, 1990, 305–341.

———. "The great ocean conveyor." *Oceanography*, Vol. 4, 1991, 79–89.

———. "Thermohaline circulation, the Achilles heel of climate system." *Science*, Vol. 278, 1997, 1582–1588.

Broecker, W. S., M. Ewing, and B. C. Heezen. "Evidence of an abrupt change in climate close to 11,000 years ago." *American Journal of Science*, Vol. 258, June 1960, 441 ff.

Bryden, H. L., and T. H. Kinder. "Steady two-layer exchange through the Strait of Gibraltar." *Deep-Sea Research*, Vol. 38, Suppl. 1, 1999, 5445–5463.

Bryden, H. L., T. H. Kinder, W. E. Johns, and P. M. Saunders. "Deep Western Boundary Current east of Abaco: mean structure and transport." *Journal of Marine Research*, Vol. 63, 2005, 35–57.

Bryden, H. L., T. H. Kinder, R. L. Longworth, and S. Cunningham. "Slowing of the Atlantic meridional overturning circulation at 25 degrees N." *Nature*, 438, 2005, 655–657.

Church, J., S. Wilson, P. Woodworth, and T. Aarup. "Understanding Sea Level Rise and Variability," *Eos*, Vol. 88, No. 4, Jan. 23, 2007.

Cunningham, S. "Cruise Report, RAPID-MOC, Spring, Western Boundary Mooring Array Refurbishment and Western Time Series CTD Section aboard NOAA ship *Ronald H. Brown*," 2006.

Curry, R. G., Bob Dickson, and Igor Yashayaev. "A change in the freshwater balance of the Atlantic Ocean over the past four decades." *Nature*, Vol. 426, 2003, 826–829.

Curry, R. G., and C. Mauritzen. "Dilution of the northern North Atlantic in recent decades." *Science*, Vol. 386, 2005, 1772–1744.

Curry, R. G., M. S. McCartney, and T. M. Joyce. "Oceanic transport of subpolar signals to mid-depth subtropical waters." *Nature*, Vol. 391, 1998, 575–577.

Dansgaard, W., et al. "Evidence for general instability of past climate from a 250,000-year ice core record." *Nature*, Vol. 364, 1993, 218–220.

Dansgaard, W., R. R. Dickson, and J. Brown. "The production of North Atlantic Deep Water: sources, rates, and pathways." *Journal of Geophysical Research*, Vol. 99, No. 12, 1994, 319–341.

Delworth, T. S., S. Manabe, and R. J. Stoffer. "Interdecadal variations of the thermocline circulation in a coupled ocean-atmosphere model." *Journal of Climate*, Vol. 6, 1993, 1193–2011.

De Ruijter, W. P. M., et al. "Observations of the inter-ocean exchange around south Africa." *Eos*, Vol. 87, No. 9, 2006, 97–101.

Drake, F. "Stratospheric ozone depletion: an overview of the scientific debate." *Progress in Physical Geography*, Vol. 19, 1995, 1–16.

Driscoll, N. W. and G. H. Huag. "A short circuit in Thermohaline circulation: a cause for Northern Hemisphere glaciation?" *Science*, Vol. 282, 1998, 436–438.

Ebbsmeyer, C. C., and W. J. Ingraham. "Shoe spill in the North Pacific." *EOS Transactions of the American Geophysical Union*, Vol. 73, No. 34, 1992, 361, 365.

———. "Pacific toy spill fuels ocean current pathways research." *EOS Transactions of the American Geophysical Union*, Vol. 75, No. 37, 1994, 425, 427, 430.

Fine, R. A., and R. L. Molinari. "A continuous deep western boundary current between Abaco (26.5N) and Barbados (13N)." *Deep-Sea Research*, Vol. 35, No. 9, 1998, 1441–1540.

Fofonoff, N. "Polygon–70: a Soviet Oceanographic Experiment" *Oceanus*, Vol. 19, No. 3, 1976, 40–43.

Fonseca, C. A., G. J. Goni, W. E. Johns, and E. J. D. Campos. "Investigations of the North Brazil Current retroflection and North Equatorial Current variability." *Geophysical Research Letters*, Vol. 31, November 2004, L21204.

Friedricks, M. A. M., and M. M. Hall. "Deep circulation in the tropical North Atlantic." *Journal of Marine Research*, Vol. 51, No. 4, 1993, 697–736.

Fuglister, F. C. "Atlantic Ocean atlas of Temperature and Salinity profiles and data from the IGY of 1957–1958." *Woods Hole Oceanographic Institution Atlas Series*, Vol. 1, 1960, 209.

Garzoli, Silvia L., Philip Richardson, Christopher M. Duncombe Rae, David M. Fratantoni, Gustavio J. Goni, and Andreas J. Foubicek. "Three Agulhas rings observed during the Benguela Current Experiment." *Journal of Geophysical Research*, Vol. 104, No. C9, 1999, 20, 971–2098.

Hacker, P., E. Firing, W. D. Wilson, and R. L. Molinari. "Direct observations of the current structure east of the Bahamas." *Geophysical Research Letters*, Vol. 23, No. 10, 1996, 1127–1130.

Hall, M. M., and H. L. Bryden. "Direct estimates and mechanics of ocean heat transport." *Deep-Sea Research*, Vol. 29, 1982, 339–359.

Hogg, N. G. "On the transport of the Gulf Stream between Cape Hatteras and the Grand Banks." *Deep-Sea Research*, Vol. 39, No. 7/8, 1992, 1231–1246.

Hogg, N. G., and H. Stommel. "On the relation between the deep circulation and the Gulf Stream." *Deep-Sea Research*, Vol. 32, 1985, 1181–1193.

Hoering, M. P., T. Xu, G. Bates, A. Kumar, and B. Jha. "Warm oceans raise land temperatures." *EOS*, Vol. 87, No. 19, 2006, 189 ff.

Hunkins, K. "Ekman drift currents in the Arctic Ocean." *Deep-Sea Research*, Vol. 13, 607–620.

Jacob, D., H. Goettel, J. Jungclaus, M. Muskulus, R. Podzum, and J. Marotzke. "Slowdown of the thermohaline circulation causes enhanced maritime climate influence and snow cover over Europe." *Geophysical Research Letters*, Vol. 32, 2005, L21711.

Johns, E., R. A. Fine, and R. L. Molinari. "Deep flow along the western boundary south of Blake Bahama Outer Ridge." *Journal of Physical Oceanography*, Vol. 27, No. 10, 1997, 2187–2208.

Johns, W. E., and F. Schott. "Meandering and transport variations of the Florida Current." *Journal of Physical Oceanography*, Vol. 17, 1987, 1128–1147.

Johns, W. E., T. J. Shay, J. M. Bane, and D. R. Watts. "Gulf Stream structure, transport, and recirculation near 68 degrees West." *Journal of Geophysical Research*, Vol. 100, 1995, 817–838.

Joyce, T. M., and W. J. Schmitz. "Zonal velocity structure and transport in the Kuroshio Extension." *Journal of Physical Oceanography*, Vol. 18, No. 11, 1998, 1484–1494.

Joyce, T. M., C. Wunsch, and S. D. Pierce. "Synoptic Gulf Stream velocity profiles through simultaneous inversion of hydrographic and acoustic Doppler data." *Journal of Geophysical Research*, Vol. 92, No. C6, 1986, 7573–7585.

Lagerloef, G. "Role of ocean salinity in climate and near-future satellite measurements." *Eos*, Vol. 87, No. 43, 2006, 466.

Lau, W. K. M., and K.-M. Kim. "How nature foiled the 2006 Hurricane Forecasts." *Eos*, Vol. 88, No. 6, Feb. 27, 2007, 105–107.

Leaman, K. D., and J. E. Harris. "On the average absolute transport of the Deep Western Boundary Current east of Abaco Island, the Bahamas." *Journal of Physical Oceanography*, Vol. 20, No. 3, 1990, 467–475.

Ledwell, J. R., E. T. Montgomery, K. L. Polzin, L. C. St. Laurent, R. W. Schmitt, and J. M. Toole. "Evidence for enhanced mixing over rough topography in the abyssal ocean." *Nature*, Vol. 403, January 13, 2000, 179–182.

Lee, T. N., W. E. Johns, F. Schott, and R. Zantopp. "Western boundary current structure and variability east of Abaco, the Bahamas, at 26.5 degrees North." *Journal of Physical Oceanography*, Vol. 20, No. 3, 1990, 446–466.

———, W. E. Johns, R. J. Zantopp, and E. F. Fillenbaum. "Moored observations of western boundary current variability and thermohaline circulation at 26.5 N in the tropical North Atlantic." *Journal of Physical Oceanography*, Vol. 26, 1996, 862–893.

Lee, T. N., and E. Williams. "Wind forced transport fluctuation of the Florida Current." *Journal of Physical Oceanography*, Vol. 10, No. 18, 1988, 937–946.

Larson, J. C., and T. B. Sanford. "Florida Current transport from voltage measurements." *Science*, Vol. 227 (4684), 1985, 302–304.

Lazier, J. R. N., and D. G. Wright. "Annual velocity variations in the Labrador Current." *Journal of Physical Oceanography*, Vol. 23, 1993, 659–698.

Lowell, T. V., et al. "Testing the Lake Agassiz Meltwater Trigger for the Younger Dryas." *Eos*, Vol. 86, No. 40, 2005, 265 ff.

Luyten, J. R., J. Pedlosky, and H. Stommel. "The ventilated thermocline." *Journal of Physical Oceanography*, Vol. 13, No. 30, 1983, 292–309.

Manabe, S., and R. J. Stouffer. "Two stable equilibria of a coupled ocean-atmosphere model." *Journal of Climate*, Vol. 1, No. 9, 1998, 841–866.

Mann, M. E., and K. A. Emanuel. "Atlantic hurricane trends linked to climate change." *Eos*, Vol. 87, No. 24, 2006, 233 ff.

Marotzke, J., and B. A. Klinger. "The dynamics of equatorially asymmetric thermocline circulations." *Journal of Physical Oceanography*, Vol. 30, 2000, 955–970.

———. "Abrupt climate change and thermohaline circulation mechanisms and predictability." *PNAS*, Vol. 97, No. 4, February 2000, 1347–1350.

McCartney, M. S., and L. D. Talley. "The subpolar mode water of the North Atlantic Ocean." *Journal of Physical Oceanography*, Vol. 12, 1982, 1169–1188.

Meinen, C. S., and L. Beal. "Preliminary Abaco cruise report." NOAA Ship *Ronald H. Brown*, September 11–24, 2005.

Meinen, C. S., S. L. Garzoli, W. E. Johns, and M. O. Baringer. "Transport variability of the Deep Western Boundary Current off Abaco Island, Bahamas." *Deep-Sea Research*, Vol. 1, No. 51, 2004, 1397–1415.

Mildrexler, D. M., M. Zhao, and S. W. Running. "Where are the hottest spots on earth?" *Eos*, Vol. 86, No. 43, 2006, 461 ff.

Milinski, M., D. Sernmann, H. J. Krambeck, and J. Marotzke. "Stabilizing Earth's climate is not a losing game: supporting evidence from public goods experiments." PNAS, Vol. 103, No. 11, 2006, 3994–3998.

Molinari, R. L., R. A. Fine, and E. Johns. "The Deep Western Boundary Current in the North Atlantic Ocean." *Deep-Sea Research*, Vol. 39, No. 11/12, 1992, 1967–1984.

Molinari, R. L., R. A. Fine, W. Douglas Wilson, R. G Curry, J. Abell, and M. S. McCartney. "The arrival of recently formed Labrador Sea Water in the Deep Western Boundary Current at 26.5 N." *Geophysical Research Letters*, Vol. 25, No. 13, 1998, 2249–2252.

Mooers, C. N. K., C. S. Meinen, M. O. Baringer, I. Bang, R. Rhodes, C. N. Barron, and F. Bub. "Cross validating ocean prediction and monitoring systems." *Eos*, Vol. 86, No. 29, July 19, 2005, 269.

Munk, W. "The evolution of physical oceanography in the last hundred years." *Oceanography*, Vol. 15, No. 1, 2002, 135–141.

Munk, W., and C. Wunsch. "Observing the ocean in the 1990s." *Philosophical Transactions of the Royal Society of London*, Vol. 307, No. 1499, 2002, 439–464.

Oey, L.-Y., H.-C. Lee, and W. J. Schmitz Jr. "Effects of winds and Caribbean eddies on frequency of Loop Current eddy shedding: a numerical model study." *Journal of Physical Oceanography*, Vol. 108, No. 610, 2003, 3324.

Oreskes, N., K. Shrader-Frechette, and K. Belitz. "Verification, validation, and confirmation of numerical models in the Earth sciences." *Science*, Vol. 263, February 1994, 641–646.

Parrilla, G., A. Lavin, H. Bryden, M. Garcia, and R. Millard. "Rising temperatures in the subtropical North Atlantic over the past 35 years." *Nature*, Vol. 369, 1994, 49–51.

Perez-Brunius, P., T. Rossby, and R. D. Watts. "A method to obtain the mean transports of ocean currents by combining isopycnal float data with historical hydrography." *Journal of Atmosphere and Oceanic Technology*, Vol. 21, 2003, 298–316.

Perry, M. J., and D. L. Rudnick. "Observing the ocean with autonomous and Lagrangian platforms and sensors (ALPS): the role of ALPS in sustained ocean observing systems." *Oceanography*, Vol. 16, No. 4, 2003, 31–36.

Phillips, T. J., K. AchutaReo, D. Bader, C. Covey, C. M. Doutriaux, M. Fiorino, P. J. Gleckler, K. R. Sperber, and K. E. Taylor. "Coupled Climate Model Appraisal: a benchmark for future studies." *Eos*, Vol. 87, No. 19, 2006, 185 ff.

Pickart, R. S., M. A. Spall, and J. R. N. Lazier. "Mid-depth ventilation in the western boundary current system of the sub-polar gyre." *Deep-Sea Research*, Vol. 44, 1997, 1025–1054.

Read, J. F., and W. J. Gould. "Cooling and freshening of the subpolar North Atlantic since the 1960s." *Nature*, Vol. 360, 1992, 55–57.

Reynaud, T. H., A. J. Weaver, and R. J. Greatbatch. "Summer mean circulation of the Northwestern Atlantic Ocean." *Journal of Geophysical Research*, Vol. 100, 1995, 779–816.

Rhines, P. "Physics of ocean eddies." *Oceanus*, Vol. 19, No. 3, 1976, 26–39.

Richardson, P. L. "On the crossover between the Gulf Stream and the Western Boundary Undercurrent." *Deep-Sea Research*, Vol. 24, 1976, 139–159.

Richardson, P. L., and David M. Fratantoni. "Float trajectories in the deep western boundary current and deep equatorial jets of the tropical Atlantic." *Deep-Sea Research*, Vol. 46, 1989, 305–333.

Richardson, P. L., and John A. Knauss. "Gulf Stream and Western Boundary Undercurrent observations at Cape Hatteras." *Deep-Sea Research*, Vol. 18, 1971, 1089–1109.

The Ring Group. "Gulf Stream Cold-Core Rings: Their Physics, Chemistry, and Biology." *Science*, Vol. 212, No. 4499, 1981, 1091–1100.

Robertson, A. R. "Eddies and Ocean Circulation." *Oceanus*, Vol. 19, No. 3, 1976, 2–18.

Rowley, R. J., J. C. Kostelnick, D. Braaten, X. Li, and J. Meisel. "Risk of rising sea level to population and land area." *Eos*, Vol. 88, No. 9, Feb. 27, 2007, 105, 107.

Schiermeier, Q. "Climate Change: A Sea Change." *Nature*, Vol. 439, January 2006, 256–260.

Schmitz, W. J., Jr. "On the basin-scale thermohaline circulation." *Reviews of Geophysics*, Vol. 33, No. 2, May 1995, 151–173.

Schmitz, W. J., Jr., and M. McCartney. "On the North Atlantic circulation." *Reviews of Geophysics*, Vol. 31, No. 1, 1993, 29–49.

Schmitz, W. J., Jr., D. C. Biggs, A. Lugo-Fernandez, L.-Y. Oey, and W. Sturges. "A Synopsis of the Circulation in the Gulf of Mexico and its continental margins." *Geophysical Monograph Series*, Vol. 161, 2005, 11–29.

Schmitz, W. J., Jr., and Philip L. Richardson. "On the sources of the Florida Current." *Deep-Sea Research*, Vol. 38, Suppl. 1, 1991, 379–401.

Schmitz, W. J., Jr., James R. Luyten, and Raymond W. Schmitt. "On the Florida Current T/S envelope." *Bulletin of Marine Science*, Vol. 53, No. 3, 1993, 1048–1065.

Schmitz, W. J., Jr., and J. D. Thompson. "On the effects of horizontal resolution in a limited-area model of the Gulf Stream System." *Journal of Physical Oceanography*, Vol. 23, No. 5, May 1993, 1001–1007.

Schmitz, W. J., Jr., J. D. Thompson, and J. R. Luyten. "The Sverdrup circulation for the Atlantic along 24 N." *Journal of Geophysical Research*, Vol. 97, 1992, 7251–7256.

Schmitz, W. J., Jr. "Weakly depth-dependent segments of the North Atlantic circulation." *Journal of Marine Research*, Vol. 38, 1980, 111–133.

Spall, M. A. "Dynamics of the Gulf Stream/Deep Western Boundary Current crossover, Part I: Entrainment and recirculation." *Journal of Physical Oceanography*, Vol. 26, 1989, 2152–2168.

Sturges, W., and B. G. Hong. "Gulf Stream Transport Variability at Periods of Decades." *Journal of Physical Oceanography*, Vol. 31, 2001, 1304–1312.

Sturges, W., and J. C. Evans. "On the variability of the Loop Current in the Gulf of Mexico." *Journal of Marine Research*, Vol. 41, 1983, 639–653.

Swallow, J. C. "Variable Currents in mid-ocean." *Oceanus*, Vol. 19, No. 13, 1976, 18–25.

Toole, J., R. Krishfield, A. Proshutinsky, C. Ashjain, K. Doherty, D. Frye, T. Hammar, J. Kemp, D. Peters, M.-L. Timmermans, K. von der Heydt, G. Packard, and T. Shanahan. "Ice-tethered Profilers Sample the Upper Arctic Ocean." *Eos*, Vol. 87, No. 41, October 10, 2006, 434 ff.

———. "Cruise Report." r/v *Oceanus* cruise No. 421, WHOI, April 5–15, 2006.

Toole, J. M., R. G. Curry, T. M Joyce, R. S. Pickart, W. M. Smethie. "Investigating the characteristics and consequences of Interannual variations in the Northeast Atlantic." DWBC, Project Summary, WHOI, 2005.

Vaughan, S. L., and R. L. Molinari. "Temperature and salinity variability in the DWBC." *Journal of Physical Oceanography*, Vol. 27, No. 5, 1997, 749–761.

Wu, Peili, Richard Wood, and Peter Stott. "Human influence on increasing Arctic River discharges." *Geophysical Research Letters*, Vol. 32, 2005, L02703.

Wyrtki, K. "El Niño—The dynamic response of the equatorial Pacific to atmospheric forcing." *Journal of Physical Oceanography*, Vol. 5, 1995, 572–584.

Yang, G., and T. M. Joyce. "How do high-latitude North Atlantic climate signals the crossover between the Deep Western Boundary Current and the Gulf Stream?" *Geophysical Research Letters*, Vol. 30, No. 2, 2003, 1070.

Zabarenko, Deborah. "U.S. Scientists, evangelicals join global warming fight." *Scientific American.com*, Jan. 17, 2007.

Personal Communication

Extended communication with Lisa Beal and William Johns, University of Miami, RSMAS; Wilton "Tony" Sturges, Florida State University; John Toole and Phil Richardson, WHOI; Molly Baringer, Chris Meinen, Carlos Fonseca, AOML at NOAA; and Jochem Marotzke, Max Planck Institute for Meteorology.

INDEX